DATE DUE

JY 3 1 01			
MY 21 '02			
AG 3			

DEMCO 38-296

MURDER IN THE NAME OF GOD

MURDER
IN THE NAME
OF GOD

THE PLOT TO KILL
YITZHAK RABIN

Michael Karpin and
Ina Friedman

METROPOLITAN BOOKS

HENRY HOLT AND COMPANY   NEW YORK

Metropolitan Books
Henry Holt and Company, Inc.
Publishers since 1866
115 West 18th Street
New York, New York 10011

Metropolitan Books™ is an imprint of
Henry Holt and Company, Inc.

Library of Congress Cataloging-in-Publication Data
Karpin, Michael I.
Murder in the name of God: the plot to kill Yitzhak Rabin /
Michael Karpin and Ina Friedman.—1st ed.
p. cm.
Includes bibliographical references and index.
ISBN 0-8050-5749-8 (hardbound: alk. paper)
1. Rabin, Yitzhak, 1922– —Assassination. 2. Israel—Politics
and government. 3. Amir, Ygal, 1975– . 4. Assassination—
Religious aspects—Judaism. 5. Judaism and state—Israel.
6. Orthodox Judaism—Israel.   I. Friedman, Ina.   II. Title.
DS126.6.R32K37   1998   98-20763
956.9405'092—dc21   CIP

Henry Holt books are available for special promotions and
premiums. For details contact: *Director, Special Markets.*

First Edition 1998

Designed by Kate Nichols

Printed in the United States of America
All first editions are printed on acid-free paper. ∞

10 9 8 7 6 5 4 3 2 1

I might show facts as plain as day:
But since your eyes are blind, you'd say,
"Where? What?" and turn away.

Christina Rossetti, *A Sketch*

CONTENTS

ACKNOWLEDGMENTS

Much of the research for this book was done in connection with the documentary film *The Road to Rabin Square*, which was the first attempt to present an in-depth picture of the campaign of incitement that preceded the assassination of Prime Minister Yitzhak Rabin. Our profound gratitude goes to the film's producer, David Mosevics, for his abiding faith and backing throughout that project. Invaluable assistance in the course of the research was provided by Navah Mizrachi, Gila Lapid, Rachel Nehushtai, Lilac Ron, Gyora Eylon, and Laurie Chock, who greatly enhanced the scope of the findings presented here.

Amnon Abramovitch was a steady source of wise counsel. Eviatar Manor and Daniel A. Ross read the manuscript and called our attention to a number of important points. Isabelle Klebanow typed parts of the manuscript with speed and accuracy, and Miriam Gillat checked various details with perseverance and care. Vered Shatil drew the map, and Nili Atzlan and Moshe Shai shot the photographs (which, unless otherwise noted, were reproduced from *The Road to Rabin Square*). We thank them all for their dedication and highly valued professionalism.

Our agents, Deborah Harris and Beth Elon, were responsible both for bringing us together at the start of this project and for shepherding us through it with patience, skill, and unflagging support. We were also most fortunate to have as our editor Stephen Hubbell, a fellow journalist whose editorial acumen was matched only by his kindness and forbearance while working within tough scheduling strictures. Lucy Albanese grappled with the technological challenges posed by the illustrations. Riva Hocherman graciously adopted the book in the production stage and, together with Carly Berwick, faithfully saw us through it. Our gratitude to them defies expression here.

Writing a book can often seem like a very lonely enterprise, even when done in concert. We enjoyed considerable aid and support from the many people mentioned here, as well as from our families and friends; nevertheless, responsibility for the final product is ours alone.

Jerusalem
July 1998

MURDER IN THE NAME OF GOD

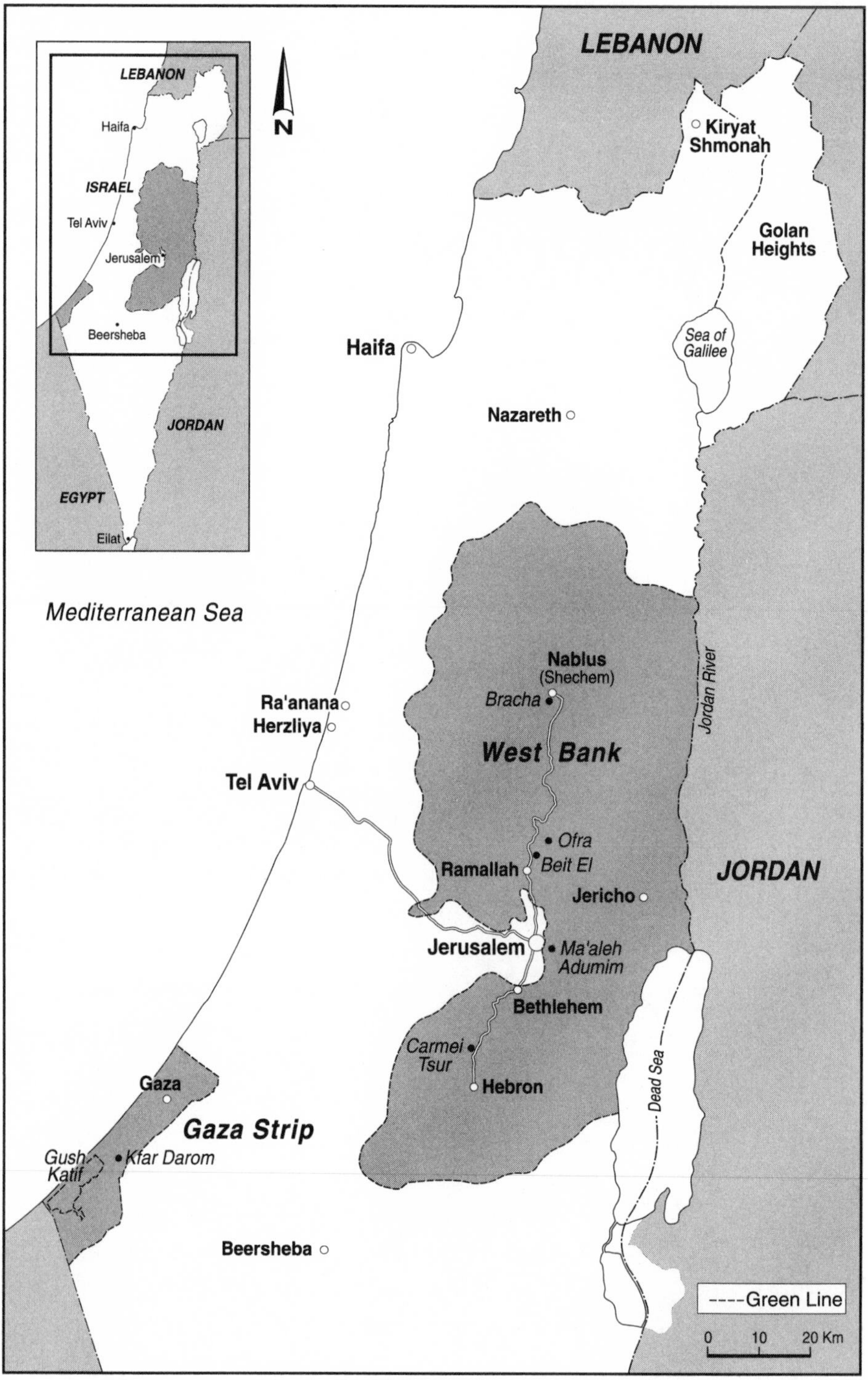

LEBANON
ISRAEL
Haifa
Tel Aviv
Jerusalem
Beersheba
JORDAN
EGYPT
Eilat
N
LEBANON
Kiryat Shmonah
Golan Heights
Sea of Galilee
Haifa
Nazareth
Mediterranean Sea
Nablus (Shechem)
Bracha
Jordan River
Ra'anana
Herzliya
West Bank
Tel Aviv
Ofra
Beit El
Ramallah
JORDAN
Jericho
Jerusalem
Ma'aleh Adumim
Bethlehem
Carmei Tsur
Hebron
Dead Sea
Gaza
Gaza Strip
Gush Katif
Kfar Darom
Beersheba
----Green Line
0 10 20 Km

PROLOGUE

In January 1994 Yehoshafat Harkabi, one of Israel's most respected intellectuals, predicted the assassination of Yitzhak Rabin. Harkabi had known the prime minister since the days they had fought together in Israel's War of Independence. Like Rabin, he had made his career in the army, retiring in 1959 as commander of Military Intelligence. His second career was as a historian and political scientist, and he had become renowned for his trenchant insights. In 1993 his country awarded him the Israel Prize, its highest honor for achievement.

Eight months before his death, to cancer, and four months after the signing of the Oslo Agreement, Harkabi sat for an interview with two younger Israeli scholars. In the sharp, somber tone that characterized his later writings, he set forth a vision of Israeli society racked by strife over Rabin's decision to compromise with the Palestinians and relinquish territory captured by Israel in 1967. "Rabin will not die a natural death," he warned. "The country will experience an intense shock."

Harkabi was haunted by the long record of Jewish fanaticism. He had written a study of one of the most traumatic chapters in Jewish history, the Bar-Kochba Revolt against the Romans in C.E. 132–135. Incited by Jewish Zealots sixty-two years after Jerusalem had been razed by the Romans in response to an earlier uprising, this second revolt raged for more than three

years and cost the lives of over half a million Jews. In the popular imagination, the Bar-Kochba Revolt was remembered as an impassioned act of
heroism and a fight for national freedom, regardless of how doomed.
Harkabi had tried to shatter its myth of glory by pointing to the revolt's
ominous implications. He quoted Winston Churchill's remark that two
ancient peoples, the Greeks and the Jews, suffered from a strong impulse of
self-destruction. Looking around him in 1994, he feared that observation
was still true.

On October 10, 1995, less than a month before Yitzhak Rabin was
assassinated, the Association of Americans and Canadians in Israel, a
mild-mannered organization of American expatriates, held a country fair
on the Mediterranean coast north of Tel Aviv. The prime minister was
invited to what was designed as a thoroughly lighthearted affair. But upon
arrival he was met by a group of raucous right-wing demonstrators shouting, "The dog has arrived!" and "Rabin go home!" One of the demonstrators, Dr. Natan Ophir, a rabbi at the Hebrew University, rushed the prime
minister, shrieking and cursing, and got as far as the bodyguard beside him.
When the guard blocked his assault, Ophir bit his hand. There had been
many demonstrations against Rabin before that day, but this was the first to
reveal his actual physical vulnerability. Shocked by the incident, Ze'ev
Schiff, the defense editor of the prestigious daily Ha'aretz, darkly described
it as "Rabin's murder—a dry run."

Two weeks before the assassination, Victor Cygielman, the correspondent of the French weekly Le Nouvel Observateur, sat down at his computer in Tel Aviv to sum up the developments of the past months. A veteran
observer of Israeli life, he recounted a series of odd and dismaying events.
Cygielman began by describing the eerie ceremony in which a small group
of religious fanatics had stood before Rabin's house on the eve of Yom
Kippur and intoned the mystical Pulsa da-Nura, a kabbalistic curse of
death. He wrote of the explicit "contract" put out on Rabin's life by rabbis
who invoked the talmudic concept din rodef, the sentence pronounced on a
Jewish traitor. Cygielman cited the handbill passed out at a mass demonstration in Jerusalem on October 5 showing Rabin in an SS uniform. And

he ended with the statement from the Shabak (Israel's General Security Services) warning that the poisoned atmosphere of incitement could culminate in an assassination. Cygielman explained that the atmosphere of violence was unprecedented in Israel. The stage was set for the murder of the prime minister, he said; an actual attempt was only a matter of time.

A technical hitch in Paris caused a week's delay in the publication of Cygielman's piece, and it didn't appear until Thursday, November 2. Two days later Yitzhak Rabin was dead.

CHAPTER 1

THE SAVIOR

The first impression Yigal Amir gives is of a polite young man, relaxed, self-possessed, almost serene. He speaks softly and laughs engagingly; in no way does his bearing suggest violence. At first he murmurs just above a whisper, forcing one to listen intently. He sounds like a missionary bent on redeeming a sinner. Those who lack faith or who fall victim to spiritual weakness are the object of his sermon, as are those who fail to grasp his reasoning and appreciate his achievement. On second glance he seems almost euphoric, at peace with himself and imbued with a sense of great power. He has no doubt whatsoever that he has accomplished the deed of the century.

Amir welcomes a battle of wits. Schooled in talmudic argument, he is an agile opponent. He never retreats when his assault is blocked, just attacks from another angle. The words flow easily off his tongue, and he even has a sense of humor, a hint of self-deprecation. At times he will giggle in discomfort, then recover and attack again, jumping from a shallow slogan to tortuous talmudic reasoning. Intoxicated by his own rhetoric, he is convinced he has won the day. His eyes shine with satisfaction as a smug smile spreads across his lips.

Amir identifies with an avant-garde of Jewish zealots: elitists in their own eyes, fanatics in the estimation of others. They have isolated themselves in small yeshivas, in settlements on the hilltops of the West Bank, in the courtyards and alleyways of Hebron, in Joseph's Tomb in Nablus. Like them, he has embraced a system of values that are messianic and anarchistic in the view of society at large. Like them, he feels only contempt for anything that smacks of the establishment, which he accuses of hypocrisy. Orthodox rabbis assail secular Jews for their crassness, Amir believes, but gladly live off their taxes. The settlers, who are widely viewed as defiant extremists, are cowed by the government, in Amir's view. "A settler wouldn't have dared to kill Rabin," he sneered to the police officer who interrogated him. "The settlers are concerned about their image. They're timid, terrified people."

Unlike the settler establishment, the zealots are unwilling to compromise. They are determined to live precisely according to their beliefs, and that is why Amir reveres them. Like them, he is prepared to obey only the law of the Torah,* for the Torah is the absolute Truth. One must never depart from its ways or appease those who deny it. Man's laws are fickle and fleeting, but the 613 commandments in the Torah are constant and eternal. At the End of Days the "believers," the Sons of Light, will defeat the heretics, the Sons of Darkness. For the believers obey the halacha, the canon of Jewish religious law, and follow God's dictates. "There's a small minority here," he says of most of his countrymen, "a small group that's completely atheistic, and its aim is to lead to an absolutely secular state," to make "Israel a nation like all the nations." This small minority, he explains, is trying to wrest control of all the instruments of power, especially the legal system and the media. The disaster looming at the gates is that the Jewish people will be destroyed by those who abhor religion. What awaits the people of Israel, Amir believes, is nothing less than a Holocaust.

One of Amir's friends, Yaron Yehoshua—himself a practicing Jew—believes that Amir's faith is particularly powerful. "I had many arguments with him about faith, and his was much stronger than mine," says Yehoshua. "I raised questions and doubts, but he argued that everything set down in the halacha must be followed." If civil law clashes with religious law, Yehoshua heard Amir pronounce, then the civil law must yield.

Amir also believes that there is only one guideline for fixing the borders

---

*The first five books of the Old Testament.

of the Land of Israel: the Divine Promise made to the Patriarch Abraham: "To your descendants I give this land, from the river of Egypt to the great river, the river Euphrates" (Genesis 15:17). Today these borders embrace most of the Middle East, from Egypt to Iraq. But the zealots read this passage as God's Will, and God's Will must be obeyed, whatever the cost. No mortal has the right to settle for borders any narrower than these. Thus negotiating a peace settlement with Israel's neighbors is unthinkable. After all, the manifest destiny of the Jewish people has not been realized, say the zealots, so what is the basis for making peace? The order of action must be reversed: First the territorial conquests must be completed, so as to bring the Divine Promise to fruition. Yet even after their territorial demands are satisfied, the zealots doubt whether it will be possible to reconcile with the Arabs. "Esau hates Jacob," says the Talmud,* and you cannot make peace with those who hate you.

Amir echoed that conviction to the Shamgar State Commission of Inquiry that investigated the circumstances surrounding the murder of Yitzhak Rabin. "There can't be peace here," he told them.

> [The Arabs are] our antithesis in every way. We can't live peacefully with them. For three years they [Rabin's government] have imposed their outlook in a way that's created new concepts. I mean, peace has received a new meaning. The word "peace" is, to me, first of all peace within the nation. You must love your [own people] before you can love others. The concept of peace has been turned into a destructive instrument with which anything can be done. I mean, you can kill people, abandon people [to their fate], close Jews into ghettos and surround them with Arabs, give guns to the army [Palestinian Police], establish a [Palestinian] army, and say: this is for the sake of peace. You can release Hamas terrorists from prison, free murderers with blood on their hands, and everything in the framework of peace.

Amir tried to persuade Shlomi Halevy, a politically liberal student of philosophy, to join the opposition to the Oslo Agreement signed by Israel

---

*Postbiblical interpretation of religious law, written both in Babylonia, after the Jews of the Kingdom of Israel were exiled there, and in the Land of Israel.

and the Palestinians in September 1993. "His line of argument is rational and devoid of emotion," Halevy said after the murder. "There's no such thing as pluralism for him, no nuance, no openness; it's all or nothing. There is only One Truth, and he is privy to it." Halevy describes Amir as "a fanatic of the holy trinity: the people of Israel, the Torah of Israel, and the Land of Israel. He hasn't much use for democracy or the secular State of Israel, its anthem, and symbols. He dismisses what the goyim [gentiles] will do or say. He says that Israel must do what it can and trust that God will take care of all the rest."

The hard-core zealots are roughly divided into two groups: vigilantes and ideologues, those who believe in direct action and those who devote themselves to philosophizing. Among the vigilantes Amir holds in esteem is Dr. Baruch Goldstein, the physician from the settlement of Kiryat Arba, adjoining Hebron, who gunned down twenty-nine Palestinians at morning prayer in the Cave of the Patriarchs on February 25, 1994. Among the ideologues, he especially admires Noam Livnat, a tall, bearded, delicate-faced settler in his forties who walks with a heavy limp (the result of a road accident that initially left him paralyzed from the neck down). He returned to religion as a youth and became intensely pious. Today his name is well known in right-wing circles and among the national religious camp.* At one point the Shabak, Israel's General Security Services, had him under surveillance. Since his sister, Limor Livnat, became a government minister in June 1996, the media have swarmed to his door. But the guarded Livnat rarely agrees to give interviews. He defines himself as a "radical right-wing messianist," and many young religious Jews regard him as a figure to be emulated. His soft voice and subdued manner stand in sharp contrast with his political image. Even right-wing radicals consider him an extremist.

Livnat is unquestionably an intellectual. He would be in his element on a university campus, lecturing on history or philosophy. Yet he is more often found in the Palestinian city of Nablus (the biblical Shechem), bent

---

*Israel's community of observant Jews is roughly divided into three camps: the *haredim*, or ultra-Orthodox Jews, easily identified by their black frocks or suits and black yarmulkes; the religious nationalists, mainly followers of the National Religious Party, who are generally identified by their multicolored, crocheted yarmulkes; and traditionalist Jews, who may or may not wear crocheted yarmulkes and who observe religious tradition but do not keep to the letter of Jewish law. Many *haredim* do not recognize the sovereign authority of the State of Israel. The religious nationalists have, over the past decades, moved far to the right.

over the Talmud in an old Arab structure—evidently the tomb of a sheikh. A late Jewish tradition identifies the site as Joseph's Tomb, for "the bones of Joseph . . . were buried at Shechem (Joshua 24:32)." It now houses a yeshiva called Joseph Still Lives (Od Yosef Chai), and gathered there each day are among the most fanatic religious settlers in the West Bank. So rabid are the students in this yeshiva that at the beginning of 1996, Rabbi Yoel Bin-Nun, himself a religious settler, warned his colleagues: "There's a potential for murder in the yeshiva in Shechem. Do not accord it your protection."

Bin-Nun, in fact, demanded that the yeshiva be closed down. He decried the racist ruling of its patron, Rabbi Yitzhak Ginzburg, that "Jewish blood and gentile blood are not the same." Ginzburg defended the act of one of the yeshiva's students who opened indiscriminate fire on Arab laborers standing alongside a highway near Tel Aviv in 1993, and he subsequently lauded Dr. Baruch Goldstein for massacring Arabs in Hebron. He wears a long black coat, dabbles in Jewish mysticism, and is a magnet for "born-again" Jews (nonpracticing Jews who have returned to religion and become radically pious).

A few years ago Ginzburg debated Bin-Nun before the small group of students at the Joseph Still Lives Yeshiva for more than three hours. He explained that he differentiates between the murder of a gentile and that of a Jew because the Torah places a "light prohibition" on the former and a "grave" one on the latter. Bin-Nun argued that murder is murder, plain and simple, and that the murder of a gentile is a desecration of the Jewish religion. Yet most of Ginzburg's students supported their rabbi's view. Some even claimed that the murder of a gentile is an act sanctified by God.

Bin-Nun was aghast. How could the Yesha* Council, which represents the Jewish settlers in the occupied West Bank and Gaza Strip, accord this racist yeshiva its auspices? Ginzburg was causing immense damage to the settlers' cause by disseminating his racist views. "I have no doubt that Rabbi Ginzburg and his doctrine are a threat to our entire enterprise: to settlement activity, yeshivas, society, the state as a whole," Bin-Nun wrote to the council, demanding that it pressure the government to dismiss Ginzburg and withhold funds from his yeshiva. "If you do not do so," he warned his comrades, "it is clear that the acts of murder will continue."

---

*Hebrew acronym for Judea, Samaria (the West Bank), and Gaza.

To this day the Yesha Council has not responded to his plea. The Joseph Still Lives Yeshiva remains open and under heavy guard. It is cordoned by Israeli soldiers who are surrounded by another belt of Palestinian policemen. The Israel Defense Forces (IDF) has allocated a considerable number to protect this group of extremists studying inside Nablus, which is controlled by the Palestinian Authority. The students are transported to the city every day, likewise under heavy guard, and evacuated again each evening.

Before transferring control of the West Bank's cities to the Palestinian Authority (as stipulated in the Interim Agreement signed on September 28, 1995), Rabin intended to close the Joseph Still Lives Yeshiva, after Chief of Staff Amnon Shahak recommended evacuating it. Then the settlers' lobby went into action, and Rabin capitulated to it. The ramifications of this decision became evident a year later, when Rabin was already in his grave and the newly elected prime minister, Benjamin Netanyahu, decided to flaunt Israel's control over all of Jerusalem by opening an exit to a tunnel adjoining the Western Wall. The Palestinians, who insisted that the tunnel undermined the foundations of the Al-Aqsa Mosque, responded with rage. On September 26, 1996, rioting broke out throughout the occupied territories, and when Israeli soldiers opened fire on the stone-throwing demonstrators, Palestinian policemen returned it.

One focus of the fighting was Joseph's Tomb in Nablus, as rioting Palestinians closed in on the yeshiva and threatened to overrun it. When the soldiers guarding it issued distress calls, the General Staff issued an order to evacuate the besieged Israelis, but the students refused to budge. Noam Livnat used his special influence with the government by calling his sister, Limor Livnat, on his cellular phone and asking her to have the evacuation order rescinded. She in turn called the office of Defense Minister Yitzhak Mordechai and was told if such an order existed, it would be canceled. Thus, instead of evacuating the yeshiva, the IDF sent in reinforcements to defend it. In the battle for Joseph's Tomb, 6 Israeli soldiers and 2 Palestinians were killed, and another 8 Israeli soldiers and 181 Palestinians were wounded. As justification for holding this isolated "position" in the heart of Palestinian territory, at such a high toll in human lives, the Yesha Council argued that relinquishing the site, marginal as it might be, would lead to the abandonment of others as well. In any event, it is doubtful that the evacuation order would have been reversed had it not been for the "hot line" between Livnat and his ministerial sister. A few months after the battle for Joseph's Tomb, Livnat told a journalist, "Thank God I have a sister who's a nationalist and that there's no dramatic gap between [our views]. I pass information on to her all the time, and she gives me feedback."

Noam Livnat was born into a family of proudly nationalist but non-observant Jews. His great-grandfather had immigrated to Palestine in 1888, and his parents had been members of the Stern Gang, a faction of the right-wing Jewish underground that fought Britain's mandatory regime in the 1940s. Noam discovered religion as a boy. He later studied under a relative, Rabbi Zalman Shlomo Orbach, the leading rabbinical authority of the *haredi* community, and became strictly observant. But although his mentor was strongly anti-Zionist, nationalism and religion merged into a potent blend of extremism for Livnat, who now lives in the West Bank settlement of Elon Moreh and is active in the messianic movement called Chai Ve-Kayam ("Lives and Endures").

One of his comrades in that group is Yehuda Etzion, who in the early 1980s headed a band of settler vigilantes that operated in the West Bank and came to be called the Jewish Underground. Amir admired Etzion, as he did all the members of the Underground. In 1984 Etzion was sentenced to seven years' imprisonment for conspiring to blow up a mosque on the Temple Mount in Jerusalem. Other members of the Underground murdered Palestinian students in Hebron's Islamic University, planted bombs in the cars of two Palestinian mayors, seriously wounding them, and planned to blow up Palestinian buses.

Etzion's plan to "purify" the Temple Mount accords with Livnat's desire to build the Third Temple there, an aim shared by the zealots of the Joseph Still Lives Yeshiva as part of their scheme to accelerate the Redemption. The First Temple was built by King Solomon in the tenth century B.C.E. and was destroyed by King Nebuchadrezzar of Babylon in 586 B.C.E. The Second Temple was restored in 520 B.C.E., rebuilt in an elaborate form by King Herod in the first century B.C.E., and destroyed by the Romans in C.E. 70. Telescoping the past three millennia, the zealots dream of rebuilding the Temple, restoring the ancient Kingdom of David, and establishing a regime based solely on Jewish religious law—a halachic state. Livnat defined the borders of that kingdom in an article entitled "Against Peace Now" published in Chai Ve-Kayam's journal, *La-Brit* ("For the Covenant"). The piece concluded that Israel should seek war with the Arabs. "Candidly speaking, we're not at all interested in peace, as this concept is understood by the general public," he wrote. "As the ultimate of radical right-wing messianists, we look forward to the Redemption, to [ruling over the] true Whole Land of Israel, from the river of Egypt to the Euphrates . . . [and] this integrity will undoubtedly be attained through conquest and wars."

Just a few years ago, when Livnat joined the zealots at the Tomb of Joseph, his vision of Redemption was considered a weird fixation. Today he believes that tens of thousands are willing to listen to him, and there are strong indications that his assessment is correct. A great change has overtaken Israeli society in recent years. Broad circles, including most of the Orthodox rabbis in Israel, are no longer reluctant to discuss their belief in Divine Redemption and will not support a government whose policy undermines it. "You can already sense the onset of the Redemption. It's just over the horizon," said Livnat as he drove the authors late in 1996 to a narrow green valley, just south of Nablus, and stopped the car between two high, rock-strewn mountains: the green Mountain of Blessing to the south; the bald Mountain of Curse to the north. "Which of them will win out?" he wondered aloud. "The Mountain of Redemption or the Mountain of Devastation?"

Livnat looks back at the last century, since Jews began returning to their ancestral homeland in numbers, and sees two parallel processes: one positive, the other negative; one congruent with God's Will, the other contrary to it. The first is the process leading to Redemption: a war to conquer the Whole Land of Israel and draw back the Jews from the farthest ends of their Diaspora. The other—the secularization of Jewish life, admiration for the vapid culture of the West, peace treaty with Egypt, relinquishment of parts of the homeland following the Oslo Agreement—only hastens the decline toward total ruin. "We, the people of Shechem, believe that Good and Evil are struggling with each other, and the outcome has yet to be decided," he said. "We, the believers, must act to manifest God's Will."

His view runs contrary to the faith of most of the nationalist rabbis. Echoing the philosophy of their mentor, the late Rabbi Zvi Yehudah Kook, they believe that even if Evil temporarily overwhelms Good, even if barriers are placed in the way of Redemption, God's Will is destined to be fulfilled without human intervention. But Livnat holds that "it's frustrating to see Jews behaving like ostriches. I know that Redemption will come in any event, but if the Oslo process takes over, the State of Israel will be a fleeting episode. It will collapse, and everything that's been accomplished in the past century will be destroyed. But if the Oslo Agreement is nullified, the process of collapse will be halted and the Redemption will move forward.

"Look at these mountains," he says, pointing to the clusters of red-roofed houses in the small, often isolated Jewish settlements of Samaria. They are set amid a sea of Palestinians and are often enclosed by barbed-wire fences, like military outposts. Day after day their inhabitants travel dangerous roads in cars reinforced to protect them from stones, firebombs, and bullets. They are determined to cling to these rock-strewn mountains even if it costs them their lives. Above Nablus lives the spearhead of the set-tler population: a few score bearded young men in tzitzit* and crocheted yarmulkes and women draped in head scarves and long dresses to conceal their allure. All are self-styled idealists, "emissaries of the people." "They are protecting the Land of Israel from the curse of Oslo," says Livnat. "You know that when the compromise was signed in Oslo, the Mountain of Curse grew higher and the Mountain of Blessing began quaking."

So says the ideologue that Yigal Amir holds in the highest esteem. His hero among the other branch of the zealot community—the vigilantes—was actually another soft-spoken man. Unlike Livnat, however, he trans-lated his beliefs into violent action and inspired others to do the same. He made his move, without warning, on February 25, 1994, during the feast of Purim. Purim commemorates the rescue of the Jews of Persia from a plot to annihilate them and is traditionally celebrated with throngs of merri-ment. But on that cold, foggy Friday morning Dr. Baruch Goldstein had another plan in mind. Waking before dawn in his flat in Kiryat Arba, a large Israeli settlement that adjoins Hebron and contains some of the most radi-cal of the Jewish settlers, the physician donned his military reserves uni-form, picked up his M-16 rifle, and rode to the Cave of the Patriarchs, a holy site shared by Muslims and Jews. A native of Brooklyn, Goldstein had been a disciple of Meir Kahane, the racist rabbi who founded the Jewish Defense League, and at one point had been the league's spokesman. That morning he was ostensibly on his way to pray with the quorum of Jewish men who meet at the holy site daily. Climbing the steps of the imposing building, Goldstein entered the hall where hundreds of Muslims were pray-ing on their knees with their heads bowed to the floor. Calmly he aimed his

*Fringed garments worn by pious Jews.

rifle at the congregation, switched the safety catch to automatic fire, and pulled the trigger. Within seconds dozens of worshipers had collapsed before him. He did not release the trigger until a number of panicked worshipers jumped him from behind, dragged him to the floor, and began beating him to death.

That morning Yigal Amir was at Bar-Ilan University studying in the kolel, a study group in which students can pursue talmudic subjects in addition to their secular education. As he sat immersed in the Talmud, someone turned on the radio. Amir listened to the report of the massacre and came away with a selective understanding of the event and its perpetrator. "People who knew him described [Goldstein] as a doctor, as a noble soul," he later told investigators from the Shamgar Inquiry Commission. "I was very intrigued by how a man like that could get up and sacrifice his life. . . . This was a man who left a family and martyred himself."

Shlomi Halevy, who was also at the university that morning, recalls that as word of the massacre spread, cries of joy were heard on the campus. "I was shocked by the response," he says. "The majority said they were against the murder but that they understood Goldstein. Yigal Amir justified his action. He said that on the previous evening cries of 'Allah-hu akbar' ['Allah is great'] and 'Kill the Jews' had been heard in the Cave of the Patriarchs. If Goldstein hadn't killed them, Amir said, the Arabs would have massacred the Jews. I was among the few who denounced the murder," Halevy said.

The Hebron massacre was a milestone for Yigal Amir. From that morning onward he concentrated his efforts on achieving the "spiritual readiness" that Goldstein had displayed. He too aspired to be an agent of God, an emissary of his people. He traveled to Kiryat Arba to attend Goldstein's funeral and meet the community in which he had lived. "I wanted first of all to get to know [them]. . . . So I went there and saw all the thousands who were at the funeral. I saw the love they had for him, and I understood that this is no simple matter. I spoke with the people and began to understand that [they are] not simply fanatic extremists. They are people who are fighting, very hard, for the nation, for whom values are very important. . . . It began after Goldstein. That's when I had the idea that it's necessary to take Rabin down. I'm sorry about the words. I'm not that kind [of person]. I had never murdered anyone before, and I love this country very much; I love this people."

Amir came to know the zealots in Kiryat Arba and Hebron. He grew close to Rabbi Moshe Levinger, a leader of the settler movement who had been convicted of killing a Palestinian and who had pronounced Rabin responsible for the Goldstein massacre. He met with members of Kahane's Kach movement. The activists of Kiryat Arba turned Baruch Goldstein's grave into a shrine. Two weeks after the massacre, when Kach and its offshoot, Kahane Chai ("Kahane Lives"), were outlawed by the government, Amir thought the country had gone mad. "They're using the Shabak against the people," he later told his interrogators. "What kind of state uses the Shabak against the people? And the media? After Goldstein, the media began a mass assault on the right, and I understood that there was a combined trend here—government plus media—to put the people to sleep, to hide things from them."

This is the intellectual and spiritual world to which Yigal Amir was drawn. These were his idols, mentors, and guides at a time of deep political turmoil. Like the soft-spoken Livnat, Amir insisted that his arguments were based on cold logic. But because he has only scant knowledge of Western philosophy, the border between reason and emotion was blurred in his mind. In conversation, he sometimes sounds as though he were delivering an oration, repeating such phrases as "an offense to the sanctity of the Land of Israel" and "an offense to the sanctity of the people of Israel." At others he chatters almost compulsively, in colloquial Hebrew peppered with "I mean" and "that is," as he struggles to explain his motives. He believes that the reason "outsiders" view him as an extremist is that few have reached his lofty level of "pure faith." He insists that his assault on Yitzhak Rabin was meant to save the Jewish people. He also claims he never planned to murder Rabin at all. He merely wanted to paralyze the prime minister, remove him from the stage, and thereby cancel the Oslo Agreement. He acted, he says, on behalf of rabbis, according to their rulings, following the commandments of the Torah.

Even as a child Amir showed signs of obstinacy. He flouted the authority of his teachers. He sought challenges, however difficult, and pursued them with tenacity. At six he entered the *haredi* Wolfsohn School near his home in Herzliya, a suburb of Tel Aviv. At twelve he concluded that his talents were not being exploited and looked for a new school. On the recommendation of friends and neighbors, he chose the Yishuv Hadash ("New Community") Yeshiva in Tel Aviv. It was an elite school, attended by the sons of proud and wealthy *haredi* families whose forebears had come from Eastern Europe and the Russian Pale of Settlement, the heartland of Jewish life prior to the Holocaust.

By contrast, Amir's family came from Yemen and lived in modest circumstances. His parents had serious misgivings about their son's decision. "My husband, Shlomo, tried to discourage him," recalls his mother, Geula Amir. "We were a bit frightened to let a twelve-year-old boy travel alone by bus to Tel Aviv and back. It was very far, and there were no school buses. When [the school administrators] laid eyes on Yigal, a dark Yemenite child, at first they refused to accept him. But he insisted and was [finally] admitted. . . . He went there alone, and after we brought him home he stayed in his room from morning till night. In the evening I said to Shlomo: 'We have no choice.' [Yigal] studied there for three years and was then accepted into its high school."

Yigal applied the same single-mindedness to Rabin's murder, preparing himself for almost two years. He says that the idea first flashed through his mind when the Oslo Agreement was signed in Washington on September 13, 1993. Watching the broadcast from the White House lawn, he was astounded to see Rabin shake the hand of PLO Chairman Yasser Arafat. "If there's no choice, it will be necessary to take down Rabin," he thought to himself. (He never used the term "murder," and even after the assassination rarely spoke of having "killed" Rabin, always preferring the idiom "I took him down," as though he had toppled the king in a chess match.)

Amir's hostility to Rabin and the notion of territorial compromise with the Palestinians had become evident years earlier, however. When he voted for the first time, in the 1992 elections, Yigal cast his ballot for the small, radical right-wing Moledet ("Homeland") Party, led by a coarse, racist retired general named Rehavam Ze'evi, who preaches the doctrine of "transfer": the expulsion of the Palestinians and annexation of the occupied territories to Israel. During Amir's service in the army, the men in his unit knew that he hated Arabs. He joined the elite Golani Brigade under a special arrangement for yeshiva students that enabled them, in return for five years' army service, to spend two of those years studying in a special *hesder* ("arrangement") yeshiva. He registered at the Kerem D'Yavneh Yeshiva, most of whose students were the sons of religious nationalist families. Until then Yigal had studied in *haredi* schools, which emphasized learning the precepts of halacha and preached contempt for the laws of the secular state. In the Kerem D'Yavneh Yeshiva, he found himself, for the first time, among religious young men whose energies were focused on settling the Greater Land of Israel.

Amir is proud of his stint in the army. He could have legally evaded the draft, for if the graduates of *haredi* yeshivas can show that they are continuing their religious studies full-time, they are exempt from military service. The parents of most *haredi* youngsters prefer their boys to exploit that option, so as to avoid "temptation" and not abandon their pious ways when they come into contact with secular youngsters. But Amir's meeting with nonreligious soldiers did nothing to undermine his faith. In the 13th Battalion of the Golani Brigade, he took pains to follow religious strictures down to the letter. He was known to argue with left-leaning soldiers, sometimes raising his voice and banging his fist. During the intifada, the Palestinian uprising in the occupied territories, Amir's battalion was sent to quell the riots. Members of his unit recalled that Yigal beat the demonstrators with relish. Yet his personal file makes no reference to any excesses, and he was promoted to the rank of corporal.

In the summer of 1992, while he was studying at the Kerem D'Yavneh Yeshiva, Amir was sent to Riga, Latvia, as one of a few hundred volunteers selected to work as counselors in summer camps for Jewish youth. He spent three months there and went on to tour in Europe. On a ferry in Germany, he struck up a conversation with some local girls and gave them his address. So strongly had this slight, swarthy Israeli impressed them that they began sending him letters.

Thus Yigal Amir had followed a typical course throughout his childhood and youth. He was not an exception among his peers, and at no point did he display signs of aberrant behavior. When Yigal was seventeen, the principal of the Yishuv Hadash Yeshiva characterized him in his personal file as "unfair, dishonest, and insincere." But no one ever discerned any emotional symptom suggesting that an assassin lay buried inside him.

In September 1993, the same month as the signing of the Oslo Agreement, Amir was released from the army, returned to his parents' home in Herzliya, and registered to study law and computer science at Bar-Ilan University. His room on the second floor of the Amirs' modest house was small and spartan, boasting just a bed, a desk, and a few books. Yigal was rarely at home during the week, as he left for school early in the morning and did not return until nighttime. But on Friday nights the entire family—Shlomo, Geula, their four sons and four daughters—sat down together for Sabbath dinner and, like so many Israelis at the dinner table, inevitably discussed the political affairs of the day. Toward the end of 1993 the hottest topic of discussion was the Oslo Agreement.

Yigal's father, Shlomo Amir, supported the peace process, insisting that Rabin be given a chance. Yigal replied angrily that Rabin was giving away the sacred Land of Israel. Haggai, the Amirs' eldest son, did not join in these exchanges. He was the mechanic of the family, a young man with skillful hands and a head for technical problems; oratory was not his forte. Geula, as usual, would follow the argument, sum it up, and declare: "Yigal is right."

It was Geula, the breadwinner, who made the decisions in the family. She was born in 1949 during a trek across Yemen to the planes that were to carry the forty-nine thousand Jews of the community, which had been cut off from the mainstream of Jewish life, out of their primitive conditions to the newly established State of Israel. Her parents named her Geula ("Redemption") because they believed they were on their way to deliverance in the Promised Land. But the reality they encountered there was a harsh one. Placed in tin huts in primitive transit camps, they froze in winter, sweltered in summer, and subsisted off the meager food rations offered by the struggling state, as it absorbed 645,000 immigrants in the first three years of its existence The Yemenite immigrants were torn between maintaining their ancient traditions of piety and blending into the modern Israeli lifestyle. Geula's father cut off his sidelocks and resolved to give his children a modern, liberal religious education. But in 1954, after the family had finally moved into a home of its own, tragedy struck. His wife fell ill and died, and emissaries of the *haredi* community came knocking on his door to offer help in the form of free schooling, room, and board for his children. The only price was relinquishing a modern way of life.

Distressed by the prospect of raising his children alone, Geula's father accepted the offer. She was sent to a school in which only religious studies—no science, no history, no literature, and certainly no foreign languages—were taught; in most of these schools the language of instruction was Yiddish, not Hebrew. At age thirteen Geula was registered by her *haredi* benefactors in a teachers' seminary whose student body was almost exclusively Sephardi young women from disadvantaged families. But Geula rebelled against their decision. She wanted to study in a different, more prestigious boarding school whose dean took few Sephardi students under his tutelage. After single-handedly arranging for a municipal scholarship, she was accepted at the Beit Ya'akov seminary and trained as a kindergarten teacher.

As a poor, orphaned girl Geula was also at the bottom of the social scale among the *haredi* community. When she was sixteen, a match was arranged for her with Shlomo Amir, another Yemenite immigrant, who studied at the elite Ponevezh Yeshiva founded by *haredi* Jews from Lithuania. A slight, gentle young man who spoke with a heavy Yemenite accent, Shlomo was seven years Geula's senior. She had hoped to find an open-minded, elegant, Ashkenazi groom, like the "Lithuanian" yeshiva boys who were modern in their outlook and impeccable in their dress. Yet Shlomo was so impressed by her that he broke his engagement to another woman and set to winning Geula's heart by writing her love letters, curling the letters like a Torah scribe and weaving biblical verses into the lines. In time Geula abandoned her dream of a modern, Ashkenazi mate and consented to the match.

Shlomo bought a small house and plot in the lower-middle-class neighborhood of Herzliya, which was populated by both Ashkenazim and Sephardim, both secular and traditional Jews. Behind the house the couple built a well-equipped kindergarten that was classified by the state as "moderately religious." Geula was a success as a teacher, and soon the list of applicants to her kindergarten grew so long that families had to register their children at birth. Most of the parents who sent their offspring to Geula's school were liberals; some were members of the Peace Now movement. Her curriculum was marked by a spirit of openness, pluralism, and tolerance, and Geula was able to relate to secular parents in a language they could understand. Rejecting the dictates of "*haredi* chic," she wore a wig, rather than the hat or head scarf preferred by many *haredi* women of her generation, and dressed in mid-length skirts and blouses with elbow-length sleeves, rather than the neck-to-ankle-covering style adopted by many of her *haredi* counterparts. Her personal lifestyle also bridged two very distant worlds. She belonged to a mixed folk dance circle, went to an exercise group, watched *Melrose Place*, followed the gossip about television stars, frequented fashionable cafés with secular women friends, and even ran for a seat on the Herzliya City Council—all rare pastimes among *haredi* women in Israel.

Shlomo Amir complemented his assertive, ambitious wife by fading into the background and letting her take center stage. Short and possessed of a soft voice, engaging smile, and wild beard that gets the better of his finely etched face, he conjured up the image of the town idler in East European Jewish folklore. Shlomo contributed modestly to the family income by working as a teacher and Torah scribe. Well versed in Jewish sources, he readily quoted from the Psalms and believed, above all, in man's insignificance before God. "Everything is in God's hands" was the fatalistic motto he aired repeatedly to his children. As a political moderate and pragmatist, he worked hard to persuade his son that the government's Oslo policy should have an opportunity to prove itself. But to Yigal's mind, there was nothing to wait for; the Oslo Agreement was an unmitigated disaster.

The prime minister had surprised Yigal Amir. Prior to the 1992 elections Rabin had been known as Mr. Security for his relatively hawkish line that Israel must not recognize or talk to the PLO, relinquish the Golan Heights, or release Palestinian political prisoners. After the results of the secret Oslo negotiations were revealed, Yigal wondered what had happened to Rabin. The very thought of surrendering any part of the whole Land of Israel and laying the foundations of a Palestinian state was sheer heresy. Amir believed that either Rabin was a callow fool who had been manipulated by the left or that he had deliberately lied to the people in presenting himself as a hawk, to win support from the moderate right. The possibility that Rabin had changed his approach to the Israeli-Arab conflict never occurred to him. In any case, Rabin's action in forfeiting parts of the Land of Israel, Yigal told his father, was strictly forbidden by the Torah.

In a conversation shortly after Oslo, Shlomo recalled, Yigal had pronounced that it might be necessary to "take Rabin down."

"Everything is in God's hands," Shlomo told his son in reply.

"But this time it's necessary to help Him," Yigal snapped.

"You're entitled to pray and hope that your prayers will be heard," Shlomo patiently instructed his son. "But you must accept the situation as it stands."

Yigal held firm. "There's a Divine Plan," he shouted, "and those who understand God's Will are obliged to help Him effect it!"

Shortly before that quarrel Yigal had read an anthology of articles by Rabbi Zvi Yehudah Kook, a philosopher and mentor of the religious settlers. It was published by two outspoken settlers, Rabbi Benny Elon and his wife, Emuna. Yigal thought that Rabbi Kook's prescriptions were too mild. But in Rabbi Elon's introduction he found an exegesis that spoke to his heart: "Contrary to the secular, activist approach, which holds that history is determined by man's actions alone, and contrary to the passive approach, which holds that Divine Will is the sole instrumentality, we must learn to fathom God's Will and 'come to the help of the Lord' [Judges 6:23] and 'act with God.' " Here was a reading he could embrace and a man willing to explicate the Divine Plan and advocate action to realize it.

The enigma of God's Will occupied Amir's thoughts. Having heard a rumor that autistic children can serve as a medium for relaying messages from the beyond, Yigal volunteered to work with them. One day, Yigal later told his fellow student Yaron Yehoshua, he had been sitting with one of the children at a computer. Yigal had asked the child whether he had been born autistic because his parents did not observe the Sabbath, and the child had directed Yigal's finger to the Hebrew letter כ for כן ("yes").

"He was obsessed by this whole business," Yaron related. "We had five conversations about it. . . . And in the end he said that he had great doubts whether the children were able to relay the Word of God."

Thus Yigal did not know precisely how God's plan for destroying the Oslo Agreement would be conveyed to him or who would tell him specifically how to "come to the help of the Lord." But he did know the basic outline of God's grand design, for the Divine Promise to the Chosen People was no secret. The technical details—how to sabotage the compromise with the Arabs; how to block the surrender of any part of the Land of Israel to foreigners; how to stop the man who was forfeiting sacred soil and endangering Jewish lives—all would come to him in God's good time. He was sure he would receive an omen. In the meantime, at one Sabbath dinner, as recounted by Shlomo, Yigal quoted the verse "act with God" and explained that its meaning was simple: Man must help God implement His Plan.

In the eyes of his friend Avshalom Weinberg, a fellow student who was arrested after the assassination and held for twelve days on suspicion of conspiring with the Amir brothers to murder released Palestinian prisoners, Yigal Amir defied classification. "He's neither black nor white," says Weinberg. "Since the murder the *haredim* have been saying that he's a religious nationalist and the religious nationalists have been saying that he's *haredi*, but he doesn't belong to either [of the camps]. He's in the middle, in the Amir camp. Once I was sitting with Yigal in a parked car, listening to the radio, when the national anthem came on the air. I stand at attention when I hear the national anthem, so I got out of the car and stood up. He turned off the radio, and I sat down again. He turned the radio on again, so I stood up again. He drove me crazy and laughed about it. He has no respect for the anthem and the flag."

Amir despaired of convincing his father of his views, but he had greater success persuading his peers. He joined a group of students who traveled on weekends to the occupied territories to witness life in the settlements for themselves. They visited the ancient synagogue in Jericho, where—even after the town had been turned over to Palestinian rule—a group of determined yeshiva students continued to study. They traveled to Gush Katif, a bloc of twelve settlements at the southern end of the Gaza Strip that remains under Israel's control. "Slowly I saw exactly the situation going on in the territories, how different it was from what people think," Amir later told his interrogators. "You live in Herzliya, which seems to you like Switzerland, I mean as though there's peace. But when you get to these places, suddenly you see that it's . . . a different country. That's just what it's like, two [completely different] countries, and neither one knows what the other is like. That's all due to the media's coverage and concealment."

Amir also began taking part in demonstrations. When students from Bar-Ilan tried to take over deserted Arab ruins on a bare mountaintop in the West Bank, he was there. In the summer of 1995, when a demonstration was organized on a bare hilltop next to the large settlement of Efrat, near Jerusalem, Amir abandoned his studies, on the eve of final exams, to join it. When he offered passive resistance, four soldiers carried him off the barren hillside. "There [in the territories], I saw an entire nation going like sheep to the slaughter," he later explained.

From a joiner Amir quickly became a leader. He wanted to imbue his fellow students with greater solidarity for the settlers, and he approached the task with vigor.

"I would talk to people. I would debate about what had to be done," he said. "But people are apathetic. . . . I decided that to arouse identification, you have to start slowly. I [said], 'Come for a Shabbat [a visit to a settlement on the Sabbath]. Not to demonstrate. Listen to a few lectures. Hear what's going on.' . . . That's how I started, going from one to the next. . . . I would walk around the university. Really, one by one. I would talk with people, persuade, argue. I have excellent powers of persuasion. Slowly I would convince people."

At first Amir made all the arrangements for these weekends—for the buses, food, housing, lectures—on his own. "The accommodations weren't the most luxurious; people slept on the floor in a large hall, boys and girls separately. At first mainly girls came, because they're always more idealistic or easier to persuade. In general, girls are far more involved in all our activities. The boys are more shallow. Career, money are more important to them. They don't have many values."

Within a few months the whole of Bar-Ilan University had heard about Yigal Amir and the group of activists that had crystallized around him. As his views became known, he drew increasingly larger groups to his Sabbath seminars. Over one weekend, 120 people traveled to the settlement of Kfar Darom in the heart of the Gaza Strip. The last weekend spent with the small Jewish community in Hebron drew five hundred participants. At each seminar Amir would organize a short tour of the settlement, a lecture on the site and its history, and discussions with right-wing politicians and rabbis.

Amir began to receive phone calls from settlers, opposition politicians, and rabbis, all promising to cover the costs if he would continue bringing students to the territories. Even the administration at Bar-Ilan offered him funding. During these weekends Amir would select a few students to cultivate. He talked with them more than with the others, gauged their reactions, decided whom to draw under his wing and whom to reject. He shared his thoughts on Rabin with his close associates, but deliberately defused their impact. "I would say: 'Rabin has to be killed,' and [then] I would smile." Predictably these announcements elicited confused reactions. "They didn't know what I meant. No one thought I would kill Rabin. Even I didn't know I would kill Rabin."

But the idea of murdering the prime minister had burned itself into his mind. He sought guidance from others in how to achieve his goal. At night, in his room, he pored over a biography of the prime minister entitled *The Rabin File*. Written by a military historian at Bar-Ilan, Uri Milstein, the book was, like its author, the subject of heated controversy. Many historians scoffed at Milstein's scholarship, but Amir decided to audit his seminar on Israeli military history. In his lectures, as in print, Milstein portrayed Rabin as a coward and a weakling, as well as an unmitigated failure as a military and political leader. Amir devoured Milstein's writings, which provided corroboration for his own devastating assessment of the prime minister, and soon recruited Milstein to his anti-Oslo campaign at Bar-Ilan. In mid-August 1995, a few months before the assassination, he invited Milstein to lecture before hundreds of Bar-Ilan students at a seminar in Jerusalem. Speaking before this supportive audience, Milstein sharply criticized Rabin, calling him a "security failure" and branding the Oslo Agreement a "big lie."*

Beyond reading Milstein's work, Yigal searched for material on the assassination of national leaders. He wasn't interested in the demented deeds of madmen; he wanted to learn from the experience of assassins driven by political motives. The model of Egyptian President Anwar al-Sadat's assassination was useless to him, for it was the work of a group of assassins, and he intended to act alone. His older brother, Haggai, and friend Dror Adani offered to help him, but Yigal did not want to endanger them; he was determined to take the full risk upon himself. "I never wanted to involve people. I would never have used my brother or anyone else. If I was going to do it, I would do it alone."

It was Haggai who told Yigal about Frederick Forsyth's thriller *The Day of the Jackal*, which was based on an attempt to assassinate Charles de Gaulle. Yigal consumed the book hungrily, fascinated by the character of the Jackal. The situation in France in the early 1960s seemed like a mirror image of what was happening in Israel, almost a dress rehearsal for the drama he was about to stage. For de Gaulle had done to France just what Rabin was doing to Israel. He had withdrawn French forces from Algeria,

---

*On November 20, 1995, Bar-Ilan University announced that Milstein would no longer be allowed to lecture on campus after he had embarrassed the university by stating in interviews that his teachings could well have helped Amir outwit the Shabak. "I gave my students, including Yigal Amir, tools to analyze a security organization and how it can ruin itself," he boasted in one interview. "With this analysis, he could have planned a way to murder the prime minister."

prompting the right to accuse him of treason. Both leaders were war heroes: de Gaulle of World War II, Rabin of the 1967 Six-Day War. Both were revered by their people as consummate patriots, though Amir, of course, thought otherwise. He identified with the French right-wing underground, the OAS, and its leader, Jean Bastien-Thiry, an officer, an intellectual, and a devout Catholic who read Christian philosophy and found in the writings of St. Thomas Aquinas the Christian equivalent of *din rodef*, the talmudic death sentence passed on Jewish informers and traitors. Three times the OAS tried to assassinate de Gaulle before he signed the agreement granting Algeria independence. All three attempts failed. The fourth, mounted a few weeks after the agreement had been signed, was Forsyth's subject in *The Day of the Jackal*. De Gaulle was saved yet again, but only a step came between him and the assassin's bullets; his wife, standing beside him, was injured.

Four times Amir tried to get within firing range of Yitzhak Rabin. He told his interrogators that he had repeatedly set out to murder Rabin but held back at the last minute, having received a "sign" that the time was not yet right. In January 1995 Rabin was scheduled to attend a ceremony at Yad Vashem, the memorial in Jerusalem to the victims of the Holocaust. Amir went to the event, but Rabin canceled. The second time Amir went to Jerusalem to target Rabin was for the Maimouna, a folk festival celebrated by Israel's Moroccan Jews on the day after Passover, April 22, 1995. Amir brought a loaded gun to Sacher Park, where Rabin was expected in the afternoon. He lost his nerve, however, and left the site. On September 11, 1995, Yigal made his way to a ceremony dedicating a new underpass along the main highway near Kfar Shmaryahu, just north of Herzliya. But he arrived too early and again lost his nerve.

On the fourth attempt, at the close of a pro-peace rally in Tel Aviv on the night of November 4, 1995, Amir surprised himself by pulling the trigger.

"It wasn't a matter of revenge, or punishment, or anger, Heaven forbid, but what would stop [the Oslo process]," he told the authors. "I thought about it a lot and understood that if I took Rabin down, that's what would stop it."

"What about the tragedy you caused your family?" he was asked.

"My considerations were that in the long run, my family would also be saved. I mean, if [the peace process] continued, my family would be ruined too. Do you understand what I'm saying? The whole country would be ruined. I thought about this for two years, and I calculated the possibilities and the risks. If I hadn't done it, I would feel much worse. My deed will be understood in the future. I saved the people of Israel from destruction."

CHAPTER 2

COLLISION

T wo worlds collided in the Kings of Israel Square in Tel Aviv on the night of November 4, 1995. Yitzhak Rabin and Yigal Amir were sons of the same modern nation and the same ancient people that had survived in dispersion for two millennia. Both were sabras, native-born Israelis, and had lived all their lives within the bounds of a small country isolated from its surroundings, struggling for its survival, dedicated to the principle of solidarity. Both cared passionately about their country's future and believed they had a prescription to shape it. Yet a sea of clashing views, myths, ideals, and aims separated them.

Yitzhak Rabin was a classic product of the Zionist revolution that began in Eastern Europe at the end of the nineteenth century and expressed its aims in Palestine during the fifty years that followed. The basic impulse of this revolution was pragmatic: to save the Jews from the ravages of anti-Semitism. Its basic prescription was political: to transfer the Jews from an inhospitable Europe to a new country of their own. Yet Zionism also saw itself as a movement of intellectual and social reform. It aspired to transform the Jews from an amorphous, dispersed "religion-civilization" into a modern sovereign nation with a common language and territory and a rational economic structure. Built into the foundations of the "Zionist idea" was a wish to rescue the Jews not only from a hostile environment but essentially from themselves. Zionism took up arms against all the putative ills of Diaspora life: insularity and conservatism; a preoccupation with religious study and ritual; and, above all, resignation in the face of recurring adversity. It offered an alternative to the enduring belief that salvation would come only from the Almighty, through the coming of the Messiah.

Zionism also rebelled against other key motifs that shaped the Jewish character. For centuries the Jews had prided themselves particularly on their differentness, on being God's "Chosen People" and thus a "people that dwells alone." But the Zionist doctrine held that the Jews had taken their differentness too far. It sought to transform them into a nation like other nations for the sake of their spiritual health as much as their physical survival. Perhaps the strongest drive behind the Zionist revolution was thus a deep thirst for normalization.

Zionism emerged at the end of a century in which European Jewry had begun to move out of its social and cultural isolation and integrate into the society around it. Two key movements during the eighteenth and nineteenth centuries had worked in tandem to bring down the physical and psychological walls of the ghetto, in which the Jews had been living for centuries. The first was the civic emancipation of the Jews in Western and Central Europe. The second was the intellectual and social movement known as the Haskalah, the Jewish Enlightenment, which flourished in Germany and Central Europe. Its thrust was the reform of Jewish education via the teaching of secular subjects such as European languages, literature, and the sciences, thus giving Jews the tools to integrate into their host societies. Exposed in this way to European culture, many Jews in Western Europe abandoned their identity altogether and assimilated into their surrounding cultures. Some even converted to Christianity to further ease their entrée into European life. But the aim of the Jewish Enlightenment was to enable the Jew to maintain his religious and ethnic identity while becoming a productive member of the modern civil state. "Be a Jew at home and a man outside" was the motto adopted by most Jews in Western and Central Europe.

The Jewish Enlightenment spread to Eastern Europe far more slowly and was initially embraced only by a thin stratum of intellectuals. The political and demographic conditions in the Russian Empire were very different from those in the West. The Jews were restricted to the Pale of Settle-ment and lacked even the most basic rights. Only in the last quarter of the nineteenth century were the limitations on their movement eased and were they allowed to study in Russian schools. They took up new occupations, gradually entered the liberal professions, and slowly penetrated the Russian intelligentsia. At the end of centuries of persecution, new horizons were opening before them, and many Jews in the Russian Empire were looking forward to full civil emancipation.

The event that abruptly shattered their optimism was the outbreak of a wave of pogroms in 1880–1881. The violence in some 160 towns and vil-lages was allowed to continue for days before the authorities intervened. When the riots were finally quelled, the government, rather than punish their perpetrators, placed new restrictions on the Jews. Devastated by the setback, the Jewish intelligentsia concluded that its faith in a future of equality in Russia had been tragically misplaced. Anti-Semitism, tacit and overt, still permeated all circles of society, and nothing the Jews could do to improve themselves would serve as a bulwark against it. "It is not the lack of higher education that is the reason for our tragedy," wrote the journalist and literary critic Moses Leib Lilienbloom, "but that we are strangers and will continue to be even if we are as full of education as a pomegranate [is with seeds]." Other assessments of the Jewish future in Europe were both apocalyptic and uncannily accurate. "Anti-Semitism will grow stronger," wrote the novelist and editor Peretz Smolenskin sixty years before the Holocaust, "and within a century will bring destruction upon the Jews of Europe."

A year after the pogroms, in a radical departure from the spirit of the Enlightenment, Leon Pinsker, a Russian Jewish physician, addressed the solution to the "Jewish problem" in purely political terms. In a pamphlet entitled *Autoemancipation*, Pinsker diagnosed anti-Semitism as a social ill-ness he termed "Judeophobia." It stemmed, he wrote, from a fear of the abnormality of Jewish life in the Diaspora. Because they lacked the stan-dard trappings of other nations—a common language, territory, and government—the Jews appeared to other peoples as a "ghostlike appari-tion," the "frightening form of one of the dead walking among the living." Since this perception and fear were irrational, it was futile to combat anti-Semitism with intellectual reasoning, as the disciples of the Enlightenment had believed. Hence it was necessary for the Jews to leave the Diaspora and live in a country of their own. Pinsker called for a Jewish national congress to unite the Jews of all lands and classes in founding that nation-state.

Autoemancipation was published in 1882 and attracted great attention in educated Jewish circles. But it was not until fifteen years later that a congress was convened, in Basle, Switzerland. It too came after a shock to Jewish optimism, this time about the future in Western Europe. This catalyst was the trial in 1895 of a French army captain, Alfred Dreyfus, an assimilated Jew who was convicted of treason on what was later exposed as trumped-up evidence. The disillusion that resulted from his court-martial rose less from the verdict itself than from the ugly outburst of a Parisian mob that coursed through the streets, shrieking, "Death to the Jews!" This flagrant expression of visceral hatred in what had been considered the most enlightened country in Europe signaled to Jews across the Continent that even total assimilation would not protect them against the ravages of "Judeophobia."

One witness to the frenzied outburst in France was Theodor Herzl, an assimilated Viennese Jewish journalist who was working in Paris as the correspondent of the liberal *Neue Freie Presse*. Herzl had written about the "Jewish problem" before the Dreyfus trial, and he had believed it could be solved by cultivating a spirit of tolerance. But the events of 1895 brought him to the same conclusion reached by Pinsker: The only solution was to settle the Jews in a sovereign state of their own. Herzl wrote up a political and financial program to translate this idea into policy. But when he sought the support of Jewish philanthropists and bankers, he was turned away empty-handed. One of his friends, a physician to whom he outlined his plan, went so far as to suggest to Herzl that he had descended into a state of dementia. Rejected in high places, Herzl decided to bring his program before the Jewish public at large and published a book entitled *The Jewish State*. The book was enthusiastically embraced by grassroots groups of Jewish nationalists that had formed in Central and Eastern Europe. Calling themselves Lovers of Zion, the groups came together at the First Zionist Congress in August 1897 and elected Herzl their leader. They established the World Zionist Organization to "establish a home for the Jewish people in Palestine secured under public law."

Like the people it came to serve, the new Zionist movement was anything but monolithic. Herzl concentrated his energies on obtaining a "charter" from Turkey for the Jews to settle in Palestine, a campaign that became known as political Zionism. But some adherents of the movement considered it improbable that European Jews would promptly flock to a desolate backwater of the decaying Ottoman Empire. Their formula for Zionism's program was to combine support for the steady settlement of Palestine with educational work in the Diaspora to prompt a Jewish cultural renaissance and create a new national Jewish consciousness. The Zionist movement proceeded along all three tracks, though the effort to gain a charter for Palestine stalled after Herzl's death in 1904.

Zionism won the support of the Eastern European Jewish intellectuals, who had become disillusioned with the promise of the Enlightenment, as well as of a remarkably broad segment of the general Jewish population. But it was far from the dominant trend in Jewish society. The Jews of Europe continued to assimilate into the societies around them or immigrated to places where they would enjoy equal rights. Toward the end of the nineteenth century there were twelve million Jews in the world, eleven million of them in Europe. Between 1882 and 1914 some three million left Eastern Europe to migrate to the Americas. Most traveled to the United States, where the principles of equal rights and the separation of church and state were enshrined in law.

In contrast with the mass movement westward, the flow of Jews to Palestine was little more than a trickle. The first wave of Jewish settlement, promoted by the Lovers of Zion societies, brought about twenty-five thousand people between 1880 and 1903. These early settlers founded the first agricultural colonies, which would have faced total ruin had they not been rescued by the philanthropy of Baron Edmond de Rothschild. The second wave (1904–1914) brought some forty thousand Jews, mostly from Russia, who had been influenced by the principles of socialism. These immigrants engaged in manual and agricultural labor in the hope of laying the foundations of a Jewish working class in Palestine. Their efforts helped establish the romantic mythology of the Zionist pioneers, which had a strong influence on generations to come. But most of them, unable to sustain themselves by their labor, left the country in despair or were expelled by the Turks in the course of World War I.

After the war Britain's Balfour Declaration and the establishment of a League of Nations mandate over Palestine rekindled faith in the viability of the Zionist endeavor. The 1920s saw two more waves of immigration that brought 100,000 Jews, laborers and agricultural pioneers, as before, but also members of the middle class who settled in the cities and founded small industries. The largest wave, 250,000 people, came during the 1930s in the form of refugees from Nazi Germany who brought much-needed capital and expanded both the business and professional classes. Yet even this dramatic influx must be seen in the broader demographic context. By 1937, of the 16 million Jews in the world, 9 million still lived in Europe, almost 4.5 million lived in the United States, and 384,000 lived in Palestine. Thus it was hard to avoid the conclusion, particularly later, after 6 million Jews had been slaughtered by the Nazis, that as an effort to rescue the Jews from persecution, Zionism was less than a resounding success.

In its parallel effort, however, to change the character and self-image of the Jew, the achievements of the Zionist revolution were far more note-worthy. Zionist newspapers, journals, pamphlets, and books, in Russian, German, Yiddish, and Hebrew, devoted enormous attention to Zionism's rejection of the Diaspora as an accident of history and a temporary aberration in which Jewish culture had become petrified. To a large degree, the Diaspora was equated with the ghetto—the dingy, overcrowded, suffocating environment that produced "puny, thin, and frail Jews" with "stooped backs and warped minds"—and with the "rabbinical culture that has shut us up in a narrow cage of [religious] laws and walls and decrees." The other enemy of the new national movement, assimilation, was equally condemned as a solution to the Jewish problem. "The emancipated [Jew] in western Europe . . . has abandoned his specifically Jewish character, yet the nations do not accept him as part of their national communities," wrote Max Nordau in his speech to the First Zionist Congress. "He flees from his Jewish fellows, because anti-Semitism has taught him, too, to be contemptuous of them, but his gentile compatriots repulse him as he attempts to associate with them."

Zionism sought to fill the vacuum between these two extremes with a renaissance of Jewish culture based on the "cult of Zion, the memories and reflections, the songs and celebrations, the signs and the symbols that bear the seal of [the Jewish homeland]," in the words of the Hebrew journalist Nahum Sokolow. It strove to create a proud, dignified, militant, "muscular" Jewry, able to work the soil and defend its land. "We national Jews must never be bookish people," said Fabius Schach, one of the early German Zionists. "Instead we must be men who relish life, who are worldly and armed to struggle for survival, to fight for their honor and for their aims." Thus the task Zionism set for itself as a national revolution was not just the political one of "taking the Jews out of the Diaspora." It was equally, and perhaps primarily, a spiritual, psychological, and cultural mission of "taking the Diaspora out of the Jews." "The Zionists know that they have taken upon themselves a task of unparalleled difficulty," Nordau wrote in 1902. "The uprooting of millions of people from different countries, peacefully and in a short time, to set them down on a different soil has never been tried before. Never has an attempt been made to turn millions of proletarians lacking skills and physical strength, shopkeepers and merchants, agents and scholars, city-dwellers cut off from Nature into farmers and shepherds, to the plow and the soil." The "new Jew," this ideal implied, would be physically strong, psychologically healthy, educated, modern, worldly, assertive, involved in the life of his country, and hence—perhaps inevitably, according to this thinking—secular.

The antireligious sentiment embedded in Zionist ideology, especially as it developed in the Palestinian Jewish community, gave rise to a new narrative that invested ancient religious symbols and elements of Jewish tradition with a new secular and national meaning. Most of the nationalist movements in Europe had employed religious motifs in forging their identities, and Zionism learned from their experience. In their schools, youth movements, and sports clubs, the secular Zionists turned the Bible, which for centuries had been regarded as the receptacle of religious law and testament of God's covenant with his "Chosen People," into a document of national history. Its divine injunctions and religious rites were completely obscured, in the new Zionist rendition, by the epic of the Hebrew nation, the saga of its warriors and kings. The prophets of Israel were sanctified not because they preached obedience to God but because some of them protested social exploitation; their religious morality was transformed into a message of "social justice." Jewish holidays were drained of their ritual content and turned into national festivals. Passover became a "festival of freedom" that marked the coming of spring. Shavuot, which for centuries had celebrated God's gift of the Torah to the Children of Israel on Mount Sinai, became a harvest festival of the "first fruits." The Song of Songs, which the rabbis had interpreted as an allegory of the love between God and his people, was read literally as erotic love poetry and drawn on as a source for folk songs and dances. In every way they could, the Zionists in Palestine, inspired by David Ben-Gurion, were determined to nationalize and secularize the ancient Book of Books. The educator Benzion Dinur summed this up in saying that Zionism would teach the Jews the "sanctification of life instead of the sanctification of God."

Toward this same end the rich history of the Jews in the Diaspora was reduced to a litany of disaster. All but erased from the new Zionist narrative were the creativity of the sages in interpreting religious law, the flowering of Jewish philosophy in the Middle Ages, the golden age of the Jews in Spain in the eleventh and twelfth centuries, and the flourishing of Jewish life in Poland from the fourteenth to the seventeenth century. In their place came a description of Diaspora history as a recurring nightmare of persecution, pogroms, blood libels, burnings, expulsions, massacres, degradation, and decline.

Zionism's appeal was based not only on the romance of its new national mythology but on its rejection of fanaticism and dogma, its stress on modernism and pragmatism, and its utter rejection of coercion. It was a lively, pluralistic movement open to socialists and the bourgeoisie, to religious believers and freethinkers, to liberals, nationalists, moderates, activists, and radicals. The one portion of Jewry that remained in active conflict with it was the majority of the Orthodox and particularly the ultra-Orthodox camp. Zionism was anathema to them on two critical counts. It defied the basic belief that God alone was entitled to redeem the Jews and return them to Zion, and it was committed to the creation of a civil, democratic state, not one ruled by religious law (halacha). "We are in [the Diaspora] for our sins . . . and must lovingly accept our sentence," wrote one representative of the rigid Orthodox line. The rabbis rejected Zionism precisely as they had rejected the Enlightenment a hundred years earlier, for they saw it as a threat to the hold of religion.

There were a few dissenters among the Orthodox from this general trend of rejection. The teachings of Rabbi Yehudah Alkalai of Serbia and Rabbi Zvi Hirsch Kalischer of Poland, precursors of the Zionist movement, provided doctrinal support for their position. Both preached that Divine Redemption would be ushered in by the voluntary return of the Jews to the Land of Israel. "The Redemption will begin with efforts by the Jews themselves," wrote Alkalai in 1843. "They must organize and unite . . . and leave the lands of exile." Kalischer expressed this idea more forcefully over thirty years before Herzl. "The Redemption of Israel, for which we long, is not to be imagined as a sudden miracle," he wrote. "Cast aside the conventional view that the Messiah will suddenly sound a blast on the great trumpet and cause all the inhabitants of the earth to tremble. On the contrary, the Redemption will begin by awakening support among the philanthropists and by gaining the consent of the nations to the gathering of some of the scattered of Israel into the Holy Land." Alkalai and Kalischer promoted plans for purchasing land in Palestine, settling Jews on it, and reviving the Hebrew language. Though vigorously assailed by most of their colleagues, they inspired groups of Orthodox pragmatists in Germany and Eastern Europe, who founded the Mizrachi movement in 1902 and officially joined the World Zionist Organization.

The members of Mizrachi were fundamentally political Zionists who opposed the secularism of Zionist culture. Nevertheless, for more than seventy years they worked hand in hand with the secularists to build and sustain the Jewish state. Their motto was "Torah and Respect," fidelity to Orthodox practice and tolerance toward other outlooks and lifestyles. So open was their movement to modern influences that its adherents even founded a number of kibbutzim, which are normally associated with socialist Zionism, and in 1948 Mizrachi supported the establishment of the State of Israel as a democracy ruled by civil law. In return, Mizrachi received from the secular Labor majority a number of concessions on the strict separation of "church" and state. Matters of personal status (marriage, divorce, and burial) remained under the control of the chief Rabbinate (as they had been under the British mandate); the Sabbath and Jewish dietary laws were observed in all government institutions, and the state educational system was divided into secular and religious streams. The full participation of these religious nationalists in the Zionist enterprise would later be praised as a historic covenant with the secular Zionist mainstream.

The rest of the Orthodox community in Palestine, ultra-Orthodox or *haredi* Jews, remained on the sidelines and stubbornly waited for Zionism to falter. The sobering tragedy of the Holocaust, which decimated the remaining Orthodox population of Europe, did induce a degree of pragmatism in part of the ultra-Orthodox camp. The Agudat Israel Party, for example, endorsed the establishment of the State of Israel and even joined successive Israeli governments. But its constituents remained convinced that the secular state was merely a fleeting episode; they believed that the moderate Mizrachi would see the error of its ways and break its covenant with the dominant Laborites. Even the sons of the secular pioneers would search for their roots and return to the "authentic" Jewish outlook. Just as the Agudat Israel Party was ruled by a council of rabbinical sages, so, in the fullness of time, the *haredim* believed, would the Jewish state be.

Decades passed, and these prophecies did not materialize. By the late 1960s it seemed clear that the Zionist movement had routed the anti-nationalist, antimodernist, narrowly religious worldview it had rebelled against less than a century earlier. The founding generation of the Jewish state had fulfilled Zionism's dream of achieving a kind of normalization. It had created a country with a democratically elected government, a powerful army, a rational (if struggling) economy, and a new Hebrew culture. Within the Israeli landscape, the much-disparaged pious, puritanical, passive "old Jew" seemed little more than a curiosity, the fading vestige of a bygone age that would soon be relegated to folklore. The old themes of mystical Redemption and the priority of religious law had been defeated by a rational, secular reality, a modern country that could take its place alongside all other nations. The revolution had triumphed, or so it appeared.

The turning point in the Zionist revolution was the 1967 Six-Day War, in which Israel defeated the combined forces of three Arab states. The victory, in which the weak prevailed against the strong and the few over the many, was perceived as something of a miracle. A generation earlier, six million blameless and defenseless Jews had been closed up in ghettos, transported in cattle cars, and systematically murdered by the Nazi genocide machine. Just over twenty years later, the soldiers of the Jewish state were able to overwhelm a far superior force in a mere six days. Euphoria swept through Israel and the Jewish world, and in its wake a seemingly antiquated but still very potent idea began to take root among a small group of religious Zionists: The messianic Redemption was finally at hand.

In purely political terms the situation Israel encountered after the 1967 war was similar to the one it had faced twenty years earlier: whether or not to subscribe to a territorial compromise that would partition Palestine, the ancient Land of Israel, between the two national movements that laid claim to it. In 1947 the circumstances had been more clear-cut. It was the United Nations that had proposed the partition of Palestine and drawn the map of the two states to be created there, Jewish and Arab, along existing demographic lines. As the Jews of Palestine had only a tenuous hold over the areas marked for the Arab state, they had little to lose by accepting the partition, even after the Palestinian nationalists had rejected it. Moreover, with tens of thousands of Holocaust survivors still languishing in displaced persons camps in Europe, the Zionist movement was under enormous pressure to fulfill its original mandate and bring them to safety in a Jewish state, however imperfect its boundaries. But when the dust had settled after the Six-Day War, the situation was strikingly different. Israel had a firm military hold over the entire Land of Israel, from the Mediterranean Sea to the Jordan River. It now had to decide whether to honor its original commitment to a territorial compromise or, if not, how to deal with the Palestinian inhabitants of the West Bank and Gaza Strip.

For a quarter of a century Israel avoided making that decision. It continued to hold on to the occupied territories but refrained from formally annexing them. It settled tens of thousands of Israelis in the disputed areas while holding out the possibility of returning them to Arab rule. Successive governments called for peace with the Arab world and simultaneously avoided it for fear of its territorial price. The nationalist right repeatedly proclaimed that it would never part with "land of the Patriarchs," the mountains of the West Bank. The secular left spoke of relinquishing the territories but only in return for a secure peace. And into this vacuum of evasion and ambivalence marched a group of "neomessianists" bent on settling the issue by dramatic means of their own.

The man largely responsible for altering the course of the Zionist revolution was Rabbi Zvi Yehudah Kook, an ascetic Orthodox rabbi who headed the Mercaz Harav ("Rabbi's Center") Yeshiva in Jerusalem beginning in 1935. An all but anonymous figure in Israel until the early 1970s, Kook imbued his students, most of whom were raised in the moderate Mizrachi movement, with a doctrine that clashed with the secular Zionist ethos. He preached that the liberation of the "land of the Patriarchs," where much of the biblical epic had been played out, was confirmation of God's intervention and a sign of the onset of the Redemption. The conquest of

Judea and Samaria, he taught, "is a determination of divine politics that no mortal politics can overcome." By bringing God into the Israeli-Arab dispute, Kook also led his students toward a new and radical position on the principle of democratic rule. "The government is illegitimate if it does not represent the desire of the people, which is Redemption by means of settling [in the territories]," he pronounced. "Those who want to withdraw from Judea and Samaria will be cursed by the Almighty. . . . We are commanded by the Torah, not by the government. For the Torah is eternal, while this government is transitory and unacceptable." Kook taught his disciples that it was their personal duty to fulfill God's vision by settling on the land, and they responded to his call with alacrity.

The "executive arm" of the Redemption, founded by Rabbi Kook's students at the end of January 1974, was called Gush Emunim ("The Bloc of the Faithful"). Its program was to bring masses of Israelis to live in the territories so as to prevent their return to non-Jewish rule. The venerable rabbi supplied the new movement with its ideological engine; the National Religious Party gave it political and logistic support. Gush Emunim's leaders, a collection of yeshiva graduates, academics, and political activists, prided themselves on being the heirs of the original Zionist pioneers and thus the new Israeli elite. They were determined to raise religion out of its disparaged role in the Zionist revolution and were prepared to sacrifice their personal ambitions and comforts to achieve their goal. They settled on remote, barren hilltops, in small clusters of trailers, to establish "facts on the ground." They also broadcast a message of deep disdain for both their nation's elected government and the Arabs among whom they had chosen to live. "For us Judea, Samaria, and the Golan [Heights] are . . . our patrimony," wrote Gershon Shafat, one of Gush Emunim's founders, in the movement's official history. "Our sovereignty over the Land of Israel is anchored in the Divine Promise, in the continuity of our presence [in the country], and in our longing for it for generations. These are what give us the exclusive right to full sovereignty and all it implies."

Two of these claims were borrowed from secular Zionism, but the most compelling one of all, the Divine Promise, was not. The members of Gush Emunim singled out one overwhelming imperative from among all the 613 biblical commandments, from Judaism's traditions and values, from all the aspirations Israelis had for their country—not least of which was peace with their neighbors after the trauma of the 1973 Yom Kippur War. That imperative was to settle the Greater Land of Israel. Their mission took on the dimensions of an obsession. They devoted themselves to pushing it to the top of Israel's agenda, thereby subordinating all other considerations to it. And to an astonishing degree they succeeded.

The first Gush Emunim settlements were founded in the West Bank in the mid-1970s against the wishes of the Labor-led governing coalition and particularly of Prime Minister Yitzhak Rabin. A former army chief of staff, Rabin did not suffer defiance gladly. But the settlers were encouraged by a mixed message coming out of the Labor establishment. On the one hand, soldiers were quickly dispatched to haul settlers off their chosen sites. On the other, a strong nostalgia for the romantic era of the early pioneers helped the Gush Emunim rebels win the sentiments of some Labor ministers and secular writers, poets, and intellectuals. Even kibbutzniks from the militantly secular far left joined the Greater Land of Israel movement, lending it a stamp of Zionist legitimacy. Gush Emunim also enjoyed the support of the political right, which had opposed the original partition of Palestine and saw the outcome of the Six-Day War as an opportunity to correct a historical mistake.

After 1977, when the right-wing Likud came to power under Prime Minister Menachem Begin, the settlement effort steamrollered forward as official government policy. No longer was it limited to small and scattered outposts held down by self-styled pioneers; whole towns were built by successive Israeli governments as fashionable suburbs. Many were populated by secular young Israelis who had felt no attachment to the "land of the Patriarchs" but were drawn into the territories by financial incentives not available within Israel. Talk of the Redemption and the Divine Promise was deliberately muted in the government's appeal for new settlers; the new slogans touted the quality of life, clean air, and breathtaking vistas. Gush Emunim was only too glad to give the settlement program an aura of mainstream respectability. Indeed, by the late 1980s even the most fervent of the messianists were ensconced in comfortable villas. The map of the West Bank changed radically. By 1992 it was dotted with 120 settlements built largely with funds that might otherwise have been channeled to Israel's decaying urban neighborhoods and neglected development towns.

The cleverness with which settlers manipulated symbols and images was particularly evident in the 1980s. The veterans of Gush Emunim, who dominated the settler lobby, had even given the occupied territories a new collective name. They called them Yesha (the Hebrew acronym for Judea, Samaria, and Gaza) and portrayed them as a kind of fantasy land of pink-roofed houses, playgrounds, and schools. Completely absent from this picture was any reference to the grim situation of the overwhelming popu-lation of the territories, the 1.5 million Arabs trapped under military occu-pation. Somehow they were expected to acquiesce mildly in the plan to turn their homeland into Greater Israel. The rabbis who championed Gush Emunim even provided a philosophical basis for this view. "The sons of Ishmael [the Muslims] among us have a right to live on the land," explained Rabbi Aviner of the settlement of Keshet. "But needless to say, this is true only on condition that they accept the Kingdom of Israel, agree that politi-cal sovereignty belongs to the People of Israel, and are prepared to be loyal and obedient citizens of the state. As Maimonides* says: 'They must not raise a head in Israel, but be submissive under [the Jews'] hand.'" When local Palestinian leaders balked at this formula, expressing their own people's desire for political independence, settler ideologists offered a simple solution. In the words of Rabbi Moshe Levinger, the leader of the Jewish settlers in Hebron, "[The Palestinian] will undoubtedly find his place in one of the Arab countries in which Arabs are the rulers." In short, submit or be driven out.

Untenable as this position may sound from a rational or moral stand-point, it gained wide currency among the religious settlers in the terri-tories. Some voices inside Gush Emunim recommended helping the Palestinians choose the option of flight by making their lives as bitter as possible. A new figure emerged in the territories at the beginning of the 1980s: the Jewish vigilante. The Likud government instituted an important change in security policy, having the army supply the settlers with arms with which to guard their own settlements as their military reserve duty. From there it was but a small step for individuals and bands of settlers to take the law into their own hands. Under the guise of performing "security operations," groups of settlers set up private militias that rampaged through Palestinian villages to take "revenge" for acts of hostility, whether actual or imagined. The Israeli authorities responded to these actions with indulgence. Time and again they found it impossible to track down the

---

*The twelfth-century Jewish physician and talmudic scholar.

vigilantes. Even when the culprits were identified, the prosecution often dropped charges before a judicial inquiry could be completed. In cases where settlers were actually tried and convicted, their sentences were often reduced or they were granted outright pardons. Reports published by the Israeli human rights organization B'Tselem and an official report issued by Israel's Ministry of Justice in 1984 clearly showed that two systems of law enforcement existed in the territories: One applied to the Palestinians; the other to the settlers. Oversight of the latter group, the official report noted, was inadequate and lax. Soon the Israeli press was referring to the hot spots of settler violence as the "Wild West Bank."

The degree to which a violent subculture had penetrated the settler community was revealed in the middle of 1984, when the Shabak uncovered a number of covert cells collectively dubbed the Jewish Underground. Composed of twenty-seven people, including prominent figures in Gush Emunim, the Underground had planned and executed a number of terrorist actions against Palestinians. The first of these operations targeted the mayors of three West Bank cities in 1980. Bombs that exploded in their booby-trapped cars severely maimed two of the mayors; one, Bassam Shaka of Nablus, had both his legs blown off. The second operation was a "raid" on the campus of the Islamic University in Hebron, during which indiscriminate gunfire resulted in the deaths of three Palestinian students. The third operation, in which members of the Underground planted bombs on Arab buses in Jerusalem, was thwarted as the devices were being set. Under interrogation some of the terrorists confessed to the most ambitious plan of all: a plot to blow up the Mosque of Omar (Dome of the Rock) on the Temple Mount in Jerusalem, to clear the way for building the Third Temple.

The exposure of the Jewish Underground focused a spotlight on the mindset of many of the settlers because its members could not be dismissed as lunatics or social misfits. To the contrary, a number of them were considered the guiding lights of settler society, and several rabbis were suspected of lending them encouragement (though none were brought up on charges). Although the members of the Underground were convicted of their crimes and sentenced to varying prison terms, the whole affair, paradoxically, actually encouraged further anti-Arab violence, because key figures on the right expressed sympathy with the terrorists. Prime Minister

Yitzhak Shamir lamented the excessive zeal of "these fine young men." Knesset members from the Likud and the National Religious Party dissociated themselves from the terrorists' actions but formed a lobby to have them pardoned. In return for expressing remorse, half the members of the Underground were indeed granted pardons by President Chaim Herzog. The double standard thus tacitly established applied not only to Jews and Arabs but to Jews living on the opposite sides of the Green Line, which divided Israel from the territories.

The Jewish Underground organized and operated during the period when Israel was withdrawing from the Sinai Peninsula, under the terms of its peace treaty with Egypt. In 1982, as the cluster of Israeli settlements built over the Egyptian border was being evacuated, the hard core of the settler movement feared that the precedent set in Sinai would weaken Israel's resolve and lead to a withdrawal from other territories occupied in 1967. The settlers read the Camp David Accords, which spoke of granting the Palestinians self-rule in the West Bank and Gaza, as an omen that obstacles were being placed in the path of the Redemption. As it turned out, the self-rule clauses of the Camp David agreement soon became a dead letter. But some of the Gush Emunim settlers decided that it was imperative to spark a crisis in the nascent peacemaking process. This was clearly one motive for the plan to blow up the Mosque of Omar.

Just over a decade later, in September 1993, when Yitzhak Rabin's government signed the Oslo Agreement, it appeared to many of the settlers that their worst fears about a withdrawal from the "land of the Patriarchs" were about to come true. Once again the notion of sabotaging the peace process took root in the darkest corners of settler society. The explosion came at dawn on February 25, 1994, when Dr. Baruch Goldstein calmly walked into the Cave of the Patriarchs in Hebron and gunned down twenty-nine Palestinians at prayer.

Like the members of the Jewish Underground, Goldstein acted out of a deep conviction that he had been chosen as an agent of the Redemption. Hebrew University Professor Ehud Sprinzak, a scholar of Jewish extremist movements, found that over a period of years—between the 1990 murder of Goldstein's ideological mentor, Rabbi Meir Kahane, and the signing of the Oslo Agreement in September 1993—"Goldstein gradually sank into a mood of messianic restiveness. His friends spoke of his growing mental turmoil in the months prior to [the massacre], of bitterness, periods of silence and isolation. Only a catastrophic act of *Kiddush ha-Shem* [self-sacrifice for the sanctification of God] and total devotion could perhaps change history and return the messianic process to its course." Goldstein, as Sprinzak described him, came to the conclusion that he, "a pure man, a physician, a pious soul with clean hands," had been chosen for the sacred mission.

Until it was appropriated by religious and political fanatics among the settlers, the notion of *Kiddush ha-Shem* had referred to the choice of death over forced conversion, particularly during the Crusades and the Spanish Inquisition. It was understood as an act of conscience and dignity, imposed on the Jew by fanatics of other faiths. It was a matter between the individual and his God that caused no harm to others. Ironically, Goldstein's distortion of this concept was quickly embraced by Jewish extremists. Extolling Goldstein as a "saint," followers of Rabbi Kahane's racist Kach movement in Kiryat Arba turned his grave into a shrine for pilgrims. They published a book entitled *Baruch ha-Gever* ("Blessed Is the Man") praising his act of "self-sacrifice" as a supreme expression of religious conviction and encouraging others to emulate it. Rabbi Elitsur Segal of the Yeshiva of the Jewish Idea in the settlement of Tapuach, a bastion of Kahane's supporters, even wrote that the rabbinical sages had never condemned the kind of suicide mission undertaken by Goldstein.

The invidious influence of Rabbi Meir Kahane's creed on the escalation of violence in the territories deserves explanation. Kahane arrived in Israel in 1971 as something of an oddity. Three years earlier he had founded the Jewish Defense League in New York as a kind of citizens' militia to protect Jews and their property from what he called the "spread of Black anti-Semitism in America." Friction between blacks and ultra-Orthodox Jews in the borough of Brooklyn had soared in that year, and the *haredi* leaders in the city welcomed his initiative. To prepare a cadre of "fighters," the JDL opened a training camp for young people in New York's Catskill Mountains and gave instruction in the use of weapons. For a year the JDL limited its activities to its original mandate, sometimes in cooperation with local authorities. But by 1972 the group's objectives had become more ambitious, and it turned its violent methods against additional targets, including Arab figures and organizations and representatives of the Soviet Union, to increase pressure for the free emigration of Soviet Jewry.

Kahane preached a line that embarrassed mainstream American Jews.

He attracted a following among *haredi* Jews in Brooklyn and Queens, but his attempts to convince his Jewish compatriots that they faced nothing short of a Holocaust in a country rife with fierce anti-Semites were rejected by the vast majority of the community. In 1971, after being convicted for making a Molotov cocktail and placed on five years' probation, he immigrated to Israel, changed the identity of "the enemy" from ubiquitous Nazis to Palestinians, and found that his vicious paranoia struck a far deeper chord in his adopted homeland. His shrill xenophobic message reminded many Jews of Hitler's rants, and again and again he was photographed in the newspapers with his face twisted into an expression of maniacal rage. Steeped in delusions of power, he announced: "When I become prime minister of Israel, many Arabs will leave of their own will and be compensated for their property. . . . All the rest I will throw out by force." Arming himself with the crudest of metaphors and playing to the basest of fears, he depicted the Arabs, all Arabs, as an "epidemic . . . germs that are poisoning us. They collaborate with the Nazis and won't leave us be until they have raped all our women and murdered all our men." In a 1985 interview he left no doubt as to how he would realize his aims. "I recognize the submachine gun's right to speak, the knife's right to speak."

With his undisguised calls to violence, Kahane at first gathered to his banner only a small group of lost souls, misfits, and Jews who had "found religion" in their teens, many of them new immigrants from the United States who had failed to find their place in Israel. But as he began to address himself to themes more familiar to Israeli ears, his following grew. "Democracy?" he declared before television cameras in 1983. "I'm no patsy. The Torah is the authority. There is a duty to [obey] a government that obeys the Torah, its laws, the Kingdom of Heaven, which is the supreme authority of the Jewish people and the government elected by it." Kahane made his greatest inroads in the ultra-Orthodox and religious nationalist communities. But his appeals did not merely reiterate established themes; they introduced new ideas that took years to germinate and then burgeoned after the Oslo Agreement.

"We face the saddest and most depressing of all decisions," he declared in 1984, "to fight fellow Jews, who, regardless of their motives, stand against Judaism, against God's decree, and, most important, therefore threaten the entire Jewish people with the collective punishment that the Almighty has warned us about. The answer lies in ridding ourselves of the extremist version of love of Jew. . . . The Rabbis of the Talmud [cited] the verse 'And thou shalt love thy fellow Jew as thyself' in order to explain why we must kill the Jew who is deserving of death in a humane way."

In 1984 Kahane ran for the Knesset at the head of the Kach Party and was elected by twenty-six thousand votes (almost enough to earn the party a second seat). His election made clear for the first time to Israeli liberals that he was a force to be reckoned with. A year later the Knesset amended the election law to bar racist parties from running for parliament, and in 1988 the Kach Party was disqualified from standing in that year's election. The decision was an important statement from a democracy increasingly concerned about the threat from within, but the change it wrought was only cosmetic. The Kach Party could no longer sit in the Knesset, but the Kach movement remained free to spread its vicious doctrine and perpetrate acts of armed assault on Arabs.

In November 1990 Meir Kahane was murdered by an Arab during a public appearance in New York. His funeral in Jerusalem was attended by an estimated fifteen thousand mourners, and he was eulogized by no less a personage than Mordechai Eliyahu, the chief rabbi of Israel, who had been his spiritual mentor. Eliyahu had also supported the convicted members of the Jewish Underground and had even founded an underground of his own, in 1951, to topple Israel's democratic government and replace it with the rule of the halacha. (He was arrested that year just hours before members of his cell were to have thrown a bomb into the Knesset.) Among others who came to pay Kahane their last respects were two ministers and a number of Knesset members from the right.

It was only after the massacre in the Cave of the Patriarchs that the Rabin government outlawed Kach and its splinter Kahane Chai ("Kahane Lives") movement, closing their offices but still not curbing their influence, which had already reached deep into the fabric of settler society. By the same token, Israel's religious establishment never acted to halt the spread of the gospel that equated murder with *Kiddush ha-Shem*, the most sinister article of faith to emerge from Israel's long and unhappy sojourn in the territories. Neither did secular Israelis demand in any concerted and sustained way that the fanaticism breeding in the territories be countered. Many Israelis preferred to view the settler violence as an inevitable part of the broad Israeli-Arab conflict that would miraculously vanish once there was peace. Even when settlers turned their wrath on Israeli soldiers, assaulting and abusing them as "Nazis," the alarm bells were quickly muted.

As the national religious settlers rose in prominence from the mid-1970s onward, the two branches of Israel's religious community began to come together. The religious lifestyle of the modern Orthodox nationalists grew more conservative, and the political leanings of the ultra-Orthodox community grew more radical until the line that distinguished them was steadily obscured.

In the *haredi* community, the hold of the aged rabbinical sages over the younger generation of their flock had weakened. As the size of the *haredi* community burgeoned, its members were becoming more involved in Israeli life and consequently more vulnerable to the competing influence of the new religious right. The Council of Torah Sages, which set policy for the *haredi* parties, held to a radical line on domestic issues but tended to be moderate on foreign affairs, including the future of the territories. Yet the affinity of the younger *haredim* for the chauvinism of the religious settlers pulled them over to the political right.

At the same time the modern Orthodox community was imbibing the fundamentalist spirit of its *haredi* counterpart. This change occurred for the most prosaic of reasons: The adherents of modern Orthodoxy had failed to train enough teachers to meet the need of the Mizrachi-style state religious schools. Because they ruled out hiring secular teachers, they were forced to employ *haredi* ones instead. And as missionaries of ultra-Orthodoxy, these educators brought the post-1967 generation closer to the stringent approach to religious practice. This process proceeded gradually, for over a generation, in the course of which mixed-gender classes were abolished and the teaching of secular subjects, such as English and the sciences, was modified in the state religious schools. Only slowly did it dawn on many modern Orthodox parents, who had been raised in a spirit of modernism and tolerance, that their children were learning a pedantic approach to ritual and an ethic of strict conformism.

In an interview published in August 1997, Yehudah Friedlander, the rector of Bar-Ilan University (which had been founded by the Mizrachi movement), cited the experience of his own family. Friedlander was particularly outraged by the emphasis being placed by teachers on the *haredi* brand of puritanism.

"Rigorous attention is paid to external etiquette, like the blanket prohibition on girls going around without socks," he said. "There is strict supervision of the length of skirts and the height of slits, with a teacher standing at the school gate and his gaze climbing up the legs of the girl students to gauge whether a slit is too high—and sending the girls home [if it is]." Fathers were barred from attending their daughters' end-of-the-school-year ceremony because it included a performance by a girls' choir. Friedlander asked indignantly, "Do they think my [sexual] desire is so potent that the voices of my daughter and her classmates would strike me as being lewd and make it impossible for me to control myself?" The principal of his son's elementary school forbade the boy to attend a summer science camp run by the Hebrew University (but eventually relented on Friedlander's insistence). Moreover, a relative of his was turned away from a state religious school because her older sister had served in the army. "A hundred years ago they didn't poke into one's [private affairs], and today they delve into every minute detail, even the most personal." Arbitrary changes in the curriculum were another target of Friedlander's ire. One Education Ministry supervisor, he revealed, had demanded that any book that had been adapted into a film be summarily removed from the reading list of the state religious schools. "I demanded a directive in writing," Friedlander said, "and asked whether this injunction included crossing the Bible off the list because of the film *The Ten Commandments.*"

The effects of this turn toward fundamentalism were felt at Bar-Ilan University itself, which was founded to serve the special needs of modern Orthodox students. At the beginning of the 1960s the student body of Bar-Ilan was 90 percent religious and 10 percent secular. By 1997 the proportion of religious students had dropped to a mere 40 percent. Two trends were reflected in this change. Bar-Ilan was no longer "religious" enough for young Orthodox Jews, and the graduates of state religious schools were turning their backs on modern scholarship in favor of yeshiva studies.

Religious Jews increasingly held similar views on another key issue: Israel's self-definition as a Jewish and a democratic state and, in the event of a clash between these principles, which of the two should take precedence. (Fifteen percent of Israel's citizens are Muslim and Christian Arabs who have called for settling this question by redefining Israel as a "state of all its citizens.") The *haredi* view on this dichotomy has consistently been that a Jewish state must, by definition, be ruled by Jewish religious law as interpreted by rabbinical scholars. Israel's secular founders had never even entertained that idea. They established the state as a democracy governed by civil law and undertook, in the Declaration of Independence, to "ensure complete equality of social and political rights to all [the state's] inhabitants irrespective of religion, race, or sex" and to "guarantee freedom of religion, conscience, language, education, and culture." But as a concession to the religious parties, they agreed to a certain blurring of the formal division between the authority of "church" and state. Thus in the early 1950s an arrangement was reached whereby matters affecting a citizen's "personal status"—essentially meaning marriage, divorce, and burial—were controlled exclusively by clerics. For Israel's Jews this means they are controlled by the Orthodox religious establishment, and over the years this arrangement has played havoc with the civil rights of countless citizens.

Because of the stranglehold of the Orthodox clerics, no Jewish Israeli, even the most confirmed atheist, can marry outside his "faith" in Israel. Should he choose to do so, he must first convert to the religion of his chosen partner or have his partner convert to Judaism. Since there is no option of civil marriage, the 20 percent of the new immigrants from the former Soviet Union who do not fit the halachic definition of being Jewish but claim no other religious affiliation are ineligible to marry in Israel at all (unless they first convert to Judaism). Neither can they be buried beside their Jewish loved ones since Israeli cemeteries are divided along sectarian lines (only recently have measures been instituted to establish "secular" cemeteries). What's more, the performance of religious conversions remains the prerogative solely of Orthodox rabbis, who require candidates to adhere to stringent standards of ritual practice before accepting them into the fold. Thousands of Israeli children who have been adopted abroad have been denied conversion to Judaism because their parents do not follow an Orthodox lifestyle. Women are categorically barred from giving testimony in the rabbinical courts that must be applied to for divorce. And these are just the most flagrant instances of official violations of common civil rights. Others are too arcane to begin to describe here.

The problems posed by these arrangements go further than personal humiliation and suffering. The blatant discrimination against the Conservative and Reform streams of Judaism, which represent the overwhelming majority of practicing Jews outside Israel, threatens to cause both an irrevocable rift with Diaspora Jewry and chaos within Israel's system of governance. Each time the Supreme Court has granted the appeals of these movements against official discrimination, the religious parties have created an uproar, threatening to leave (and possibly topple) the government if the court's ruling is honored. Recently they have even called for legislating curbs on the Supreme Court's powers or for laws making it possible to "bypass" the court's rulings when they are not to Orthodox tastes. In the past decade the friction over which system of law should prevail has grown increasingly acute, with the religious right demanding that democratic values be subordinated to Jewish law and the secular left demanding that in the absence of a formal constitution, the Knesset should at least legislate a "bill of rights."

The most sinister development in this trend has been the call by forces on the right to strip non-Jewish Israelis of equal political rights. Since the signing of the Oslo Agreement, some hard-liners have demanded that any government decision fateful to the country's future should require a "Jewish majority" to be ratified by the Knesset. The implication is that when the tally of votes is taken in parliament, those cast by the parties representing Israel's Arab citizens should simply be disqualified. Although it originated among the religious right, this demand has been echoed by leading figures in the Likud, including Benjamin Netanyahu. As a frontal attack on the principle of democratic rule, it is unquestionably the most frightening expression of the identity crisis that has been brewing in Israel since 1967.

While the outlook of Israel's religious community was growing increasingly chauvinistic and insular, secular Israel was turning outward, particularly toward the United States. Until well into the 1970s Israeli society remained culturally secluded. The Beatles were banned from touring there in the 1960s; television was not introduced until 1968. Even afterward, Israel remained a "mobilized society" in terms of its nationalist values and semi-socialist policies. But in the past generation the growth of the economy, the development of communication, and the greater mobility of Israelis exposed the public to an array of new values and lifestyles. In some sections of Israel's secular, affluent society, the rebellion against the personal sacrifice preached by the founding generation reached the point where it became fashionable to evade serving in the army. Some on the left spoke of Israel's having entered the post-Zionist era, in which it is destined to shed its institutionalized attachment to both religion and a militantly national ideology, as befits a modern, Western state.

Thus by the early 1990s it seemed that the secular and religious camps had moved so far apart, and become so inimical to each other, that they no longer shared a common language. The strains between them were viewed as political differences of opinion because they found their strongest expression in the debate over the peace process. In fact they ran much deeper, down to the very heart of the Zionist ethos. For if most of secular Israel regarded the peace process as the crowning stage of the Zionist quest to accord the Jews physical security, as a prerequisite to developing a new national and cultural life, most of the religious community perceived it as a plot to destroy Israel's essential Jewishness. Hillel Weiss, a scholar of Jewish thought at Bar-Ilan University and spokesman of the religious right, describes the peacemaking effort thus:

> The world's attempts to erase the results of the Six-Day War also gave rise to the peace process, which is not just a process of making peace between enemy countries or peoples but a mythological process of tearing down Jewish uniqueness. . . . Halting the process . . . will evidently be a great disappointment to some of the Arabs and nations that expect the accelerated secularization of the Jewish people, that is, abandoning the marks of its authentic identity that bind it, emotionally and experientially, with its land and memories.

Weiss's chief complaint, however, is not against the hostile gentile world but against the very success of the Zionist revolution. "It is actually the Jew who has turned into an anti-Semite," he says of Israel's secular majority. "[He] perceives himself as an autonomous Jewish man entitled to decide whatever he chooses. He tries to dissociate himself from being different in favor of normalcy." Mocking the secular Israeli as content to "wade off the beaches in Tel Aviv" rather than "climb up the mountain" to settle in the West Bank, Weiss continues: "The Six-Day War entangled the Zionist thirsting for normalization in the continuation of the struggle for the Land of Israel, and he doesn't want to be a part of it . . . [because it represents] the menacing link between secular Zionism and the Return to Zion as a process of religious redemption."

And here, to illustrate the yawning gap between the two camps, is how the late political science professor Yehoshafat Harkabi described the crisis awaiting Israeli society, precisely because the "continuation of the struggle for the Land of Israel" was fueled by differentness stretched to the point of chauvinism, raised irrational expectations, and was allowed to continue for so long:

> The fact that the public must recognize its political mistake [in settling in the occupied territories] and repent for it is not new in history. . . . Our political mistake was not short-lived . . . [and cannot] be erased by focusing on a particular elite and punishing it as a scapegoat. It is a *structural* error in our national culture connected with basic patterns in it. . . . Peace with the Palestinians will not bring an end to the internal debate in Israel . . . [and] a peace about whose benefit a part of the nation has doubts, or persists in seeing as wrong, cannot become established. . . . Therefore, *without almost general remorse that a misguided Zionism grew strong among us, the peace will not be stable.*

Here, then, lies the true fault line in Israeli society a century after the birth of Zionism. On one side of it stands a community that sees clericalism, messianism, and ethnocentrism as the continuation of the Zionist revolution toward a purer expression of "authentic" Jewish values. On the other stands a community that sees the rejection of modernism, pluralism, and pragmatism as a throwback to the ills that Zionism emerged to cure. These were the two worlds that collided on November 4, 1995, when one young man deluded himself that by a single act of violence he could settle the struggle between them once and for all.

CHAPTER 3

ACTION HEADQUARTERS

A t 10:00 P.M. on June 23, 1992, Israel television's Channel One announced to a tense State of Israel that a clear electoral upset had just taken place. The polls had closed an hour earlier, and as the tally of the votes streamed into the station's computers, the full significance of the evening's events began to sink in across the country. After fifteen years of languishing in opposition or being locked in an uneasy alliance with the Likud, Yitzhak Rabin's Labor Party had returned to power under extraordinary circumstances. Labor alone was in a position to form a government. Together with three smaller parties to its left—Meretz, the Democratic Front for Peace and Equality, and the Democratic Arab Party—Labor commanded a one-vote blocking majority of 61 of the Knesset's 120 seats. In building a coalition, Rabin was not obliged to cater to the demands of the religious parties, which had been members of every government since the founding of the state. He did not have to solicit the support of the Likud or the smaller Tsomet Party on the moderate right. Even if he did not choose to invite the two small Israeli Arab lists into his coalition (and he did not), as long as he was able to maintain their backing for his policies, his government stood secure. Never was the split of the Israeli public into two almost equal political camps more graphic than on the night of June 23. And never since the Six-Day War had any Israeli prime minister been in a better position to tackle the issue his country had studiously avoided: deciding the future of the occupied territories.

For seven years, between 1984 and 1990, Israel had been ruled by two National Unity governments in which Labor and the Likud had effectively neutralized each other on this very point. While the settlement of Israelis in the territories steadily proceeded, Labor blocked the possibility of annexing the West Bank and Gaza Strip. Right-wing activists prophesied that a million Jews would flow into the West Bank from the Diaspora to redress its lopsided demographic balance, predictions that were scoffed at in most circles as demented fantasies. Dire warnings from the left that the high Palestinian birthrate would turn the Jews into a minority in the Greater Land of Israel by early in the twenty-first century were repeatedly met with a shrug. Even the outbreak of the intifada, the Palestinian popular uprising, in December 1987 did not force a thorough reassessment of national policy. It did, however, have a profound influence on the thinking of Yitzhak Rabin.

As defense minister in the Likud-led National Unity government, Rabin had responded to the runaway violence in the territories by dismissing it as an outburst of anger that would be quashed quickly. He would be proved wrong. Israel's army was trained and equipped to fight other sovereign armies, not rioters armed with stones and Molotov cocktails, and the violence did not abate. After ten weeks of pitched battles in the winter of 1987–88, which evoked the struggle between David and Goliath, Rabin still had no answer to the military challenge. But he had come to some far-reaching political conclusions.

"I've learned something in the past two and a half months," the frustrated defense minister confided to a closed meeting of Labor Party colleagues in February 1988. "You can't control a million and a half Palestinians by force." Rabin did not offer any clear formula at that meeting. However, he did rule out both the political options being aired as alternatives to relinquishing the territories to Palestinian control. "Transfer [the mass expulsion of the Palestinians] has been used up till now against Jews. We can't forget that," he said. "And if we annex the territories and grant the Palestinians Israeli citizenship, they will have between twenty-five and thirty seats in the Knesset. If we don't [grant them citizenship], we will be a racist state, not a Jewish one."

Rabin also shared his thinking with the settler leadership. At the height of the intifada, when the heads of the Yesha Council were holding a hunger strike in Jerusalem to protest the government's failure to provide for their security, Rabin agreed to talk with them on condition that they would not publicize the meeting. When they gathered at his office in Tel Aviv, he gave a long speech on his plan to accord the Palestinians self-rule. Uri Ariel, the head of the Yesha Council, was astonished. "We held the hunger strike over the matter of security, and he sat and talked for twenty minutes, perhaps longer, about self-rule. . . . We concluded that we had made a mistake in not expressing our opposition to his ideas more forcefully. Perhaps the seeds of the Oslo Agreement were planted in [Rabin's mind] at that time; perhaps this was the conclusion he had drawn from the intifada. Later on I feared that Rabin had come away from that meeting with us with the impression that we were not vehemently opposed to Palestinian self-rule."

In any event, at the end of six months of punishing clashes with the Palestinians and a steady accumulation of bad press for the Israeli Army, Rabin moved a giant step away from government policy during an appearance on ABC's *Nightline*. He announced that he would be willing to enter into negotiations with the PLO if it met three basic conditions: revoking the Palestinian Covenant (which negated Israel's right to exist), accepting Security Council Resolutions 242 and 338,* and bringing all terrorist activity to a halt.

This was in fact the broad outline of the deal Yitzhak Rabin concluded with Yasser Arafat five years later, in September 1993, spelling out Israel's terms for recognizing the PLO. But first Israel had to undergo a slow and difficult process of adjusting its perceptions. As the intifada ground on month after month, sapping the IDF's strength and eroding international support for Israel, the strains within the National Unity government grew sharper until it collapsed in March 1990. For the next two years Yitzhak Shamir remained at the head of a right-wing government that dug in its heels, stepped up settlement activity, and stood determined to maintain the status quo in the territories at all costs.

But history was against Shamir, and events elsewhere would steadily influence public opinion in Israel. One after the next, the peoples of Eastern Europe turned out their authoritarian regimes. The ideologically and

---

*Passed by the Security Council after the 1967 Six-Day War, Resolution 242 called for the "withdrawal of Israel armed forces from territories occupied" in that conflict. Resolution 338 was passed toward the end of the 1973 Yom Kippur War and called for the start of negotiations "aimed at establishing a just and durable peace in the Middle East."

economically bankrupt Soviet Union dissolved into its member republics, radically changing the global geopolitical balance that had prevailed since World War II. The 1991 Gulf War also changed the political alignments in the Arab world, as the one remaining superpower built a coalition of moderate Arab states to face down Saddam Hussein's aggression against Kuwait. At the same time, a flood of hundreds of thousands of immigrants to Israel from the former Soviet Union demanded new investment capital and a change in the country's economic priorities. Yet through it all, the government remained bogged down in the historical, political, and economic anomaly of a colonialist venture in the post–Cold War world: the obstinate struggle to hold on to the Greater Land of Israel.

Finally, in October 1991, eight months after the Gulf War, the Bush administration was able to persuade Shamir's government to participate, however reluctantly, in the Madrid Peace Conference on a comprehensive solution to the Arab-Israeli conflict. Nevertheless, Shamir's rigid policy on the territories and cavalier attitude toward the Palestinians ensured that the subsequent negotiations remained fruitless. So in June 1992, when Labor and its allies achieved their electoral upset, *The New York Times* captured the new situation succinctly in writing: "The real winner was pragmatism and the big loser uncompromising ideology."

Still, when Yitzhak Rabin walked up to the Knesset podium to present his government on July 13, 1992, his countrymen were not sure what to expect. An old soldier who had led Israel to its lightning victory in 1967, Rabin had proceeded cautiously in the negotiations on an interim agreement with Egypt in the mid-1970s and had dealt harshly with the Palestinians during the intifada. He had never shown himself to be a leader of soaring vision or charisma. A shy, gruff, prudent man, he was stingy with sentiment and best known for his dry but trenchant analysis of strategic affairs. Categorized as a hard-liner on defense issues, he had been dubbed by the press as Israel's Mr. Security, and his countrymen instinctively trusted him not to lead them into any reckless adventures. Thus his reputation for toughness made his forthright call to break free of worn mythologies, mystical dreams, and self-delusion and face up to the reality of the times all the more compelling.

In the last decade of the twentieth century, the atlases, history, and geography books no longer present an up-to-date picture of the world. Walls of enmity have fallen, borders have disappeared, powers have crumbled and ideologies collapsed, states have been born, states have died, and the gates of emigration have been flung open. And it is our duty, to ourselves and to our children, to see the new world as it is now—to discern its perils, explore its prospects, and do everything possible so that the State of Israel will fit into this changing world. No longer are we necessarily "A people that dwells alone," and no longer is it true that "The whole world's against us." We must overcome the sense of isolation that has held us in its thrall for almost half a century. We must join in the international movement toward peace, reconciliation, and cooperation that is spreading over the entire globe these days—lest we be the last to remain, all alone, in the station.

Taking the first step in that journey, Rabin turned to Israel's closest neighbors, the Palestinians, in a tone of surprising empathy. No Israeli prime minister had ever addressed them directly or spoken of their leadership, the PLO, with anything more than rude contempt. Golda Meir had denied that there was any such thing as a Palestinian nation. Menachem Begin had called Yasser Arafat a "two-legged animal," and to this day Yitzhak Shamir likens him to Hitler. But Rabin that day treated the Palestinians as he had his own countrymen, inviting them to take a hard look at their own reality:

> To you, the Palestinians in the territories, I wish to say from this rostrum: We have been fated to live together on the same patch of land, in the same country. . . . One hundred years of your bloodshed and terror against us have brought you only suffering, humiliation, bereavement, and pain. You have lost thousands of your sons and daughters, and you are losing ground all the time. . . . You who have never known a single day of joy and freedom in your lives: Listen to us, if only this once. We offer you the fairest and most viable proposal from our standpoint today—autonomy, self-government— with all its advantages and limitations. You will not get everything you want. Perhaps neither will we. So once and for all, take your destiny in your hands. Do not lose this opportunity that may never

return. Take our proposal seriously, to avoid further suffering and grief, to end the shedding of tears and blood.

Finally, he addressed the settlers in the territories with words of assurance and warning:

... It is only natural that the holding of talks on [Palestinian self-rule] creates concern among those of us who have chosen to settle in Judea, Samaria, and the Gaza District. I hereby inform you that the government, by means of the IDF and the other security services, will be responsible for the security and welfare of the residents of Judea, Samaria, and the Gaza District. At the same time, however, the government will refrain from any steps and activities that would disrupt the proper conduct of peace negotiations.

Not since Egyptian President Anwar Sadat's journey to Israel fifteen years earlier had such words been heard in the Knesset. Rabin made it clear that "we do not intend to lose precious time" in getting down to the work of peacemaking, and within days he fulfilled that promise. Having announced "a change in priorities," his government blocked the massive flow of funds that the Likud had allocated for expanding the settlements in the territories. A month later Rabin released eight hundred Palestinian security prisoners, as a gesture to Palestinian public opinion, and in December 1992 an unofficial back channel was created for exploratory talks with the PLO. After nine months of secret negotiations in Norway, in August 1993 it produced the Oslo Agreement, a program for granting the Palestinians self-rule in the West Bank and Gaza Strip.

The notion of Palestinian self-rule was not an invention of the Rabin government. It had actually been agreed upon fifteen years earlier in the talks between Prime Minister Begin and President Sadat that produced the 1978 Camp David Accords. Like that original autonomy proposal, the Oslo plan was a graduated one to be carried out over a five-year interim period. It was also an open-ended blueprint, committing the sides to reach a permanent resolution of their conflict by a set date but making no reference to what the nature of that settlement was likely to be.

Nevertheless, the Israeli right responded furiously to this change in the government's attitude toward the Palestinians. "You are worse than Chamberlain," Likud Chairman Benjamin Netanyahu shouted at Foreign Minister Shimon Peres during the first Knesset debate on the agreement. The future prime minister accused the government of agreeing to the establishment of a Palestinian "bridgehead" that would be used to destroy the State of Israel. His colleague Tsachi Hanegbi went a step further by threatening that if Israel handed military positions in the West Bank town of Jericho over to members of the Palestinian police force, as called for in the initial stage of the autonomy plan, he would mobilize fifty thousand Jews to prevent it. A third Likud deputy, Yehoshua Matza, outdid them both in charging that the government was "illegitimate" because its majority was based on the votes of those "who are not of the Jewish race" (meaning the two Arab parties in the Knesset). "Should we go on merely appealing to the nation [to oppose the government], or should we try to incite the nation to revolt?" Matza cried in a meeting of the party's Knesset faction.

Rabin heard the outcry and was not deterred. On September 10, 1993, in a modest ceremony in the Prime Minister's Office, he signed a letter to Yasser Arafat officially recognizing the PLO. Three days later he shook Arafat's hand at the signing of the Oslo Agreement on the South Lawn of the White House in Washington. And for the next two years he kept the Oslo process moving forward, despite disappointments, setbacks, and crises. It was a bold policy born not of weakness or sentiment but of a sober assessment of the possible, of the bitter lessons learned during the 1980s about the limitations of military power, and of a realistic view of Israel's place in a region in flux.

From the moment the details of the Oslo Agreement had begun leaking out in Israel late in August 1993, it was clear to the political opposition that the real struggle to block the implementation of the new policy would have to be waged beyond the parliamentary arena. Within the Knesset, barring an unlikely upheaval within the Labor Party itself, the government's majority appeared to be unassailable. At first leaders of the opposition competed over who could come up with the most apocalyptic rhetoric and the most drastic appeals for action. They called for their supporters to lay siege to the Prime Minister's Office, declare a tax strike, and bring life in the country to a halt. All eyes naturally turned to the Likud, the second-largest party in Israel and head of the opposition, for initiative and leadership. But the Likud was in an embarrassing bind. Beyond being saddled with a crushing debt, which made the financing of sustained extra-parliamentary activities impractical, the party found itself in a state of internal disarray. Its young and ambitious new leader, Benjamin Netanyahu, was still in the process of establishing his supremacy over a collection of fractious and far more experienced politicians. The veterans resented his leapfrog ascent to power, which they blamed on the Likud's "shopping mall members" (enrolled, just before the party's first popular primary, by Netanyahu supporters at stands set up in shopping centers).

Worse yet, the Likud knew that it lacked foot soldiers to wage a battle for public opinion on the street. Most of its constituents were secular, lower-middle-class Israelis who backed the party's tough line on security but felt little attachment to the notion of a Greater Land of Israel. In general they identified as members of the political center and much preferred a cozy evening in front of their television sets to the rigors of raucous demonstrations. Many party stalwarts from poorer urban neighborhoods and outlying development towns resented the vast resources the Likud had invested in the territories at their expense. There were also deep divisions over the peace process, even among the party establishment. Three Likud Knesset members broke ranks and abstained in the vote on the Oslo Agreement rather than vote against it. A number of Likud mayors, who were thought to be in closest touch with the popular mood, argued for giving Palestinian autonomy a chance. As the press quoted Likud voters expressing their relief at not having to do any further military reserve duty in Gaza and advocating a wait-and-see philosophy, Netanyahu himself became so worried about the gap between his firebrand rhetoric and the feelings of his constituents that he backed away from his initial demand to hold a national referendum on the agreement.

For these reasons the leading party in the opposition was forced to rely on the fervor and organizational talents of the two sectors of the population that viewed the Oslo Agreement as a direct challenge to their ideological and religious identity: the settlers (and their national religious supporters within the Green Line) and the *haredim*, who had consistently turned out in large numbers at antigovernment demonstrations from July 1992 onward. Tactically, Likud's decision to join forces with these two exceptionally cohesive sectors of Israeli society was a wise one. For despite their relatively small numbers (the settlers, for example, constituted some 2 percent of the Israeli population), the forces that waged the extra-parliamentary battle against the Oslo process would prove to be the largest and most effective popular coalition ever to operate in the Jewish state. An umbrella organization coordinated the activities of three other bodies responsible for the planning and execution of the opposition's policy. The Joint Staff was the umbrella construct, the Political Guidance Headquarters set the goals from inside the Knesset, the Yesha Council established the operative program, and the hard, day-to-day work of implementing the antigovernment campaign was done by the Action Headquarters.

The Joint Staff was a loose coalition of grassroots protest groups that spanned the spectrum of the political right, from *haredi* to secular and from moderate to extreme. Each of its member groups was free to decide whether or not to participate in the activities it sponsored collectively. This flexible arrangement obscured the degree of legal responsibility that the Joint Staff bore for the actions of its more extreme members and made it convenient for the moderates to place blame for excesses on a small number of "hooligans." Each of these groups was funded by contributions raised in Israel and abroad, while the costs of specific joint events were subsidized by the Yesha Council.

The Political Guidance Headquarters consisted of a group of right-wing politicians who reviewed and approved the operations proposed by the Joint Staff and Yesha Council and helped defray their costs from the funds allocated to their parties by the national treasury (under the Parties' Funding Law). Its weekly meetings, held in the Knesset, were attended by permanent representatives of the four right-wing parties (the Likud, Tsomet, National Religious Party, and Moledet), who were occasionally joined by representatives of the *haredi* parties. Each party's financial contribution to the extra-parliamentary effort was proportional to its representation in the Knesset. Michael Eitan, the head of the Likud faction in the Knesset, was responsible for coordinating with the other representatives in the Political Guidance Headquarters; Likud Knesset member Tsachi Hanegbi was the liaison between the headquarters and the extra-parliamentary bodies.

The members of the Yesha Council consist of the leaders of Jewish local government in the territories (from the city and regional councils) plus

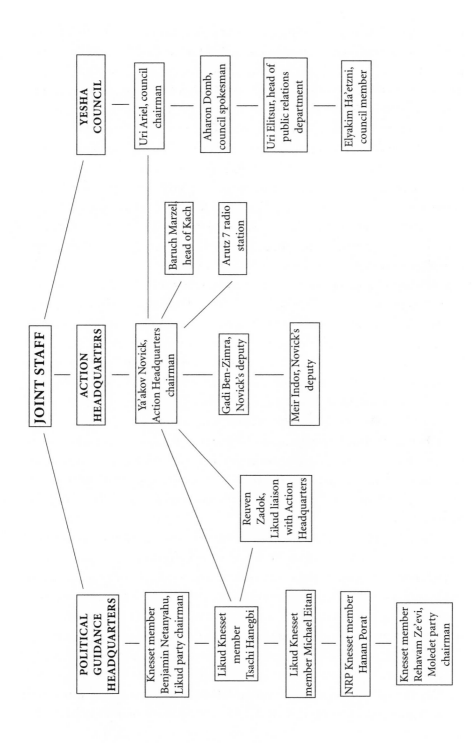

seven "representatives of the public." Founded at the end of the 1970s as an arm of Gush Emunim, the council later replaced that movement as the settlers' lobby and chief liaison with the government and the Knesset. The Yesha Council runs independent fund-raising campaigns in Israel and abroad, but its primary funding comes from each of the local councils in the territories, which in turn obtain part of their budgets from government ministries. At its discretion the Yesha Council could, and did, use the funds at its disposal to pay for the activities of both the Joint Staff and the Action Headquarters. Thus perhaps the most ironic paradox of the protest campaign was that, by circuitous channels, the Israeli government largely financed the political struggle against its own policy and prime minister.

The fourth body in this constellation, the Action Headquarters, functioned as an organizational subcontractor for the other three. A nonprofit organization originally established by one of the leaders of Gush Emunim, it excelled in its ability to activate masses of people quickly, bringing tens of thousands of demonstrators onto the streets, arranging torchlight parades, and dispatching smaller groups to hold vigils on street corners and road intersections throughout the country. Efraim Cohanim, the treasurer of the Yesha Council, credits the Action Headquarters' remarkable access to manpower to its "direct ties with yeshivas, religious seminaries for women, religious neighborhoods, and settlements." The organization was run by a small paid staff aided by volunteers drawn from these quarters. The cost of its operations—including the printing of leaflets, handbills, posters, placards, and bumper stickers, the hiring of buses to transport protesters, and other logistics for vigils and demonstrations—was largely defrayed by the Yesha Council.

The recruitment and direction of local activists were handled by a network of cells built throughout the country by the Yesha Council and Action Headquarters. Known as the Cities Headquarters, this network was responsible for mobilizing participants for local and national rallies, demonstrations, vigils, lectures, conclaves, and tours in the territories. It functioned like an organizational octopus, with small core groups of dedicated activists reaching out to hundreds of sympathizers according to specially compiled lists. In the city of Rehovot, south of Tel Aviv, for example, the head of the City Headquarters was Susie Dym, a member of the militant group known as Women in Green (established by immigrants from the United States and France). For three years Dym organized small biweekly vigils, manned tables for distributing protest literature, sent clusters of pro-testers to harass visiting left-wing politicians, plied the press with news items, sent faxes to government ministries, and traveled every month to demonstrate in Hebron.

Activities were organized along similar lines in other cities and towns. Protest vigils were posted almost every day at key intersections in four neighborhoods in Jerusalem. A permanent "protest tent" was set up at the Golani Junction, a main intersection in the Galilee. Other vigils, replete with banners, large posters, and placards, were held at major intersections throughout the country. Hard-core activists carried protest kits in their cars, ready to whip out signs and banners wherever the prime minister's cavalcade was scheduled to pass. By the summer of 1995 Yitzhak Rabin could hardly move anywhere in Israel without encountering at least a small group of protesters. His aides and bodyguards believed that the same few people were following him from place to place, but the truth was that at each appearance he was awaited by activists of the Cities Headquarters, and only a few "regulars"—mostly from the fanatic Kach and Kahane Chai movements—stubbornly dogged him.

This ramified network grew out of a number of similar constituencies that gathered at joint events and functioned largely by fax and word of mouth. The hallmark of its strategy was sheer persistence—a quality often lacking in Israeli protest movements—making its achievements all the more impressive. A few hundred determined people managed to create the impression of mass and unflagging protest throughout the State of Israel.

While it is impossible to cite exactly when the protest campaign against the Oslo Agreement turned into an incitement campaign against Prime Minister Rabin, it is clear that the idea behind the shift emanated from the Yesha Council. The opposition began its struggle to halt the peace process by sharply criticizing the government's policy but not the competence or motives of its sponsors. Admittedly, some of the language employed by the critics of the Oslo plan was caustic from the very start. "We are witnessing an act of national treachery," Tsomet Knesset member Moshe Peled announced to the press after the first sketchy details of the Oslo Agreement became known on August 30, 1993, "and in treachery the tools and rules are broken. The government has lost its legitimacy, and therefore we will not accept any decision or agreement that it signs." A few similarly drastic declarations were voiced by leading figures in the Likud. Ariel Sharon demanded that the party announce that any future Likud government would not honor the Oslo Agreement. But such statements were countered by admonitions from other party leaders, particularly Knesset members Ze'ev Benyamin ("Benny") Begin and Dan Meridor, to distinguish between the government's policy, however misguided, and the legitimate right to pursue it as long as it enjoyed a parliamentary majority. Begin even called upon the Likud to boycott a forthcoming demonstration because the ad announcing it included the sentence, "The people are up in arms against the treason of Rabin's government against the State of Israel."

At the end of 1993 the Yesha Council looked into the possibility of taking a different tack. Rather than assail the Oslo policy, the council discussed mounting a crusade to discredit Rabin personally, crush his spirit, and drive him to resign. To assess the potential of such a strategy, it invited a select group of psychologists, public opinion analysts, an advertising executive, and a public relations expert to participate in a closed, professional, and detailed discussion. The unofficial title of the agenda was How to Break Yitzhak Rabin.

"At Yesha Council staff meetings there was explicit talk of a campaign [directed] personally against the prime minister," Rabbi Yoel Bin-Nun, a member of the council, revealed after the assassination. "I heard such discussions with my own ears. To my regret, I was present in the room. The model was the late Prime Minister Begin, and the aim was to bring Rabin down by abuse, just as the left had broken Begin."

The parallel between the two leaders was patently far-fetched. Menachem Begin had abruptly resigned as prime minister in August 1983, in the middle of his second term, after gathering his aides in his office and telling them, "I cannot go on." He then withdrew to his home in Jerusalem and remained there in seclusion until his death nine years later. In all that time Begin never explained his decision to the Israeli people, leaving the matter a lingering enigma. Talk had it that he had sunk into a deep depression set off by the death of his wife, Aliza, in November 1982. But because of his enduring silence on the matter, press speculation was rife that Begin had gradually become overwhelmed by the calamitous results of the IDF's 1982 incursion into Lebanon that had snowballed into a costly war.

Touted at its start as a limited military operation to push the PLO's military forces in south Lebanon out of rocket range of Israel's northern towns and settlements, Operation Peace for Galilee expanded, incrementally, until Israel's troops had moved as far north as Beirut, laid siege to the western half of the city, and ravaged it with artillery and air strikes. The nadir of the war came in September 1982—after the PLO had withdrawn its forces from Beirut—when the Lebanese Christian Phalange militia allied with Israel secretly entered Sabra and Shatilla, two Palestinian refugee camps in West Beirut, and massacred some eight hundred civilians under the noses of Israel's troops. Reports of the slaughter brought an estimated four hundred thousand Israelis out to protest the runaway course of the war and demand an official commission of inquiry into Israel's culpability in the massacre. For months thereafter, a vigil stood guard outside the prime minister's official residence in Jerusalem. Outraged by the rising death toll of IDF soldiers, the protesters shouted "Murderer!" at Begin's windows.

During the opening days of the operation a sanguine Begin had promised the Israeli people that "the land will be peaceful for forty years." But with the Christian Phalange alliance unraveling, with Muslim guerrillas attacking the invasion force, and with Israel unable to extricate itself from what had become a political and military quagmire, it was not unreasonable to conclude that if Begin had succumbed to depression, it was due in no small part to the fiasco for which his government was responsible.

In the autumn of 1993 Yitzhak Rabin found himself in very different circumstances. He had engaged his country not in an unpopular war but in a credible bid for peace. The world applauded the Oslo Agreement and his courage in taking what he called risks for peace. The plan was certainly not a miracle cure for the Israeli-Palestinian conflict, but Rabin had never portrayed it as such. Moreover, there were signs that as a result of the understanding with the PLO, the Arab world was slowly opening its doors to Israel, leading the majority of the Israeli public to receive the Oslo plan with at least cautious optimism.* Nevertheless, the notion deliberated within the Yesha Council was the incongruous aim of "driving Rabin to resign, to get up and say, 'I cannot go on,'" as Bin-Nun described the gist of the group's discussions. "[The idea was] to break Rabin, those around him, his legitimacy, his image. There was an orderly discussion about attacking

---

*A poll published by the Guttman Institute of Applied Social Research on September 12, 1993, the day before the signing of the Oslo Agreement, showed 62 percent of Israeli Jews in favor of the plan, with 71 percent prepared to cede anywhere from a small part to all of the West Bank in return for peace agreements with the Arab states.

Rabin alone. If both [Rabin and Foreign Minister Shimon Peres] were attacked, the campaign would become diffused and Rabin would get off, because public opinion would blame Peres."

Uri Ariel, the secretary of the Yesha Council, confirmed that two discussions were devoted to exploring ways of undermining Rabin's emotional and political stability. "We asked what should be done so that Rabin, who was the dominant figure and exuded an air of self-confidence, would falter," he explained. The answers from the experts varied. Eyal Arad, the public relations expert who participated in these sessions, recommended that Rabin be singled out but attacked in "a dignified and legitimate" manner. "I wanted to portray Rabin as a man who had succumbed to [pressure from] the left," he recalled. He proposed stressing the prime minister's weakness rather than his genuine change of heart on dealing directly with the PLO. Uri Elitsur, the head of the Yesha Council's public relations department, similarly pressed for a depiction of Rabin as a dupe of the leftist elements in his government but wanted the line of attack to be "aggressive, on the border of violent." "The basis of the discussion was my assessment that Yitzhak Rabin was a 'screen' behind which forces [on the left] were operating and . . . if we succeeded in removing that 'cover,' they would fail," Elitsur later explained. "From our standpoint, it was quite legitimate to assume that if it were possible to mount a campaign [focused] on Rabin, we might be able to turn the wheel back. [Our] professional opinion was that this was legitimate and permissible, and if we were able to smear [Rabin], we should."

Others who participated in those discussions favored a bolder and more hard-hitting offensive. One of them was Elyakim Ha'etzni, a sixty-seven-year-old lawyer, founder of the Yesha Council, and former Knesset member from the defunct radical right-wing Tehiya Party. Ha'etzni lived in the settlement of Kiryat Arba and had a well-earned reputation for bluster and hyperbole. During Rabin's first term as prime minister, Ha'etzni had kindled his anger against Gush Emunim by shouting the derisive epithet "Jew boy" at Henry Kissinger, when the American secretary of state was mediating the interim agreement between Israel and Egypt in 1975.* Ha'etzni was later the mastermind behind some of the most provocative

---

*It is interesting to note that Rabin's sole reference to Gush Emunim in his 1979 autobiography, *The Rabin Memoirs*, concerns this incident. He also revealed in that account that Rabbi Kook had referred to Kissinger as "the husband of a gentile woman."

anti-Oslo bumper stickers. In November 1993 he was also one of three former Knesset members who signed an open letter calling upon soldiers and police to defy orders to evacuate settlements (should such an order ever be given) and warning that relinquishing any territory to the Palestinians would spark a civil war. In March 1995 he again tried to spur the army to revolt by telling the head of the IDF's Central Command, during a heated meeting with settlers in Hebron: "In Hitler's Germany there were officers who understood that their government was leading the German people to oblivion, and they stood up and threw down their insignia and paid for it with their lives. Here too the government is leading the people to oblivion."

Ha'etzni also harped on the alleged parallel between Rabin's government and the collaborationist Vichy regime in France during World War II. "Those loyal to the Greater Land of Israel have the right to declare a government that gives up territory as an illegal one, just as de Gaulle declared the Vichy government illegal," he proclaimed repeatedly. He even drew a direct parallel between Rabin and Vichy leader Marshal (Henri-)Philippe Pétain, saying: "We will treat [the signing of the Oslo agreements] as collaboration with the Nazis was treated in occupied France. . . . This is an act of treason, and it's unavoidable that the day will come when Rabin is tried for this act just as Pétain was." In the Yesha Council consultations he called for appending the adjective "traitor" to Rabin's name as standard usage.

When Ha'etzni was interviewed by *Village Voice* reporter Robert I. Friedman in March 1994, Friedman compared him with "the French officer who conspired to assassinate de Gaulle for ending the French occupation of Algeria." "Unless Rabin faces down fanatics like Ha'etzni," Friedman added, "Israel will be hijacked by the zealots."

The two Yesha Council consultations were, in the strictest sense, only an informal sharing of views. No vote was taken at the close of the discussions, and no specific directive was given to the Action Headquarters to target Rabin directly. But word of the meetings was brought to the Action Headquarters by a settler from Hebron who took part in both sessions. "Lots of suggestions were raised during those discussions," he reported, "and more than one participant said that there should be no qualms about portraying Rabin as a traitor." Thus the message conveyed to the Action Headquarters, however informally, was that the Yesha "establishment" favored a strategy of aiming attacks directly at the prime minister and couching them in the most savage of terms. Both tactics were gladly embraced by the Action Headquarters, thanks to the temperament of its staff.

The director of Action Headquarters, forty-two-year-old Ya'akov Novick, who ran the organization out of a dilapidated house in an Orthodox neighborhood of Jerusalem, was a prime example of the new breed of *haredi* nationalists. Novick supported his wife and eleven children on his salary from the Action Headquarters, where his greatest talent was in organizing large-scale events. At his command were three printing presses for producing posters, placards, and stickers, as well as a fleet of cars (provided by the Yesha Council) and a small army of volunteers, mostly *haredi* yeshiva students. To the police Novick was also known as a hot-tempered man who was reckless enough to threaten Jerusalem Police Chief Aryeh Amit during the dispersal of a violent demonstration near the prime minister's residence. Summoned for questioning and issued a stern warning about his behavior, Novick replied that he intended to deal with Amit within the "framework of the law." The police were not reassured. A few days later Novick was arrested for ignoring a summons to appear at police headquarters for calling a demonstration without first obtaining the required permit. He angrily complained of being persecuted as a right-wing activist, but he received no more than the same slap on the wrist meted out to many agitators at the time. No charges were brought against him, and he returned to organizing demonstrations.

Novick's deputy was Gadi Ben-Zimra, another *haredi* nationalist who lived in the West Bank settlement of Ma'aleh Levonah and studied in the Joseph Still Lives Yeshiva in Nablus under the racist Rabbi Yitzhak Ginzburg. In 1989, at the height of the intifada, Ben-Zimra participated in a "hike," along with some thirty of the yeshiva's students, through the Palestinian village of Kifl Harith. The purpose of such outings, which were encouraged by the Gush Emunim philosophy, was to show the Palestinians that the settlers were the true "lords of the land." In the course of the march a clash broke out. The local residents complained that the hikers had rampaged through their village, while the settlers held that they had been attacked without provocation and had fired in the air to ward off their assailants. One of those shots killed a thirteen-year-old Palestinian girl, and the ballistic tests showed that it had come from Ben-Zimra's gun. Charged with manslaughter, he opted for a plea bargain, was convicted of aggravated assault, and was sentenced to eight months in prison. Ben-Zimra's special talent at the Action Headquarters was mobilizing settlers and yeshiva students, and among the people he brought in was his brother, Moshe, a member of the Jewish community of Hebron.

The number three man in the Action Headquarters' hierarchy was forty-six-year-old Meir Indor, who had been a founding member of Gush Emunim. Indor is best known today as the head of a small but strident group called Victims of Arab Terror (VAT), which began demonstrating against the Israeli-Arab peace process well before the Oslo Agreement. (VAT recognized Baruch Goldstein's family as victims of Arab terror.) Indor was responsible for producing a number of provocative placards that appeared at antigovernment demonstrations. One showed Rabin in a keffieh (traditional Arab head scarf) and bore the caption "Liar." Another merged the famous photograph of Rabin shaking Arafat's hand at the signing of the Oslo Agreement with a dictionary entry defining AIDS as "a disease that sometimes results when educated people give their impulses free rein and behave irresponsibly and without due caution."

Indor's chief contribution to the incitement against Rabin, however, was being the first demonstrator to carry a placard baldly branding him a traitor. He brandished the sign at a demonstration in the northern town of Afula following a terrorist attack in April 1994. Indor had not consulted with his associates in the Action Headquarters in advance, and they did not censure him afterward. On the contrary, once the precedent had been set, Action Headquarters' placards reading RABIN IS A TRAITOR became a standard feature at vigils and demonstrations.

The fourth member of the Action Headquarters' hierarchy was the most notorious, which is undoubtedly why he took pains to keep his association with the organization secret. Thirty-nine-year-old Baruch Marzel, a veteran of Meir Kahane's Kach movement, had ample reason to remain in the shadows. Having served as Kahane's parliamentary assistant in the mid-1980s, he went on to become the most prominent Kach activist after Kahane's death. After the signing of the Oslo Agreement, Marzel declared, "We are planning to do everything we can to halt the peace process. Peres's fantasies will be washed away in a river of blood." Indicted eleven times for acts ranging from disturbing the peace to rioting, assault, and vandalism, he was described in a 1994 police intelligence report as "violent and dangerous." He drew much of his power from his close association with Rabbi Moshe Levinger, who had led the first settlers to Hebron in 1968, and was sentenced to five months' imprisonment for killing a Palestinian shop-keeper in Hebron's marketplace in 1990. In 1985, irked by the government's decision to release Palestinian prisoners, Marzel was photographed damaging Palestinian cars at an intersection in Hebron, while Levinger, armed with his rifle, provided him with cover. Marzel also had powerful supporters in the *haredi* community, including close associates of Rabbi Mordechai Eliyahu (who eulogized Kahane at his funeral in Jerusalem).

It was not until March 1994, after the Kach movement had been outlawed, that the authorities took firm steps to curb Marzel's thuggery by placing him in administrative detention* for nine months and then keeping him under house arrest for two years. Despite the limitations on his movements, however, he was a driving force behind the Action Headquarters' incitement campaign. He had long been a key figure in a group called the Hebron Headquarters, where he had learned propaganda skills that proved useful in his new capacity.

Marzel moved to Hebron, a city of eighty thousand Palestinians and some five hundred Jews, in the early 1980s and became a leading member of the local settler community. For twenty-five years the settlers there had hammered away at the claim that Hebron was a "Jewish city," and their high-profile concentration in three locations there had rendered Hebron the most celebrated hot spot in the territories. The model of Jewish vigilantism was established there, as settlers from Hebron and the adjoining settlement of Kiryat Arba periodically took "revenge" on the Muslim population by overturning stalls in the vegetable market, trashing Arab cars, and even firing at Palestinians, whose resentment at their presence and preferred treatment by the Israeli army fueled anti-Jewish attacks. After violent incidents (including the massacre of twenty-nine Palestinians in the Cave of the Patriarchs by a settler from Kiryat Arba), it was the eighty thousand Palestinian residents of the city who were invariably placed under curfew, playing havoc with the city's already depressed economy, while the settlers were allowed to pursue their lives as usual.

The bitterness generated in Hebron over thirty years appears to defy resolution. Yet the tension seemed to energize the settlers and strengthen

---

*Incarceration without trial, provided for by the 1945 Emergency Regulations issued by the British mandatory government and retained by Israel after 1948. These same regulations define "incitement" as "anything that causes hate against the government or ministers," but Israeli Jews have rarely been indicted under this law.

their resolve, turning their community into the best-organized and most generously funded settlement in the territories. During the two years between the signing of the Oslo Agreement and the murder of Prime Minister Rabin, their Hebron Headquarters brought around a million Israelis and Jewish tourists to the city for briefings on why the peace process must be halted. It organized seminars in which tens of thousands of high school, university, and yeshiva students were taught the Jewish history of Hebron. The group flooded synagogues in Israel and abroad with books and pamphlets, produced countless posters and bumper stickers with the slogan "Hebron ... once and forever," and, together with the Action Headquarters, set up a news service called A Voice from the Field.

Marzel was involved in all these activities and many more. When not engaged in acts of violence or evading capture by the police, he initiated propaganda programs, dreamed up slogans, lobbied politicians, fed items to A Voice from the Field, and organized summer camps in which settler children were indoctrinated in Kach's Arab-baiting ideology and taught to carry out vigilante actions. During the period when he was under house arrest, Marzel also remained in phone contact with Ya'akov Novick a number of times a day, discussing ideas and offering advice but always being careful to keep his involvement covert so that there would be no direct connection between the activities of the legitimate political opposition and the outlawed Kach movement. Once the right was back in power, he would become less circumspect about admitting to his connections. "Paradoxically," he revealed in an interview in October 1996, "Kach was integrated within the public bodies and the activity [against Rabin]. I won't say exactly where, because not everyone [involved in that activity] is interested in having it be known that they were working with Kach people." Efraim Cohanim, the treasurer of the Yesha Council, confirmed this relationship: "Baruch Marzel [was] the Action Headquarters of Hebron, but quietly. Novick [was] his cover."

Thus there was a traceable line between the "violent and dangerous" Kach leader Baruch Marzel and the coalition of forces that waged the anti-Rabin campaign. Each time violence marred their demonstrations, the leaders of the Likud and the Yesha Council insisted that they had tried to keep extremists at bay. Yet it was a gallery of known extremists like Ben-Zimra, Indor, and Marzel who were piloting the opposition campaign. "We all understood that if we didn't adopt very radical methods, we would lose the public," Marzel explained. "There was an understanding about this in all the circles [involved in the anti-Rabin effort]."

The liaison between the politicians and the Action Headquarters was Uri Ariel, the forty-one-year-old secretary of the Yesha Council. Known as a decisive and cool-headed pragmatist, Ariel, as head of Gush Emunim's settlement arm in the 1980s, had been personally responsible for the creation of many of the 140 settlements in the territories. A founder of Gush Emunim and an officer in the reserves, he was often seen in the corridors of power, barking out orders and trying to persuade ministers and officials to expropriate more land and budget additional resources for the settlers. He was also a man of considerable physical courage. On two occasions when demonstrations spun out of control, he personally stood in the path of a frenzied mob to block its advance. The first incident occurred at the King David Hotel in Jerusalem, where Secretary of State Warren Christopher was staying at the time, and the second took place when a crowd tried to rampage through the alleys of the walled Old City of Jerusalem following a demonstration. Had he so chosen, Ariel could have ended the Yesha Council's collaboration with the Action Headquarters, especially after a number of his colleagues warned him about the makeup of its staff and of Novick's connections with Marzel. But he heeded neither their warnings nor the frightening evidence of what the incitement was capable of spawning.

Two of Ariel's associates, Rabbi Bin-Nun and Aharon Domb, then the spokesman of the Yesha Council, were particularly concerned about the Action Headquarters' inflammatory influence on the public campaign. After the demonstration in Afula where Indor introduced the placard calling Rabin a traitor, Bin-Nun phoned Ariel and urged him to crack down on the use of incendiary language before it spread. But Ariel had his own bone to pick with the prime minister, and his reply was emphatic: "Because Rabin is ignoring us and attacking [us] at every opportunity, I'm not going to intervene."

"I wasn't prepared to be the one who threw the extremists out," Ariel later explained. "There's such a thing as the police, and they knew about the demonstrations. So my policy was let the police do it. We tried to influence what was printed on the placards, and we ourselves never produced a sign reading 'traitor' or 'murderer.' The 'traitor' placard wasn't coordinated with us in advance; it [came out of] the Action Headquarters. We spoke with them [about it], but we never gave them an ultimatum to remove the signs."

The deeper reason for the Yesha Council's reluctance to intervene was explained by Aharon Domb, who cited the daunting effect of social pressure within the settler society and an overriding desire to preserve unity within the ranks. "The settlers live in a constant state of paranoia that the whole world's against them, and this feeling leads people to the edge," he explained. "There's [a strong tendency toward] conformist thinking, and it's unacceptable to speak out against the 'camp.' Mutual criticism is not tolerated among us; you're immediately accused of supplying ammunition to those who wish us ill. . . . [So] to avoid quarreling, we turned a blind eye to the activities that sometimes went to extremes. I was strongly opposed to treating the problem this way, but I knew that I wouldn't prevail."

Even when individual members of the Yesha Council tried to bring the Action Headquarters into line, Novick rebuffed them by sneering that they were impotent without him. "*You'll* bring in money and get people onto the streets?" he said mockingly during a particularly tense meeting with some of the Yesha leaders. "We're the only ones capable of doing that!" In one confrontation, Bin-Nun recalled, he pointedly reminded Novick that only the Yesha Council was entitled to set policy. Novick's response was to laugh in his face. "They were contemptuous of the Yesha 'idlers' and 'political hacks,'" Bin-Nun said. "It was all a sham. The Yesha Executive pretended it made the decisions and directed [the campaign] when exactly the opposite was happening."

Ariel himself apparently grew uneasy about the alliance with the Action Headquarters. He feared that Novick and his people would embarrass Knesset members active in the Political Guidance Headquarters and shatter the consensus in the "national camp." "Uri knew that they would create discord," recalled one parliamentarian. "The Action Headquarters people complained to him a number of times about not being invited to [our] meetings until finally they came to the Knesset and sat down in the room without being invited." Thus Novick and Indor, who had printed the placards calling Rabin a traitor and whipped up feeling on the streets, sat with Benjamin Netanyahu and other members of the parliamentary opposition crafting the campaign.

In fact Ariel could have spared himself the effort of keeping Novick and his assistants away from the Political Guidance Headquarters; a direct connection already existed between its Likud representatives and the Action Headquarters. That link operated through two people: Knesset member Tsachi Hanegbi and Reuven Zadok, the head of the Likud Operations Division.

Hanegbi, among Netanyahu's closest and most trusted allies, was an excellent choice to work with Novick and company, if only because of his own colorful history of political and personal dirty tricks. An ardent secular nationalist, Hanegbi was raised on the classic ideology of the Israeli right. His mother, Geula Cohen, had fought in the Stern Gang (the more radical of the two prestate right-wing underground movements that practiced terrorism against the British mandatory regime). She was a founder of the settler-supported Tehiya Party, established to outflank the Likud on the right, and demonstratively walked out of Yitzhak Shamir's government to protest its attending the 1991 Madrid Peace Conference.

Cohen's son directed his political passions into less orderly outlets. As a Hebrew University student in the early 1980s, Hanegbi had earned a reputation for pugnacity as the leader of a campus group that actively sought violent confrontations with Arab students, at one point lashing out at several of them with chains. When Israel was completing its withdrawal from the Sinai Peninsula in 1982, he joined a group of fanatics who fortified themselves in a bunker in the town of Yamit and threatened to commit suicide if the pullback was not halted. His behavior did not improve when he entered the political arena. Over ten years later, when he was already a member of the Knesset, he drew a gun during an argument with a taxi driver over a parking spot. Moreover, as late as October 1995, just a few weeks before Rabin was assassinated, Hanegbi tapped into the public-address system as the prime minister was about to give a speech, cut Rabin's microphone off, and broadcast anti-government propaganda to the stunned crowd. (These incidents might have faded from public memory had Netanyahu not appointed Hanegbi to the highly respected post of justice minister in November 1996.)

In 1994 Hanegbi was Reuven Zadok's superior in the Likud's chain of association with the Action Headquarters, supervising him on a daily basis. Zadok described those contacts as follows:

The activities with the Action Headquarters took place on two levels. On the higher level, representatives of the opposition parties met [to set down] principles. Our representative there was Tsachi

Hanegbi. They discussed plans down to the level of the placards. The lower level, that of coordination, was comprised of Novick, Reuven Cohen [the head of the City Headquarters], and me as the representative of the Likud. Our meetings took place in Novick's office or mine. We would coordinate everything down to the smallest detail ... [and] after a meeting with the Action Headquarters' people, I would present a work plan and budget to the Likud Executive. Bibi [Netanyahu] participated in and addressed all the demonstrations that we initiated with the Action Headquarters.

One particularly rabid demonstration was held in Jerusalem's Zion Square on July 2, 1994, the day after PLO Chairman Yasser Arafat had arrived in the Gaza Strip to assume control over much of that area, along with the West Bank town of Jericho. One hundred thousand protesters listened as patriotic music blasted out of the loudspeakers and bands of Likud and Kach supporters plied their way through the crowd, waving flags and shouting, "Rabin is a homo!" and "Rabin is the son of a whore!" Knots of demonstrators periodically broke into chants of "Death to the Arabs," and megaphones were used to lead the chant "In blood and fire we'll drive Rabin out," as pictures of Arafat and a Palestinian flag were burned. Above a balcony of the Ron Hotel, on which the speakers positioned themselves, was a large printed sign proclaiming THE BATTLE FOR THE DEFENSE OF JERUSALEM, a motto ostensibly inspired by reports, which were denied by the government, that Arafat would be coming to the Israeli capital to pray at the Al Aqsa Mosque.* But draped from the balcony's railing was a huge banner hand-painted in blood-red letters with the visceral message that was the real crowd pleaser: DEATH TO ARAFAT. In addressing the protesters, Netanyahu issued the most apocalyptic warnings he could convey. "We are here for three reasons: Jerusalem, the Galilee, and the Negev. . . . This base murderer [Arafat] is now being carried along by the present government of Israel, which in its blindness, is allowing him to carry out the first stage of

---

*During the life of the Labor government, Yasser Arafat was in fact permitted to enter sovereign Israeli territory only once, after Rabin's murder, to pay a condolence call on the prime minister's family in Tel Aviv. He was not even invited to the ceremony marking the signing of the Jordanian-Israeli peace treaty, in October 1994, held on the border between the two countries north of the Red Sea.

his plan: the destruction of the Jewish state," he called out. The crowd repeatedly halted his speech with a chorus of *"Rabin boged!"* ("Rabin is a traitor!").

Netanyahu did not require the setting of a heated demonstration to pound away at his message that Rabin was soft on the Palestinians. Three months later, on October 19, 1994, a Hamas suicide bomber blew up a crowded bus on Dizengoff Street in Tel Aviv, killing twenty-two people and wounding dozens of others. The sight on the street was appalling. Scenes of the charred corpses in the mangled remains of the bus and of chunks of raw flesh hurled onto the upper stories of surrounding buildings plunged the country into shock and panic. Soon after the blast a visibly shaken Rabin arrived to survey the devastation personally. The bus bombing was the second spectacular reminder in less than a week of Israel's vulnerability to terrorism (a week earlier an Israeli soldier had been killed by his Hamas captors), and its shattering psychological impact called for the nation's leaders to show their mettle. Netanyahu chose it as an opportunity to make political capital. Arriving on Dizengoff Street just after the prime minister had left, he stood before television cameras and held Rabin personally responsible for the attack, charging, "The prime minister has chosen to prefer Arafat and the welfare of the residents of Gaza over the security of the residents of Israel."

Netanyahu never repeated that performance. Flayed by the press for his self-serving behavior in an hour of national crisis, he heeded the counsel of his public relations adviser to project an image of mature restraint. But he did not withdraw his forces from the fray; bands of young Likud stalwarts continued to augment the hecklers organized by the various City Headquarters. Uri Aloni, the head of the Young Likud, was ordered to form a task force whose mission was to turn Rabin's life into a nightmare. Posing as journalists to obtain information about the prime minister's schedule, Aloni and his crew lay in wait at Rabin's engagements to rattle him with shouts of "Traitor!" and "Murderer!" "We wanted to crush his self-confidence," Aloni later boasted, "and each time I saw his face redden when we put him under pressure, I knew we had succeeded."

For his part, Rabin did his best to show that they had not. "I feel contempt for them," he said of the hecklers and chanters in a television interview in August 1994. "Who are they? Have they fought in combat as I have?

Are they responsible for the State of Israel's achievements in the realm of security, as I am?" The dismissive response was typical of Rabin, who was generally poor at hiding his disdain for his detractors. Although he did not know that the Yesha Council had discussed a strategy for driving him to despair, he intuitively sensed a guiding principle behind the relentless harassment. "They're on the prowl for me; they want to break me," he told two journalists from *Yediot Ahronot* in an interview published on November 19, 1993, two months after the signing of the Oslo accord. "It's not by chance that they call me a traitor. [But] I'm no Begin; it won't do them any good."

Time and again Rabin was advised to soothe the settlers' anger by displaying more understanding for their anxieties. But he perceived them not as hapless victims of the peace process but as formidable ideological foes. He also had a long, mutual account with Gush Emunim, going back to the days of his first prime ministry in the mid-1970s. In a series of meetings with settler leaders in 1974, he told them that "settlements do not determine the borders of the state" and that "[we must not allow] settlement in areas densely populated by Arabs." Few on the right forgot or forgave his bitter characterization of Gush Emunim in 1975 as a "dangerous political movement."

When the settlers went back on the attack in 1993, Rabin struck a pose of impassivity. From time to time, however, his temper betrayed him, and he lashed out at his tormentors with stinging rebukes of his own. Irked by a twenty-day hunger strike and subsequent demonstration by settlers from the Golan Heights, he mocked the protesters by sneering, "They can spin in their demonstrations like propellers. It won't do them any good." He once referred to the West Bank settlers as "crybabies" and "not real Israelis" and took another much-resented swipe at them after the signing of the Oslo II Agreement (which turned over 27 percent of the West Bank to autonomous Palestinian rule) by telling American Jewish leaders that Israel had "chosen Jewish values over real estate." After the Zion Square demonstration in July 1994, he went so far as to charge that there was "an evil, wicked circle of partnership between the Hamas murderers and the [Israeli] radical right" against the Oslo Agreement, prompting a howl of outrage from the opposition.

Surprisingly, Rabin never considered a possible structural connection between the hecklers who dogged him and the opposition parties or the Yesha Council. (It was not until the beginning of 1995 that the Shabak traced the ties among the Political Guidance Headquarters, the Yesha Council, and the Action Headquarters.) Even when the details of these links were brought to his attention, Rabin brushed the information aside, saying, "They don't bother me." He continued to receive the leaders of the Yesha Council, with whom he had worked closely as defense minister during the intifada, and they continued to keep up the appearance of a respectful attitude toward him. Only in the summer of 1995, as the conclusion of the negotiations on the Oslo II Agreement drew near, did the Shabak approach Rabin to express concern for his safety after the Yesha Council had published a "personal warning to all those who have a hand in bringing additional grief, destruction, and loss on Israel." "You will bear personal responsibility," the communiqué read, "each man according to his position and his degree of involvement. You will not be absolved of the disgrace." Among the people to whom the warning was directly addressed was Prime Minister Yitzhak Rabin.

Taking its cue from Rabin, perhaps, the Israeli media also failed to pay appropriate attention to the fury of the incitement and its possible consequences. Demonstrations were regularly covered by Israel's two main television channels. Yet the most shocking clips of the crowd were filmed by foreign news organizations and aired abroad, while the Israeli crews usually stood at the edges of the crowds and missed the agitation within. It is also possible that reporters and their editors heeded requests from the Prime Minister's Bureau not to amplify the incitement by broadcasting it. There's little question that the media in general favored Rabin's policy of compromise with the Palestinians and may, wittingly or otherwise, have skewed their coverage accordingly. Or it may be that the sheer persistence of the demonstrators' hounding of Rabin prompted editors to reject the story in favor of fresher and thus more enticing material.

The demonstrators wanted as much coverage as possible and regularly complained at being shut out by the press. To win a spot on the evening news, Women in Green took to producing street theater that portrayed Palestinians in the crudest cultural stereotypes. After airing a few such

pieces, news editors became wary of events obviously staged for their benefit. One way or another, by paying only perfunctory attention to the persistent vilification of the prime minister, the mainstream media helped the
Israeli public ignore the phenomenon.

At the same time, the media outlets of the right wing were actively
engaged in spreading the incitement. One was the pirate radio station
Arutz 7 ("Band 7"), which broadcast from a ship its owners claimed to be
anchored outside Israel's territorial waters (though Israeli naval radar
photographs reported that the craft routinely anchored a mile off the port
city of Ashdod) and from a studio in the West Bank. Established in 1988 as
a counterweight to what rightists have long decried as the "leftist Mafia"
dominating the Israeli media, Arutz 7 patterned its operation on the Voice
of Peace, another pirate station that had broadcast from beyond the twelve-
mile limit. Neither station was licensed by the Israeli government, making
its broadcasts illegal. Both proved to be highly popular, though to very different audiences. The Voice of Peace drew a following of secular young
Israelis with its popular music programs. Arutz 7's regular listeners (polled
as 7.2 percent of the national audience in February 1993) were for the most
part settlers, other religious nationalists, and *haredim*. Its fare consisted of
exclusively Israeli folk music, programs on religion and Jewish tradition,
rabbinical sermons and lessons, and right-wing political commentary.

After the election of the Labor government in June 1992, the station
inaugurated a special news division. It was directed by Haggai Segal, a
member of the Jewish Underground who had been sentenced to three
years' imprisonment for his involvement in booby-trapping the cars of
three West Bank mayors. Like A Voice from the Field, Arutz 7 served as an
alternative source of news with an antigovernment spin, supplemented by
commentary and interviews with leading right-wing politicians. Ariel
Sharon, Yitzhak Shamir, and Rehavam Ze'evi (of the ultra-right Moledet
Party) were frequently tapped as analysts. Netanyahu lent the station his
high-profile support in August 1995 by leading a small delegation of opposition Knesset members out to the ship in a show of solidarity after the
Communications Ministry had impounded its transmission equipment.
(Arutz 7 purchased new equipment and was back on the air a week later.)

An efficient tool for promoting the activities sponsored by the Yesha
Council, the Joint Staff, and the Action Headquarters, Arutz 7 was also a

prime channel of venomous incitement against Rabin and his government. One of its more popular broadcasters, the television director Adir Zik, regularly and unabashedly called Rabin a traitor during his weekly program, *Adir's Fireworks*. Defining a "traitor" as one who "jettisons his loyalty, a man who works against his comrades, against his people, or against his country and aids the enemy," Zik added slyly: "So what do you have to say about Rabin?" When he wasn't bashing the prime minister directly, Zik focused on the government. "This is a government out to destroy Judaism," he charged in one of his more memorable harangues. "They're eradicating everything Jewish. . . . This government lacks legitimacy. It is a government that has betrayed me, my ideas, and my principles with its [one-vote] majority and a few traitors."

Like Israel's state-run radio stations, Arutz 7 gave its audience an opportunity to express their views on the air. But unlike the licensed stations, it did not intervene when callers advocated violence. Speaking in American-accented Hebrew, one caller, who was careful to identify himself only by his first name, delivered the following plaint on January 24, 1995, almost a year after the Kach and Kahane Chai movements had been banned:

> The right here is impotent. Each time I come to another demonstration in Jerusalem, I leave frustrated. What good does it do to stand for half an hour with a few thousand people, sometimes hear a speech by Netanyahu, and go quietly home? No wonder Rabin says these demonstrations don't move him. If thousands of people were to break into [the Prime Minister's Office], grab Rabin, and drag him out, that would move him! In the 1970s I was a member of the Jewish Defense League in New York, led by Meir Kahane, may the Almighty avenge his blood. We weren't ashamed to use methods like that. . . . It's time to remove the gloves and deal with Rabin properly.

When a photomontage of Rabin in an SS uniform circulated at a mass demonstration in Jerusalem early in October 1995, many on the right felt that the crusade against the prime minister had gone too far. Arutz 7, however, broadcast the comments of the seventy-four-year-old novelist Moshe Shamir, an Israel Prize laureate:

No, Yitzhak Rabin is not a Nazi officer, as he was portrayed in that picture. But Rabin is a collaborator with thousands of Nazi officers he is bringing into the heart of the Land of Israel, turning it over to them under the command of their leader, Adolf Arafat, in order to advance the plan of destroying the Jewish people. . . . The government is committing another Nazi-Bolshevik act when it spreads slander about the national camp—as though [it] were planning to harm the prime minister [physically]—in order to lay the groundwork for its repression. This blood libel is a Nazi act in the fullest sense of the word. The national camp must close ranks to topple the government of collaborators led by Rabin.

The owners of Arutz 7 acted against these excesses only after the damage had been done. Immediately after the assassination they worried that they would be held accountable for incitement and took the station off the air. It resumed broadcasting after the official seven-day mourning period but initially limited itself to music programs. As it gradually returned to regular programming, Arutz 7's broadcasters remained far more circumspect in their use of language.

The same cannot be said of the *haredi* weekly *Hashavua* ("The Week"), which was used by its publisher, Asher Zuckerman, to wage a vicious crusade against Rabin. The magazine regularly called the prime minister "a *Kapo*," "an anti-Semite," "ruthless," and "a pathological liar." Emboldened by the lack of objection to such epithets, the weekly (which is read by close to 20 percent of Israel's *haredi* community) published a symposium on the question of whether Yitzhak Rabin deserved to die and the appropriate means of executing him. It also described the prime minister as mentally ill and suffering from alcoholism. "Senior figures," a lead article stated in March 1995, "report signs of a deterioration in the emotional condition of Prime Minister Yitzhak Rabin." The magazine even regularly reported that Rabin had been hospitalized for mental instability.

In March 1994 *Hashavua* published an interview about Rabin's mental health with Neta Shuv, a clinical psychologist who knew Rabin only from afar. "The diagnosis of Rabin, arrived at from the map of his personality and behavior, is that he is schizoid," she pronounced. "We're talking about a man cut off from reality. His understanding of others is very flawed, as is his judgment."

"Is this related to his drinking?" the *Hashavua* reporter asked, invoking rumors that had been spread to tarnish Rabin's image during the 1992 election campaign.

"The schizoid becomes addicted to things."

"Are people of Rabin's type placed in mental hospitals?"

"In cases of a worsening of the condition, yes."

"Throughout the world, do we often come upon leaders suffering from emotional problems?"

"Here and there, there are such cases."

"Surely Hitler, may his name be blotted out, was one?"

"Definitely. There were also others."

"Given an emotional map like Rabin's, could he go so far as to dismantle the state?"

"Yes," Dr. Shuv replied without reservation.

Hashavua also printed interviews with right-wing politicians that cast aspersions on Rabin's loyalty to his country and even suggested that he was a "member of a satanic cult." Ariel Sharon spoke of the Oslo peace policy as "graver than what Pétain did," adding, "It's hard to use the word 'treason' when speaking of Jews, but there's no substantive difference. They're sitting with Arafat and planning how to deceive the citizens of Israel." Netanyahu was apparently leery about being published in *Hashavua* in a question-and-answer format, but at the end of March 1995 Zuckerman wrote of a talk he'd had with the Likud's chairman in an article entitled "Bibi Speaks." "Rabin charges that he's called a terrible word, 'murderer,'" says Netanyahu in Zuckerman's rendition. "But with all the unpleasantness [implied by such terms], he has no reason to complain. Whoever is aware that the fetters he places on soldiers' hands have led directly to the murder of a large number of Jews has difficulty refraining from use of the terrible word 'murder.'"

By the critical summer of 1995 *Hashavua* had cast aside all caution. An editorial published at the end of August 1995 charged that Rabin and Peres "are leading the state and its citizens to annihilation and must be placed before a firing squad." And in the issue published on Friday, November 3, 1995, the day before the assassination, Zuckerman (under the pen name A. Barak) offered his readers the forecast that "The day will come when the Israeli public will bring Rabin and Peres into court with the alternatives being the gallows or the insane asylum. This nefarious duo has either lost its mind or is flagrantly treasonous."

Like the broadcasters on Arutz 7, Zuckerman and his magazine were never called to account as purveyors of incitement. Unlike the radio station, however, even after the assassination *Hashavua* continued to slander the new prime minister, Shimon Peres, claiming, inter alia, that he had been convicted of bribery and black-market dealings. Then, after Peres had been defeated in the May 1996 election, it trained its sights on a new and no less eminent figure, Supreme Court Chief Justice Aharon Barak, deriding him as a threat to democracy in a piece headlined THE TARGET: BARAK. "The shells must not be scattered," the article advised. "The battle must be focused on this man who is highly dangerous to democracy and liberty." Upon receiving death threats, the chief justice was added to the list of Israeli leaders protected by bodyguards around the clock. Attorney General Michael Ben-Ya'ir contemplated but ruled out taking legal measures against *Hashavua*, citing, paradoxically, both the importance of freedom of speech and the fear that a trial would give people like Zuckerman an additional platform from which to disseminate their views.

What did spur the legal authorities into action was a series of demonstrations that forced them to address the question of when incitement becomes sedition. In August 1995, as negotiations with the Palestinians on self-rule in the West Bank shifted into high gear, the antigovernment campaign escalated when an energetic group of militants, called Zo Artzenu ("This Is Our Country"), went into action. Sensing that the Yesha Council was tiring, the leaders of the new movement forged a daring strategy that had never before been tested in Israel: to win over the public and thwart the government through civil disobedience.

Two of the three leaders of Zo Artzenu were relative unknowns. Born into a family that had emigrated from Australia, thirty-five-year-old Moshe Feiglin was a reserve officer in the Engineering Corps, owned a computer company, and lived in the prosperous settlement of Karnei Shomron. His neighbor and deputy, Shmuel Sackett, was a native of New York who had settled in Israel in 1990 and was active in Kahane Chai while working as a marketing manager for the electronics division of the Israel Postal

Authority. The two joined with Rabbi Benny Elon, the soft-spoken son of a retired Supreme Court justice who lived in the West Bank settlement of Beit El and headed the Beit Orot Yeshiva (set in the heart of a Palestinian neighborhood of Jerusalem in a building purchased by Dr. Irving Moskowitz of Miami). Elon was the only one of the three familiar to the Israeli public from the ongoing demonstration he had led outside Orient House, the center of Palestinian activity in Jerusalem. He was also an out-spoken champion of the argument that a "Jewish majority" be required to ratify key decisions in the Knesset. All three men based their call for civil disobedience on the claim that the government was "illegitimate" because it rested on the votes of Israeli Arabs. "Hitler also rose to power in democratic elections," Feiglin told the daily *Ha'aretz*, "[and] Rabin is the *Judenrat* putting us on the trains."

Zo Artzenu's operative program was frightfully simple: to cripple the government by bringing life in Israel to a halt. In its first major demonstration, held on August 8, 1995, an estimated seven thousand demonstrators—yeshiva students, settlers, and their supporters inside the Green Line—blocked some eighty road junctions at the height of the after-noon rush hour. Two weeks later Zo Artzenu organized a second action to block the main Jerusalem–Tel Aviv highway and lay siege to the Prime Min-ister's Office. As the police halted the buses carrying demonstrators to the capital, Feiglin directed his "troops" from a rented helicopter and issued regular reports to Arutz 7. "The police are trying to stop us," he declared. "They're not interested in the law, and we won't place any limitations on ourselves either." In the course of that day's operations Jerusalem Police Chief Aryeh Amit came under bodily assault from a crowd of rioting protesters near the Knesset. Yet when thirty people trying to block traffic in central Jerusalem were injured in a clash with police, Zo Artzenu com-plained bitterly of police brutality, insisting on its right to disrupt life in the country. Feiglin justified his refusal to apply for the police permits required for demonstrations by proclaiming that "the government is illegitimate and has lost its authority to demand our obedience."

Zo Artzenu also devised a plan to challenge the government on the set-tlers' home turf by organizing groups to seize and occupy land adjoining fifteen West Bank settlements. When soldiers were sent to evacuate these makeshift encampments, Women in Green, a kindred movement that encouraged its members to bring their children to demonstrations, led the passive resistance. The tactic backfired. News clips of a mother sitting obstinately on the ground clutching her infant and of toddlers wailing in terror as their parents were carried off to detention drained whatever public support for Zo Artzenu remained. Worst of all, the land-grab operation ended in tragedy when a Palestinian counterdemonstrator who rushed the encampment outside Beit El was shot dead by a settler.

Zo Artzenu's civil disobedience campaign lasted a little more than a month and attracted considerable media coverage. But its bid for mass support foundered. The movement's call on the public to display such innocuous signs of solidarity as turning on headlights, honking horns, and blacking out their homes at an appointed hour, to show the vast scope of antigovernment feeling, won only a marginal response. Zo Artzenu even failed to garner the backing of the Yesha Council, which continued to exercise the strongest influence over the settler community. In a bitter debate on how to relate to the civil disobedience campaign, Uri Elitsur, the head of the council's public relations division, argued for joining it. But sensing the strategy's negative impact on broad public opinion, Uri Ariel came out firmly against the descent toward anarchy, and in the end his position won the day.

Thus, despite assistance from the ever-resourceful Action Headquarters, Zo Artzenu was a short-lived phenomenon. It had its moment of fame but misjudged the essentially conservative instincts of the Israeli public. The leaders of the right-wing establishment, from political parties to the settlers' lobby itself, tended to view civil disobedience more as a threat to their standing than a boon to their ideological cause. By mid-September, therefore, the leadership of the antigovernment campaign reverted to the institutionalized channels of Yesha Council and Action Headquarters, working in tandem with the opposition leaders in the Knesset.

It is noteworthy that of all the forces involved in the two-year effort to delegitimize the Israeli government and its prime minister, only Zo Artzenu's leaders were brought to trial. Feiglin, Sackett, and Elon were indicted on a list of charges, including sedition, suborning to commit crimes, and attempting to suborn to commit armed extortion. Because of the gravity of these charges (this was the first sedition indictment ever brought against Jewish citizens of Israel), the defendants were tried by a special three-judge panel of the Jerusalem Magistrate's Court.* The prosecution introduced into evidence publications distributed by Zo Artzenu. One of these, entitled *In the Long Run*, openly proclaimed the movement's aim as breaking the "obedience barrier" in the public's attitude toward the government. Another directed protesters not to bring their identity cards (which must be carried by citizens at all times) to demonstrations and to refuse to identify themselves or answer any other questions while under detention.

Feiglin and Sackett tried to belittle the import of these publications by calling them "a gimmick to draw people to demonstrations." The court took a far less clement view, and Feiglin and Sackett were convicted, in the summer of 1997, of fomenting rebellion and issuing seditious publications. The court ruled that the pamphlets promoted "a systematic violation of the law" and denied "the legitimacy of the regime based on a belief that it is permissible to violate the law in order to bring the government to capitulation." The publications, the court ruled, contained "seditious messages" designed to "force the government to change its policy, under threat, and attack the government's legitimacy by means of illegal acts." In issuing these leaflets, the judges wrote, the defendants had "posed a threat . . . to the fabric of public life and social stability . . . out of a desire to topple the government and create a threat to the stability of the state."

The conviction of Feiglin and Sackett was the only instance during, or after, the two years of persistent incitement against Rabin and his ministers in which the Israeli legal system addressed the question of when radical protest becomes rebellion against the state. Zo Artzenu's leaders were certainly not alone in carrying out actions against the government. But they suffered from two cardinal drawbacks. Like the members of Kach and Kahane Chai, they lacked the support of any element within the political establishment. They also erred in spelling out their program, while more sophisticated groups were careful to deliver their messages in veiled language.

The more cautious approach was adopted by Knesset member Ariel Sharon, for one, in an article published in the Likud journal *Hayarden* ("The Jordan") in June 1995. Sharon was careful to calibrate the vehe-

---

*The indictment against Elon was placed in abeyance in June 1996, after he was elected to the Knesset on the ticket of the Moledet Party and acquired parliamentary immunity. In January 1998 the case against him was dropped altogether.

mence of his attacks as circumstances dictated. Beginning soon after the 1992 election, he characterized the government's policies as "dangerous" and compared them with those of the British government's 1939 White Paper (which heavily restricted Jewish immigration and land acquisition in Palestine). Later, after others had raised the rhetorical stakes, he likened the government to the *Judenräte* in Nazi-occupied Europe. His *Hayarden* article accused the government of collaboration with the enemy, stating that it was "turning settlers over to the armed bands of Palestinians"—a patent distortion of the terms of the Oslo Agreement. With this incendiary portrayal of the situation Sharon tried to stir his party colleagues out of their lackadaisical attitude: "We have voted no-confidence [in the government] countless times. They keep going on. Hence the time has come to stop talking. The time has come to act. . . ." Precisely how he intended to act was prudently left up to the reader's imagination.

The clause of the Penal Code under which Feiglin and Sackett were convicted describes sedition, inter alia, as "causing hatred, contempt, or disloyalty toward the ruling authorities." By this standard, any number of people involved in the incitement could well have been charged with the same crime. They were not. Even in the case of Feiglin and Sackett, the court sent a mixed message by passing a mild sentence of six months' imprisonment and a year on probation on Feiglin and four months' imprisonment and eight months' probation on Sackett. The judges further suggested that the two might be permitted to serve their sentences by performing acts of public service, rather than spend them behind bars. The sentencing was announced two years after Rabin's murder, when the results of such inflammatory language were no longer a matter of conjecture. But in Israel's overheated political climate, the lethal potential of words was still not taken seriously.

Twice in the course of October 1995, the month before the assassination, individual demonstrators who managed to get near the prime minister tried to assault him.

The first incident occurred on October 5, 1995, at the annual memorial ceremony for the fallen of the Yom Kippur War held at the Mount Herzl military cemetery in Jerusalem. There were no protesters present to mar the solemnity of the occasion. But suddenly, as Rabin was walking from his car to the site of the ceremony, a man flew out of the crowd, shrieking, "Murderer! Traitor!" He got within a few steps of the prime minister before being blocked. Standing beside Rabin that morning was the head of the Shabak, Carmi Gillon. As he witnessed this breach of the prime minister's security cordon, Gillon was convinced that the public warning he was about to issue on the possible consequences of the ongoing incitement was not in the least exaggerated.

The second instance, cited in the Prologue, was on October 10 at an open-air event for English-speaking immigrants held at the Wingate Institute. As Rabin was walking toward the speakers' platform, a man in a crocheted yarmulke suddenly rushed from a group of raucous protesters dressed in Kach and Zo Artzenu T-shirts. He got to within a yard of his target before being deflected by one of the prime minister's bodyguards. Meanwhile, the attacker's cohorts shouted, "Rabin is a traitor, Rabin is a murderer," as they pushed their way toward the knot of guards around the prime minister and spit at them. "You won't stop me from saying what I have to say," Rabin shouted back at his tormentors as his car drove up to extricate him from the fracas. The incident shocked most Israelis, especially when it came out that the man who had tried to attack the prime minister was none other than a rabbi at the Hebrew University, forty-two-year-old Natan Ophir.

Likewise in October, on the eve of Yom Kippur, a very different sort of incident had taken place in front of the prime minister's official residence in the quiet residential neighborhood of Rehavia. Wrapped in prayer shawls, a handful of Meir Kahane's disciples had stood in a circle on the sidewalk reciting an ancient execration known as the *Pulsa da-Nura* ("Lashes of Fire"). According to a tradition dating to the Middle Ages, if ten rabbis cursed a man by invoking the formula, he would meet his end within thirty days. The leader of the strange group was Avigdor Eskin, a thirty-five-year-old businessman who had come to Israel from the Soviet Union in the early 1970s and been drawn into Kahane's circle. Unlike his infamous mentor, Eskin was glib and polished, an accomplished demagogue who insisted that violence was abhorrent to him. Rocking back and forth on the sidewalk that day, he raised his eyes to the prime minister's house and solemnly intoned the words: "I deliver to you, the angels of wrath and ire, Yitzhak, the son of Rosa Rabin, that you may smother him and the specter of him, and cast him into bed, and dry up his wealth, and plague his thoughts, and scatter his mind that he may be steadily diminished until he reaches his death." As Eskin declaimed the Aramaic text, the men around him chimed in: "Put to death the cursed Yitzhak, son of Rosa Rabin, as quickly as possible because of his hatred for the Chosen People." For the finale Eskin filled his lungs and shouted up at the building: "May you be damned, damned, damned!"

A woman who happened to be walking down the street during the odd performance stopped beside the group and scolded, "How dare you curse the prime minister? You should all be ashamed of yourselves!" Eskin looked her straight in the eye, his lips forming a cynical smile, and continued: "Damned are you, Rabin. Damned, damned, damned!" It was then that the police officer posted outside the residence felt obliged to intervene by walking over to the group and gently pushing the outraged woman to move on.*

These incidents, however, paled in comparison with the drama that unfolded on the evening of October 5, when the Knesset was scheduled to vote on ratifying the Oslo II Interim Agreement, a complex plan for turning areas of the West Bank over to the Palestinian Authority. Maps of the first stage of the Israeli pullback covered an entire wall of the Knesset lecture hall. General Uzi Dayan, the commander of the IDF's Planning Branch and one of the key negotiators who had hammered out the critical security clauses of the agreement, stood before the maps, explaining their meaning. In that first phase, the West Bank was to be divided into three parts. Six Palestinian cities (Area A) would be transferred to the exclusive control of the Palestinian Authority (as Gaza and Jericho had been sixteen months earlier). Most of the Palestinian towns and villages (Area B) would be controlled jointly by the Palestinian Authority (managing civil affairs) and the Israeli Army (retaining responsibility for counterterrorism). Control over the city of Hebron was to be divided between Israel and the Palestinian Authority according to the location of their relative populations. The rest of the territory (Area C), which comprised 73 percent of the West Bank and included all 140 Jewish settlements, was initially to remain under full Israeli

*In May 1997 Eskin was convicted of violating the Prevention of Terrorism Act for giving an interview on television in which he expressed his satisfaction with the efficacy of the curse on Rabin. Sentenced to four months' imprisonment, he was released pending the hearing of his appeal and was again arrested in December 1997 on suspicion of a plot to throw a pig's head onto the Temple Mount during the Muslim holy month of Ramadan, which would undoubtedly have sparked an outburst of violence in Jerusalem and the territories.

control. Additional areas of the West Bank would later be transferred to the Palestinians in three "further redeployments" to take place over a period of eighteen months. Precisely which and how much territory would be ceded to the Palestinians in these subsequent redeployments were left to Israel's sole discretion. In no case, however, would it include any of the Israeli settlements. And in no case would any Israeli anywhere in the West Bank, resident or visitor, be answerable to the Palestinian civil authorities or police. To ensure their protection further, the government was paving a number of "bypass roads" so that Israelis could travel freely in the West Bank without having to pass through Palestinian-held areas.

This was the gist of the Oslo II Agreement, a diligently detailed arrangement designed to free Palestinians of Israel's suffocating control while providing for the safety of Israelis. On the Knesset's agenda that day lay the question that Israel had evaded for twenty-eight years: whether to opt for a peace based on territorial compromise or cleave to the Greater Land of Israel, regardless of the consequences. Two years after the dramatic breakthrough of the first Oslo Agreement, the opposition's view remained as firm as ever.

"It's madness!" Netanyahu muttered to his colleagues as they listened to Dayan's explanation of the new accord. "They're giving the City of the Patriarchs [Hebron] to Arafat's terrorists!"

"The people will resist," Yitzhak Shamir forecast darkly. "This is a recipe for a Palestinian state in the Land of Israel."

Outside the lecture hall the Knesset was a hive of activity as settler and *haredi* lobbyists stalked Labor backbenchers in the hope of persuading them to defeat the agreement. It was no secret that there had been considerable political jockeying in the previous days, with Rabin finding himself in the unpleasant position of having to court votes among the least illustrious members of the Knesset. Two Labor deputies had already announced that they would vote against the agreement and bolt the party to set up their own Knesset faction. Two others made it well known that they were wavering. Moreover, to Rabin's considerable discomfort, the outcome of the vote would probably depend upon the whims of two delegates from a tiny faction that had earlier split from the right-wing Tsomet Party and crossed the aisle to join his coalition. At one point the Labor leadership hoped it would not be necessary to have the agreement ratified by the Knesset at all. But the opposition had done its homework and obtained a

Supreme Court ruling blocking the implementation of the accord until the Knesset approved it. To aggravate the tension, the verdict on Oslo II was declared a confidence vote. Therefore, if the government lost, Rabin stood not only to suffer excruciating embarrassment (the agreement had already been signed in a ceremony at the White House attended by Jordan's King Hussein and President Hosni Mubarak of Egypt) but to lose power as well.

Thus tempers were already at the flash point when the debate opened in the Knesset plenum. Taking his turn on the rostrum, Netanyahu berated Rabin for his lack of Jewish pride. "There has never been a government more removed from Israel's heritage," he cried. Rabin waved his hand in a typical gesture of dismissal, but Netanyahu pressed on. "You, Mr. Prime Minister, have said that the Bible is not our land registry. . . . It's no wonder you've relinquished the heart of the homeland with such astounding ease. A man should not give up his country and his home with that kind of ease and joy. Only one who feels like an invader and thief behaves in such a fashion. . . . How can a nation that does not recognize its right, a nation that has lost the dream, continue to defend [itself] and struggle for its existence?"

Netanyahu cannot seriously have expected to shame the prime minister with his scolding, for Rabin's intent was clearly to safeguard Israel's existence by a pragmatic compromise. The head of the opposition undoubtedly had a different purpose in mind. Aware that the Knesset session was being broadcast live, he was essentially addressing his troops in the field, warming them up for the other battle that would be fought that day: the one about to unfold in the streets.

By early evening tens of thousands of right-wing protesters had made their way to Jerusalem's Zion Square for a demonstration called by the opposition parties, the Yesha Council, the Joint Staff, and the Action Headquarters. As similar demonstrations had been held over the previous two years, no one could have doubted what its tone would be like. In an earlier protest rally, held in Tel Aviv, a line of *haredim* stood at the front of the crowd blowing rams' horns to bring down Rabin's government, just as Joshua had brought down the walls of Jericho. A bearded young man in a yarmulke was caught on tape holding a picture of Rabin in one hand and beating it with his fist while shouting at the camera in French, "Because of this dog, this country is going to be destroyed. He's a bastard, a liar, and a cheater. He must be thrown out." The microphone caught a voice saying, "Instead of filming, will you come to the funeral? Will you come to the funeral tomorrow?"

Thus the scene in Zion Square that evening had been played out before. As loudspeakers blasted patriotic songs, the crowd began working itself up to a frenzy even before any of the scheduled speakers had begun to address it. Wild young men in yellow Kach T-shirts carried Meir Kahane's son, Benyamin, on their shoulders as a trail of youngsters ran after him, stretching out their arms to touch him. Supporters of the Likud set Rabin's portrait on fire. Two bearded young men hoisted a banner reading "Rabin, Arafat's dog." Standing near them a woman waving a blue and white Likud flag shouted, "Death to Rabin!" over and over like a mantra. Shouts of "Nazis!" "Collaborators!" and *Judenrat!* were leveled at the cordon of policemen stationed around the crowd. Overlooking it all, on the balcony of the Ron Hotel, stood a gallery of right-wing politicians gazing with satisfaction at the maelstrom below. Benjamin Netanyahu waved his hand at the demonstrators in encouragement. Ariel Sharon, Tsomet's Rafael Eitan, and Rehavam Ze'evi—all masters of anti-Arab and antigovernment invective—flanked him. Tsachi Hanegbi, Netanyahu's liaison with the Action Headquarters, stood beaming with pride at the turnout and tenor of the crowd. The heart of the capital had been turned into a scene of fevered abandon.

Not all the opposition leaders on the balcony were welcome that night. As the Knesset member (and former foreign minister) David Levy made his way to the microphone, an angry rumble passed through the crowd. Levy had never been an outspoken champion of the Greater Land of Israel movement. He represented a constituency of mostly working-class Sephardi Jews who were generally traditional in their approach to religious practice and of a moderate political bent. Since an ugly clash with Netanyahu over the Likud party's chairmanship more than a year earlier, Levy had spent much of his time avoiding contact with Netanyahu. His appearance at the demonstration thus came as something of a surprise. In any event, the crowd didn't want him there. "Levy is a bastard," a chorus called out as he approached the microphone, and cries of "Levy is a traitor!" and "Get out of here, collaborator with the left!" rose out of other parts of the square. Levy was furious at the offense to his dignity. "Shame on you!" he bellowed into the microphone. "You're a threat to democracy!" But the jeers continued, and none of his colleagues moved to quiet them, until Levy stalked off the balcony in a rage.

The climax of the evening was Netanyahu's speech. When the emcee extended his hand toward the head of the opposition and told the crowd, "Greet the next prime minister of the government of the Jews," the throng in the square broke into a chant of "Bibi! Bibi!" and a large banner was raised with the words: OUR FATE [TO BE DECIDED] BY A VOTE OF JEWS ALONE. Netanyahu latched on to the theme. "Dear Jews," he called out to the crowd, and was rewarded with an explosion of applause and chants of "Rabin is a traitor!" He delivered the same pernicious message that had been touted by the leaders of Zo Artzenu. "This government has a non-Zionist majority," Netanyahu cried out. "This government rests on five Arab deputies who are identified with the PLO! I want to remind Yitzhak Rabin that their children don't serve in the IDF, and he nevertheless rests on them and builds his distorted majority on them."

Throughout the speech the violence kept escalating. Demonstrators threw lit torches at policemen. Groups of Kach supporters jumped up and down screaming, "Rabin is a dog," and the chant "In blood and fire we'll drive Rabin out" rippled from one section of the demonstration to another. At one point Netanyahu wagged his finger at the chanters, but that was as far as his expression of disapproval extended. "Today the agreement of capitulation called Oslo II has been brought before the Knesset," he thundered. "The Jewish majority of the State of Israel has not approved the agreement. We will fight, and we will bring the government down."

Suddenly a new chant rose out of the center of the square: "Rabin is a Nazi!" It was inspired by a handbill being circulated among the demonstrators showing a photomontage of Rabin dressed in an SS uniform. The image had been prepared by two *haredi* youngsters, and a video camera caught several young men waving it and gleefully tearing it into shreds. One of the protesters, a veteran right-wing agitator named Avishai Raviv (who later became the subject of national controversy), took the trouble of bringing the handbill to the reporter covering the demonstration for television's Channel One.

In this way the picture became known to the entire nation, including the group of political figures who were watching the demonstration on TV in one of the rooms off the balcony of the Ron Hotel. Word of the handbill quickly spread to the leaders out on the balcony, but no one saw fit to comment on it to the crowd. Only David Levy, smarting from his treatment at the hands of the demonstrators, made reference to the handbill before leaving that night. "Tonight will be remembered as one of the darkest and most dangerous in the history of the State of Israel," he huffed to television reporters. "Disgusting! There were swastikas there and the figure of an SS officer—things which have no place in our country—and no one bothers to deplore something like that!"

The evening was still young, however. Following the demonstration, thousands of demonstrators set out from Zion Square on a torchlit march to the Knesset. Heading the procession was Rabbi Benny Elon surrounded by young men screaming, "Death to Rabin." At one point a group of Kach activists rushed ahead of the line to reach the Knesset first. They included twenty-year-old Itamar Ben-Gvir, who on that night already had 120 complaints lodged against him, as well as twelve criminal indictments. Days earlier he had been shown on the news informing his cohorts of Rabin's schedule and directing them to wait at each stop and shower him with abuse. Now he spearheaded the group that charged the line of policemen protecting the gate to the Knesset plaza. As the rest of the marchers reached the fence surrounding the parliament, they too surged toward the live blockade of police officers. At the ready inside the Knesset compound were mounted policemen and water cannon to repel the mob as it tried to scale the gate.

In a fluke of timing, the marchers closed in on the Knesset just as the prime minister's Cadillac was passing. By the time Rabin's driver, Menachem Damti, grasped what was happening, a number of demonstrators had identified the car and begun banging on the hood, doors, and windows with fists and sticks. Howling with rage, Mike Gozovsky, the head of Kahane Chai in New York, led the assault as Ben-Gvir pounced on the front of the Cadillac and wrenched its symbol off. A third man clambered onto the hood, blocking Damti's line of sight and pounding on the windshield with his fist, while others hurled burning torches at the vehicle. Damti continued to inch the car forward as policemen struggled to drag the demonstrators out of its path. The doors were locked, the bulletproof windows were closed, and, most important of all, Rabin was not in the car. But the demonstrators were unaware of this. At that point, appalled by the wanton violence loosed at a demonstration sponsored by the Yesha Council, Uri Ariel climbed onto the roof of a squad car and shouted into a megaphone: "Friends, I ask you to maintain your self-control! I ask you to move back in the direction of the main road. Friends, please, move away from the Knesset!" It was a belated and futile exercise in leadership; his shouts were smothered by the racket of the rioting crowd.

As the gates of the Knesset parking lot finally closed behind Rabin's car, another vehicle began moving up the same access road. In it sat Housing Minister Benyamin Ben-Eliezer, a figure who had worked closely with the settlers in the 1980s, in his capacity as the coordinator of activities in the territories, but was now the symbol of the Labor government's construction freeze in most of the settlements. TV cameras caught the trapped minister pale with fright as the rioters surrounded the car and rocked it from side to side like a ship in a tempest. One rioter who was being taken into custody screamed at the police: "Rabin is murdering the homeland and you're arresting *me*?"

"He's right!" Rabbi Elon called out. "The traitor is inside [the car]. He's the one who should be arrested!"

When he reached the safety of the Knesset building, the shaken Ben-Eliezer set out in search of Netanyahu. "I've never experienced anything like it!" he told colleagues along the way. "I've fought in all [of Israel's] wars and seen death before my eyes. But never was I so close to death as I was tonight." Finally collaring Netanyahu in one of the corridors, Ben-Eliezer warned him loudly: "You'd better restrain your people. Otherwise it will end in murder. They tried to kill me just now!"

Embarrassed by the scene, Netanyahu responded with a grin of discomfort.

"I suggest you wipe the smile off your face," Ben-Eliezer barked at him. "Your people are mad. If someone is murdered, the blood will be on your hands!"

Again Netanyahu chose not to respond, but Knesset member Hanan Porat of the National Religious Party could not resist the temptation to do so for him. "What do you want of those people?" he sneered. "If the prime minister wasn't selling out the Land of Israel, they wouldn't be behaving this way."

"The settlers have gone crazy," Ben-Eliezer shot back, "and someone will be murdered here, if not today, then in another week or another month!"

By then the debate in the plenum was in its twelfth hour and the Knesset was abuzz with reports of what had transpired in Zion Square and outside the gates of the parliament itself. Especially distressed by the accounts was the speaker of the Knesset, Professor Shevach Weiss, a Holocaust survivor who felt that the matter could not be allowed to pass in silence. Calling a halt to the proceedings, he grimly announced that he wished to make a personal statement.

"I have received a description of what happened today in Zion Square and then of what befell Minister Ben-Eliezer," he began, "[and] I want to say that what happened tonight in Zion Square, when an effigy of the prime minister as a Gestapo trooper bearing a swastika was displayed, is the embodiment of calumny and infamy. I personally, to my regret, knew these types in Europe during the 1930s," Weiss commented, careful to make only oblique reference to Nazi Brown Shirts, lest he himself be accused of practicing incitement. "This is a spreading stain, an infectious and cancerous wound . . . and a threat to the democratic way of life. It is an anti-Jewish and antihuman incident. I call upon all the factions in this house and the whole of the political leadership to emphatically condemn this phenomenon, drive it out of our midst, and tear it out from the root. . . ."

"What do you expect of them?" Rabin called out, pointing to the opposition benches. "They organized the demonstration!"

"Mr. Speaker," Netanyahu cried, jumping to his feet, "I would like to make a statement."

Weiss granted the request, much to the annoyance of the coalition deputies, who cried, "Don't let him speak!" In response, opposition members shouted, "Stop gagging us!" Rising out of his chair, Rabin joined in the verbal volley, demanding, "What's going on? Why must he speak?" Weiss asked him not to interrupt, which only infuriated the prime minister further. "This is scandalous," he scolded the speaker. "This man is the chief inciter!"

"*You're* the greatest inciter of all!" Likud deputy Michael Eitan bellowed at Rabin. "Shame on you!"

"You're giving the Land of Israel to the murderers of children!" howled his colleague Yehoshua Matza. Seeing Rabin flush with anger, Matza pointed his finger at the prime minister and jeered, "He's had too much whiskey. The prime minister is drunk!"

Meanwhile, Weiss fought desperately to restore order. Rabin, however, had already lost his patience and was walking toward one of the exits from the hall, with a number of Labor deputies following him.

"Leave, coward!" came shouts from the opposition benches. "You're losing your wits!"

Rabin stopped just outside the hall, lit a cigarette, and waited within earshot while Netanyahu made his statement. Adopting offense as the best defense, the Likud chairman began with a reprimand of the prime minister.

"I think that the members of the house who walked out, and the prime minister in the lead, should sit quietly and listen. I want to say that the first condemnation came immediately when I heard about this abuse during the demonstration, [as I stood] facing a handful of hooligans who belong to some illegal movement."

This was to remain Netanyahu's consistent reply to charges that he had acquiesced in the incitement against Rabin. It in no way satisfied the prime minister. Three times Weiss implored Rabin to return to the hall before he finally relented. But he did not let the matter drop. "The chairman of the Likud, Netanyahu, has asked for a meeting," he fumed in a televised interview the following day. "It would be folly on my part to play along with the hypocrisy of the Likud chairman. He was there [in Zion Square] and gave his address [facing] the pictures of the Gestapo, and he's suggesting that we meet?"

Weiss was similarly unimpressed by Netanyahu's attempt to portray himself as a man of principle. Shortly after the Knesset voted to ratify the Oslo II Agreement (by a majority of 61 to 59) and the meeting was adjourned, Weiss called the head of the opposition on his cellular phone. "I have a suggestion for you, Mr. Netanyahu," he said coldly. "Stop going to these fascist demonstrations."

The ominous events of October 5, 1995, carried into the following day, when yet another direct threat was issued against Rabin. Itamar Ben-Gvir brazenly appeared in front of the Prime Minister's Office, proudly displaying the Cadillac symbol he had torn off Rabin's car, and told the journalists gathered there, "Just as we got to this symbol, we can get to Rabin." (The boast got Ben-Gvir arrested, but he was promptly released on bail.)

Meanwhile, some supporters of the peace process were not prepared to cede the fight for public opinion. Among the first to speak up were French businessman Jean Friedman, a close friend of both Rabin's and Peres's, and former Tel Aviv Mayor Shlomo Lahat, who had begun his political career in the Likud but steadily moved away from the party and ultimately ran for mayor as an independent. Both men came from outside the Labor Party, which was slow to grasp what was happening. Friedman and Lahat proposed holding a pro-peace and antiviolence rally in Tel Aviv as a response to the incitement campaign. At first Rabin balked at the idea. He feared it would be seen as a sign of weakness for the parties in power to solicit an active show of public support between elections. He may also have feared an anemic turnout. There were, after all, no lack of extra-parliamentary movements on the left that could have sponsored such a rally. Yet they seemed to take the peace process for granted or at least had not felt moved to organize their own expression of support for Rabin. But Friedman and Lahat persisted. They were confident that numerous Israelis were interested not just in affirming their faith in the government's policy but in venting their disgust at the fanaticism that had become the hallmark of the opposition's crusade. After a while they succeeded in allaying Rabin's qualms and scheduled the rally for Saturday night, November 4, in the Kings of Israel Square in Tel Aviv.

During the days leading up to the event, the incitement machine shifted back into high gear. Itamar Ben-Gvir announced plans to disrupt the rally in the hope of deterring participants with the threat of violence. Broadcasting on Arutz 7, Adir Zik took a similar line, warning: "Whoever conducts a media festival in favor of the PLO and Hamas will receive an appropriate answer." Two weeks before the rally a death certificate bearing Rabin's name was circulated in the settlements in Samaria. Under the clause "Cause of Death," the certificate read "Suicide," and the date was left blank with the accompanying comment, "Rabin, fill in the date soon, and we will remember you as the prime victim of peace." Friday-afternoon demonstrations outside Rabin's home in the northern Tel Aviv neighborhood of Ramat Aviv became more acrimonious. On November 3, the day before the peace rally, the group standing outside the apartment building contained a mixture of people in Likud T-shirts, members of Women in Green, settlers from the West Bank town of Ariel, a few Kahane people, and Yigal Amir and his brother Haggai. Every week a group stood vigil outside the building shouting offensive slogans. The citizens of Ramat Aviv grumbled about the noise but had no stomach for confronting the protesters and demanding that they leave. Neither did the Labor Party send out its Young Guard to stage counterdemonstrations.

On that particular Friday afternoon, Leah Rabin arrived home first and, walking from her car to the building's entrance, heard a protester shout, "Next year we'll hang you like they hanged Mussolini and his mistress!" Shaking with rage, she took the elevator up to the family's penthouse flat and tried to find refuge in her husband's study. But the chorus of "Death to Rabin" penetrated this sanctum as well. "Why do they allow it?" she brooded in frustration. "Why don't his supporters come out to answer them?"

"When Yitzhak would come home, I'd ask him, 'Where are our people? Why don't they come and drive them away?'" she recalled in an interview after the assassination. "And he would say, 'What can I do?' He tended to make light of them, not accord them any importance, not give them the satisfaction [of sensing] that they angered and upset him."

By the time Rabin reached home at five o'clock on that Sabbath eve, the demonstrators were gone. His wife again raised the issue of the unbearable disturbance, and this time he picked up the phone and complained to someone. Leah Rabin doesn't know who was on the other end of the line, but she heard her husband say, "I don't pay any attention to them, and I don't care what they do to me. But I won't put up with the incessant affront to Leah's dignity."

A few miles away in the Kings of Israel Square, preparations were being completed for the peace rally that was to begin soon after the Sabbath ended the following evening. Earlier that day quiet preparations had also been made by the indefatigable Action Headquarters. Spotted in the square by a reporter from Israel television's Channel One was Ya'akov Novick, who had received a permit to hold a small counterdemonstration—of up to three hundred people—nearby.

"What will your three hundred people do at the demonstration tomorrow?" the reporter asked him.

"They will express their position," Novick replied tersely.

"In what way?" she pressed him.

"Come and see for yourself" was all the secretive head of the Action Headquarters was prepared to say.

CHAPTER 4

DIN RODEF

R abbi Yoel Bin-Nun still remembers with a thrill the day on which his beloved mentor, Rabbi Zvi Yehudah Kook, gave his poignant talk in the Mercaz Harav Yeshiva. It was on a Sunday evening, May 14, 1967, as outside, on the streets of Jerusalem, Israelis had begun celebrating the state's nineteenth Independence Day in song and dance. Rabbi Kook had his own way of observing the event. He gathered his students in the yeshiva's large central hall for a session of personal reflections. The elderly Kook reminisced about another day of national celebration twenty years earlier, November 29, 1947, when the United Nations General Assembly voted on whether to partition Palestine into a Jewish and an Arab state.

As the roll was being called in New York, the 660,000 Jews of Palestine sat huddled around their radio sets, drinking in every word of the live broadcast and recording the replies, country by country: yes, no, abstention. When the tally was counted, their homes echoed with cries of joy. The United Nations had approved partition; finally the Jews would have their independence. On that day too, Rabbi Kook recalled with muted nostalgia, the streets had filled with people eager to celebrate the triumph of their bitter struggle against British rule. Kook remembered wanting to join them but feeling overwhelmed by melancholy over the cost of that victory: The heart of the Land of Israel was to fall under alien rule. As though again tasting the bittersweet savor of that hour, Rabbi Kook fell silent. Then the small, frail man raised his eyes heavenward and let out a terrible wail of pain. "Where is our Shechem?* Can we forget her?" he cried. "Where is our Hebron? Can we forget her? Where is our Jericho? Can we forget her? And where is our Trans-Jordan?† Can we forget her?"

The very next day history began moving in a new direction. As Chief of Staff Yitzhak Rabin stood on a reviewing stand in Jerusalem, accepting the smart salutes of his troops, he received word that Egypt had placed its army on alert and was sending its soldiers into the Sinai Desert toward the border with Israel. Rabin immediately began mobilizing the Israeli Army, and for the next three weeks the Middle East rolled inexorably toward a war that would provide unexpected answers to Kook's anguished questions. Fighting broke out on the morning of June 5, and within four days the IDF had captured Nablus and Hebron, Jericho and Bethlehem, together with the eastern half of Jerusalem. On June 7 Yoel Bin-Nun's reserve battalion of the IDF's Paratroop Brigade penetrated the walled Old City, and after a bitter battle he found himself standing next to the Western Wall, the only remnant of the holy Second Temple complex destroyed by the Romans two millennia earlier. His brigade commander, Mordechai ("Motta") Gur, announced over the communications network, "The Temple Mount is in our hands!" and like a latter-day Joshua, the IDF's chief rabbi, Shlomo Goren, blew a ram's horn to mark the magnitude of the occasion. Bin-Nun stood there trembling, with tears in his eyes. "We felt a sense of being overwhelmed by this meeting with Jewish history—the Temple Mount, the Western Wall, the huge mass of Jewish history that seemed to bear down on us, regardless of political outlooks—together with the experience of war, and death, and the shock of battle."

Twenty-nine years later Rabbi Bin-Nun still spoke with a tinge of awe in his voice in recalling Rabbi Kook's speech on Independence Day 1967 and the dramatic chain of events that followed. To the twenty-one-year-old yeshiva student, the turnabout was no mere twist of fate. God's hand was apparent in the victory of the few against the many, Kook taught his students, and when he called upon them to return to their ancient

---

*Biblical name of Nablus.
†East bank of the Jordan River, where the biblical tribes of Reuben, Gad, and part of Manasseh settled.

patrimony, Bin-Nun gathered up his family and went off to found the settlement of Ofra, north of the Palestinian city of Ramallah. He was an eager and active leader of the settlement movement. His comrades fondly called him "the ideologue." In 1974 Gush Emunim was founded in his living room.

A bearded teacher and preacher whose brow is deeply etched with wrinkles, Yoel Bin-Nun was born in Haifa two years before the establishment of the State of Israel. He attended a religious school but unlike many of the religious boys of his generation never suffered from a feeling of inferiority. While secular youngsters volunteered to serve in combat units and for dangerous missions, the boys raised in crocheted yarmulkes usually served in the military rabbinate or other noncombat units. But Yoel served in the Paratroops before entering the Mercaz Harav Yeshiva.

Though driven by the same messianic fervor as the other founders of Gush Emunim, Bin-Nun possessed a rare ability to appreciate other views and counted secular intellectuals among his friends. He also maintained contacts with Israel's secular political establishment while winning the trust of even the most zealous settlers. Where others preached a doctrine of force, he remained a staunch champion of dialogue. His virtues made him a great asset to the settler community. After the Oslo Agreement was signed in September 1993, for example, Bin-Nun was chosen to serve as the liaison between the Yesha Council and the Prime Minister's Bureau. It was precisely because of his close acquaintance with both sides of the Israeli political divide that with each passing year Yoel Bin-Nun grew increasingly alarmed about how wide the chasm between them had grown.

Throughout the 1980s Bin-Nun watched with mounting dismay as his countrymen resorted to violence to settle their differences and achieve their ideological goals. He was badly shaken in February 1983, when Yonah Abrushmi, an embittered young man fired by reckless right-wing rhetoric, threw a hand grenade into a crowd of Peace Now demonstrators, killing one protester, Emil Grunzweig, and injuring eleven others. Just over a year later, in April 1984, shock hit closer to home when Bin-Nun discovered that one of his friends, Yehudah Etzion, was a leader of the Jewish Underground and had planned to blow up a mosque on the Temple Mount. He knew that Etzion was impatient to find a shortcut to Redemption, and more than once they had argued over Etzion's radical views. But he never imagined that a man of Etzion's sterling background and standing in Gush Emunim was capable of such a fanatical act. Bin-Nun was troubled by the extent of admiration for the Jewish Underground within the national religious camp. He tried to rally his colleagues to condemn the extremist rabbis who were encouraging attacks on Arabs, warning, "The longer the rabbinical establishment avoids facing this problem, the more it's likely not only to undermine the settlement enterprise in Yesha but to jeopardize the standing of the rabbinical world as a whole." He also demanded that his comrades in Gush Emunim take a close look at their values and admit to their mistakes. But the settlers refused to acknowledge that there was any cause for self-scrutiny.

By the middle of the decade Bin-Nun was beset by doubts about the moral course on which the settlement movement was headed. The racist doctrine of Rabbi Meir Kahane was poisoning the minds of many of his comrades. He shuddered at reports of covert cells being formed by religious fanatics who believed themselves above the rule of law and flaunted their contempt for democracy as a "Western" value that had no place in Judaism. As the incidence of Jewish vigilantism spiraled during these years, he repeatedly noted that religious and political leaders turned a blind eye to the violence or even commended it. Convinced that the preoccupation with the sanctity of the Land of Israel was alien to Jewish life, Bin-Nun stressed the premium that Judaism had always placed on the sanctity of life. "There is no land without a people," he preached to the contracting circle of those willing to listen. After the massacre in the Cave of the Patriarchs, he denounced the praise that fellow rabbis were heaping upon Baruch Goldstein as "a desecration of the Almighty and a disgrace of the Torah." Such utterances made Bin-Nun suspect in the very movement he had helped found and nurture, to the point where grumbling was heard in some of the Gush Emunim settlements that he was "collaborating with the leftists."

Hence Yoel Bin-Nun's standing among his fellow settlers was already seriously undermined when reports began to reach him, late in 1994, that a new and particularly pernicious idea was overtaking the religious community. Orthodox rabbis in Israel and abroad had revived two obsolete halachic precepts—*din rodef* (the duty to kill a Jew who imperils the life or property of another Jew) and *din moser* (the duty to eliminate a Jew who intends to turn another Jew in to non-Jewish authorities)—and were seriously debating whether these antiquated religious laws should be applied to the prime minister of Israel. Until that time the two injunctions had been studied only in yeshivas. For all practical purposes they were a dead letter, no more relevant to contemporary life than the laws on animal sacrifice detailed in the Bible. Yet suddenly rumors circulated that highly respected rabbinical scholars had ruled that because his policies placed the lives and property of the settlers in peril, Yitzhak Rabin was a *rodef* and a *moser* and thus deserved to be put to death.

The pronouncement of the death sentence was a rare occurrence in Jewish history. The automatic license to kill a *rodef* is essentially an extension of the right to self-defense. It derives from the Mishnah,* which cites not only the right to protect oneself against harm but also the duty to save the life of any Jew who is being persecuted by another with the intent to kill. With laudable wisdom, the twelfth-century rabbinical scholar Maimonides, who is revered as the most brilliant and authoritative interpreter of the halacha, established that it was necessary to catch a *rodef*—not summarily to murder him—in order to foil his plan. Should that prove impossible, one was obliged to stop him by wounding him, beating him, cutting off his hand, breaking his leg, or blinding him. Only if all these means failed was it a duty to kill a *rodef*. As these restrictions imply, *din rodef* applies to a situation of pursuit in which there is imminent danger to the target's life. Such a notion was taken from Jewish criminal law, and the extension of its pertinence to the political sphere was patently absurd. Even were it not outlandish, Orthodox Jews are well aware of the prohibition on committing violence against their rulers. They still mark by a day of fasting the assassination of Gedaliah Ben Ahikam, a Jew who served King Nebuchadrezzar of Babylon as the governor of Judah after the destruction of the First Temple in 586 B.C.E. (Jeremiah 41:1–3). Nevertheless, there were Orthodox rabbis who, through a broad extrapolation of *din rodef*, reached the conclusion that relinquishing territory in the West Bank and Gaza Strip to non-Jewish rule endangered Jewish lives, making *din rodef* applicable to anyone who did so.

---

*The basic codex of Jewish law, containing the core of the Oral Law, compiled and edited at the beginning of the third century C.E. by Rabbi Judah Hanasi.

There was a similar restriction on the execution of *din moser*. According to the Babylonian Talmud,* before one takes action against a person suspected of intending to deliver a Jew into the hands of non-Jews, it is necessary to admonish him by saying, "Do not inform." Only if there is evidence that he persists in his plan is it a duty to kill him, and, the injunction adds, "the sooner the better." Born in an age of foreign domination over the Land of Israel, *din moser* remained relevant in the Diaspora, particularly to situations in which state authorities were hostile to the Jews or unable to accord them sufficient protection from their enemies. In no way could it reasonably be extended to life in modern democracies and certainly not to life in a democratic Jewish state. Nevertheless, certain Orthodox rabbis linked its relevance to the political situation in Israel after 1993. By relinquishing rule over parts of the Land of Israel to the Palestinian Authority, they argued, the head of the Israeli government had become a *moser*. And by so branding Rabin, they effectively declared open season on his life. Any Jew who was faithful to the halacha was entitled, if not actually obliged, to kill him.

It might be assumed from the way these concepts were used in Israel that they were deeply rooted in Jewish culture. Yet they were so obscure (except to those who had a thorough grounding in the Talmud) that until they first appeared in press reports, most Israelis had never even heard the terms *din rodef* and *din moser*. This was not true of Yoel Bin-Nun, however. He was painfully aware of their implication and found the phenomenon of invoking these antiquated concepts to serve political ends absolutely chilling. "Hundreds of people heard the word *rodef* used in connection with the late prime minister months before and around the time of the murder," he lamented in an interview. "The fact that these discussions leaked out and [inspired a] heated public debate in the religious community turned the obsolete notions of *rodef* and *moser* into household words."

Indeed, from the beginning of 1995 onward the popularization of the words *rodef* and *moser* nourished the belief in religious circles that a consideration of whether they could be applied to Rabin was legitimate. Yeshiva students asked their teachers to explain these principles. Congregants made similar requests of their rabbis. Before long Orthodox rabbis in Israel and the United States were consulting one another, orally and in

---

*Two great compilations, the Babylonian Talmud and the Jerusalem Talmud, contain the exegesis of Jewish law by ten generations of scholars and jurists who lived from the third to the sixth century C.E. The term *halacha* refers to the Torah, Mishnah, and Talmud together.

writing, about whether Rabin fell into the category of a *rodef* or a *moser*. In the United States hundreds of Orthodox rabbis signed a statement declaring that he did. In Israel the subject was discussed secretly, lest the clerics expose themselves to charges of incitement to murder. When asked for a ruling on the subject, some pronounced that Rabin clearly fitted the definition of a *rodef*. Others approached the subject warily, stipulating that the two laws were outdated, so that even though Rabin could be considered a *rodef* or a *moser*, he would be punished by Providence, not mortal men. A few rabbis proposed that he be tried by a panel of rabbinical judges; one or two favored suing him in a civil court. Yet in each case the intent was the same: to frighten the prime minister into halting the peace process.

How much practical weight did rulings sanctioning the murder of the prime minister actually hold with religious Jews in Israel? The answer is far from clear. Contemporary Judaism has no central rabbinical institution that determines or interprets religious law; nor is there any supreme rabbinical authority that all believing Jews are obliged to obey. These roles were fulfilled until the destruction of the Second Temple in c.e. 70 by the high priest and a legislative-judicial body called the Knesset Gedolah ("Great Assembly") in the First Temple period (eleventh–sixth century B.C.E.) and the Sanhedrin during and after the Second Temple period (fourth century B.C.E. to first century c.e.). But after the Sanhedrin had lost its power under Byzantine rule in Palestine in the fifth century c.e., no central Jewish authority ever evolved to replace it. The last halachic authority to be accepted by all the Jewish communities of the Diaspora was Maimonides (1135–1204), whose commentary on the Talmud, the Mishnah Torah, attained the stature of a codex of Jewish law. After the establishment of Israel a number of rabbis proposed that the Sanhedrin be restored as the ultimate arbiter of religious law. But by then the schism among the Orthodox, Conservative, and Reform streams of Judaism was too deep to make the initiative viable. The closest thing to a preeminent body of rabbinical authorities today is an ad hoc collection of halachic scholars regarded as *poskim* ("decision makers"), who are consulted by the rabbis of individual communities for judgments on specific halachic issues.

Any Jew with a question about the labyrinth of laws and conventions collectively called the halacha is entitled to ask the rabbi of his choice for enlightenment. Having sought rabbinical counsel, however, a practicing Jew is morally obliged to follow it. "Choose yourself a rabbi and rid yourself of doubt," goes an oft-quoted saying from the Mishnah, and asking for rabbinical judgments on matters large and small is integral to the Orthodox and especially to the *haredi* way of life. Rabbis may also publish unsolicited rulings—and regularly do so in Israel—but they are not binding upon anyone beyond their circle of avowed followers. If a rabbi has doubts about how to rule on a specific issue, he must consult with a higher or more experienced rabbinical authority.

The consequence of this system, inherited from centuries of autonomous communal life in the Diaspora, is that the hundreds of thousands of Israeli Jews find themselves caught precariously between the dictates of man's law and of God's, as interpreted for them by their rabbis. Throughout the history of Israel, the civil and rabbinical establishments were keenly aware of the potential conflict between the two canons of law and did their utmost to avoid it through a combination of compromise and self-restraint. In the early years of the state, when the religious community was relatively small and politically weak, it was unthinkable that rabbinical leaders would force their followers to choose between their fidelity to religion and to the state, especially on issues of an obviously political nature. But that changed dramatically after Oslo as prominent members of the religious establishment began brazenly challenging the regime on the core question of who holds ultimate authority in matters of national policy: rabbis invoking the halacha or the elected government of Israel.

The first open clash came at the end of March 1994, six months after the signing of the Oslo Agreement and a month after the massacre of twenty-nine Arab worshipers in the Cave of the Patriarchs in Hebron. For weeks after the slaughter, the eighty thousand Palestinian inhabitants of Hebron were kept under a twenty-four-hour military curfew for fear of violent retaliation against the city's 450 Jewish settlers. In response, the PLO had suspended the negotiations on implementing the Oslo accord and demanded the removal of the settlers from Hebron. Rabin was caught in a dilemma. His chief concern was to reduce the friction in the city and ensure the security of Jews and Arabs alike. But he also had to consider the immediate and long-term effects of dismantling any Jewish settlement so early in the peace process.

Two proposals were placed before him. The first was to relocate all the fifty or so Jewish families living in Hebron to the adjoining settlement of Kiryat Arba. The second was to evacuate only the seven Jewish families (including that of Kach leader Baruch Marzel) living in caravan homes in the neighborhood of Tel Rumeida, which was isolated from the other two concentrations of settlers in Hebron. The decision was all the more perilous because Rabin's chief security advisers were divided among themselves. IDF Chief of Staff Ehud Barak was in favor of removing the Jews from Tel Rumeida, but the head of the Shabak, Ya'akov Perry, feared that an attempt to remove Jewish settlers from anywhere in Hebron would be met by violent resistance. Perry predicted that citizens would open fire on the troops sent to evacuate them and might even stage Masada-like acts of mass suicide. "The scenes will be horrific," he warned.

The predicament was a grave one for the Israeli government. Though the security situation in Hebron was volatile and the Palestinians could not be kept closed up in their homes indefinitely, it seemed equally clear that the militant settlers would brook no change in the status quo without a fight. When word leaked of the possible evacuation of the Jewish families from Tel Rumeida, the Hebron Headquarters declared a hunger strike and called upon Israelis to descend upon the city for a mass rally in support of the Jewish community. The army responded by imposing a closure on Hebron to prevent demonstrators from entering the city. It was in this already charged atmosphere that a group calling itself the Rabbinical Council for the Land of Israel convened in Kiryat Arba on March 29 to deliberate whether it should publish a halachic ruling forbidding Israeli soldiers to obey any order to evacuate Jewish settlers. Never had such a direct challenge to the authority of the Israeli government even been contemplated by Israeli clerics.

The sages who took counsel in Kiryat Arba could not be brushed off as misguided or overzealous. Heading the group was eighty-one-year-old Rabbi Avraham Shapira, the former Ashkenazi chief rabbi of Israel, who enjoyed the backing of two other highly distinguished colleagues: eighty-one-year-old Rabbi Moshe Zvi Neria, an Israel Prize laureate in education and leader of the national religious Bnei Akiva Yeshiva network; and eighty-five-year-old Rabbi Shaul Yisrael, an Israel Prize laureate in Jewish studies and Rabbi Kook's successor as dean of the near-sacrosanct Mercaz Harav Yeshiva. Paragons of the national religious establishment, all three men had become more radical as they aged. Rabbi Neria was so offended by the signing of the Oslo Agreement that he actually wrote a new version of the official prayer for the welfare of the State of Israel, imploring the Almighty to "protect it from its leaders, officers, and counselors."

For hours the rabbis gathered in Kiryat Arba agonized over what action to take. Their concern was not the justice of the proposed ruling. All agreed that any soldier who felt himself subject to the halacha was duty bound to defy an order to evacuate any settlement. Rabbi Kook himself, citing Maimonides, had already determined that Jewish law forbids the cession of any part of the Land of Israel to non-Jewish rule. But some of the participants went further, arguing passionately that when a practicing Jew is forced to ignore or contravene a religious injunction, he is obliged to *resist*. The more moderate members of the forum shrank from a clear-cut ruling for fear of creating mass dissension within the army and thus weakening the very branch on which Israel's control of the territories rested. Instead, they proposed that any religious soldier who could not carry out an order in good conscience should ask to be released from doing so on the grounds of conscientious objection.

In any case, it was not clear what effect a blanket ruling would have on military discipline, and the rabbis' aim was not to precipitate anarchy in the army but to intimidate the prime minister. "This is the one thing that can unnerve Rabin," Rabbi Shapira told his colleagues, arguing that religious soldiers would understand the tacit convention (known in religious circles as the difference between the Oral Law and the Written Law) that when a rabbi of Shapira's or Neria's stature issues such a ruling, he does not expect it to be taken literally. The most the rabbis intended was for soldiers (some of them settlers themselves) to seek a discreet way out of an unpleasant situation.

Rabin may have suspected what the rabbis were up to, but he found it difficult to gauge the seriousness of these men, who were so closely identified with the settlers and the National Religious Party. "Are they mad?" he fumed to his advisers. "Do they really intend to have soldiers defy their commanders?" Others much closer to the national religious establishment were similarly uncertain how the test of wills would end. Yoel Bin-Nun rushed to Tel Aviv to see Chief of Staff Barak and warn him that the territories would explode if the government tried to remove the settlers from Tel

Rumeida. Nevertheless, when the prime minister held a second round of consultations, Barak still backed the evacuation plan, while Perry reiterated his disaster scenario, and Rabin remained loath to decide between them.

In the meanwhile, the rabbis issued their ruling that "It is a duty to reject an order to evacuate any settlement in the Land of Israel." Oddly, the sharpest reaction to it came from within the religious community itself. Although the National Religious Party issued a typically equivocal statement opposing the defiance of military orders "as long as the orders in question are not patently illegal," Colonel Eliezer Stern, the modern Orthodox commander of the IDF's Officers School, denounced the three rabbis who signed the ruling, and he was joined by Bin-Nun. But Rabbi Shapira only poured scorn on his critics, calling them "*Rebbelach* ['little rabbis'] who fawn before the government" and publishing a communiqué of unprecedented defiance that pronounced: "The decision of the secular regime cannot oblige a Jew when it runs contrary to [religious] law."

Stunned by the vehemence of the declaration, Rabin decided to respond cautiously. He asked Barak to evaluate the response to the ruling within the army, and within twenty-four hours a survey had been conducted among religious officers from the rank of major upward. All but two of the dozens of officers declared that they would faithfully carry out their orders, thus assuring Rabin that he would not face a mutiny if he called the rabbis' bluff. Nevertheless, he decided against evacuating the settlers from Tel Rumeida. Though confident of the army's loyalty, he was justly apprehensive of the settlers' reaction to such a move—particularly of the specter of violence directed against Israeli soldiers. Three days after the provocative ruling, he also tried to lessen the tension created by the recalcitrant rabbis by sending Deputy Minister of Defense Mordechai Gur to coax Shapira into retracting or at least modifying the ruling. Shapira would not be moved, however, and the matter was allowed to pass without any further action.

That was a decision Rabin would have cause to regret, for it emboldened an even larger contingent of the Rabbinical Council for the Land of Israel to endorse a far rasher ruling in the tense summer of 1995. This time Rabbis Chaim Druckman, Nachum Rabinovitch, Eliezer Waldman, and Dov Lior—among the most outspoken and influential rabbis in the national religious camp—appended their signatures to a ruling issued by Shapira and Neria that went far beyond forbidding soldiers to evacuate settlements. "We rule that there is a prohibition forbidding the evacuation of IDF bases and the transfer of the areas to non-Jews," the rabbis announced on July 12, 1995, explaining that "a permanent IDF base is actually a Jewish settlement" and that "it is forbidden for any Jew to participate in any way in the closing of any Jewish settlement, base, or outpost." To enhance the impact of their decision, they reminded the public of Maimonides's injunction that even the command of a king must be disregarded if it requires a Jew to violate the law of the Torah.

The terms of the Oslo II Agreement were still being negotiated at the time. But whatever its ultimate details, all Israelis knew that its thrust would be the transfer of parts of the West Bank to Palestinian self-rule. The point of the latest rabbinical edict was thus to preclude the document from ever being signed. Since many of the IDF's installations were in Palestinian cities and towns, even if not a single settler was to be uprooted as a result of the agreement (and the fact is that no settlements or settlers were moved under any of the three agreements signed between Israel and the Palestinians between September 1993 and September 1995), by prohibiting the shutdown of army bases the Rabbinical Council was effectively ordering the government to halt the peace process.

This time Rabin's response was emphatic. "This is a call to violate the law," he declared to the press, and he ordered Attorney General Michael Ben-Ya'ir to determine whether the rabbis who signed the ruling should be charged with sedition. Sharp reactions also ensued from President Ezer Weizman, Ashkenazi Chief Rabbi Yisrael Meir Lau, and former Sephardi Chief Rabbi Ovadiah Yosef, who as mentor of the Shas Party wielded considerable political clout. Yosef was quoted as fearing that the judgment would lead to civil war. Yet not even such reproof from within the religious community stopped Shapira and Druckman from meeting in Kiryat Arba on September 21 to reiterate the ruling, declare the Oslo II Agreement "null and void," and proclaim: "We are not going to leave any place in Judea and Samaria." Still, no action was taken against any of the rabbis. The attorney general made it clear that "Whoever complies with the [rabbinical] ruling is liable to three years' imprisonment" but took no measures against the clerics themselves, citing the hallowed principle of free speech.

Rabin never pressed the issue. Though angered by the rabbis' presumption, he was apparently convinced that they posed little threat and that the worst course would be any move that suggested he took their power seriously. The more Rabin's "battle for peace" progressed from one agreement to the next, the clearer it became that the nationalist rabbis had failed in their efforts to win the obedience of Israel's soldiers.

The revival of the laws of *din rodef* and *din moser* was a far more insidious threat, for it left behind no evidence, beyond rumors and hearsay. In only one instance did a trio of rabbis leave a paper trail of their involvement with the subject, which was at any rate never used against them in a criminal proceeding. In January 1995 the rabbis sent a letter from the small West Bank settlement of Bracha, above Nablus, soliciting the considered opinion of forty Orthodox rabbinical scholars in Israel, the United States, Belgium, and Canada on two questions: whether, in light of the Oslo agreements and the IDF's withdrawal from Jericho and most of the Gaza Strip, Prime Minister Rabin and the members of his government were considered *mosrim* and, if so, whether it was necessary to warn them of the punishment they risked if they did not mend their ways. The author of the letter was Rabbi Eliezer Melamed, the thirty-four-year-old dean of the yeshiva of Har Bracha who doubled as the secretary of the Rabbinical Council of the Land of Israel. His cosigners were Rabbi Dov Lior of Kiryat Arba and Rabbi Daniel Shilo of Kedumim, one of the early Gush Emunim settlements. Their letter implied that these questions were being asked throughout the Jewish world. And while the signers conceded that they were taking a risk by posing their query in writing, they justified it by saying that "the voice of the people murdered by Palestinian terror rises up from the ground, and it is impossible to remain silent." The wording of their questions also left little doubt about the verdict they were seeking on "this evil government and its head."

> Is it possible to consider them accomplices to the terrorists' acts of murder; and should they, according to halacha, be placed on trial; and what should their punishment be in the event that they are found to be accomplices to murder? Is it incumbent upon [rabbis], at this difficult hour, to warn the prime minister and his ministers that, given the bitter experience with the [Oslo Agreement] . . . if they continue to implement it throughout Judea and Samaria,

it will be necessary ... to treat them according to the halachic law regarding a *moser*, who turns Jews and their property over to gentiles?

The forty rabbis were asked to send their replies to Rabbi Melamed in Bracha, where they would be collected by Melamed's wife, Inbal. Eleven rabbis responded. Two confirmed that *din moser* was applicable to Rabin and that he should be warned of his precarious position, seven gave an equivocal reply, and two chastised the authors of the letter for mixing halacha and politics. One of them warned: "You're playing with fire."

After the assassination, when word of the letter to the forty rabbinical sages became known, the police summoned Rabbi Melamed for questioning. Fearing that he would be charged with sedition, he consulted with a more senior colleague. Then he carefully explained to the police that the letter's sole intention had been to inquire whether "it was necessary to place Rabin on trial" and that it "had made no mention of a death sentence." When the interrogators asked to see the replies, Melamed claimed that he had destroyed them. His house was not searched, and the two letters confirming that Rabin was a *moser* were never uncovered. At the end of the interrogation, the case was nonetheless passed on to Attorney General Ben-Ya'ir, who at the end of March 1996 published his decision that since the query requested rather than stated a halachic ruling, it did not constitute incitement.

"We wanted to place Rabin on trial, and we did not speak about a death sentence," Melamed repeated in an interview at the end of 1996. "From my viewpoint, merely raising the question was sufficient [to make the point]."

From the standpoint of halachic law, however, the situation was more complex. The punishment due a *moser* need not be determined by a court, and the ruling Melamed and his two colleagues received from two of the sages was sufficient to justify their own determination, should they choose to make it, that Rabin was subject to an automatic death sentence by any Jew who deemed himself bound by the halacha. Yoel Bin-Nun understood this fact when he characterized the very posing of the question to the rabbinical sages as "appalling."

The letter to the forty rabbis was not Melamed's only connection to the discussion of *din moser* and *din rodef*. Six months before the assassination he received a visit from thirty-two-year-old Rabbi Shmuel Dvir of the settlement of Carmei Tsur, north of Hebron. A teacher in the Har Etzion Yeshiva in Gush Etzion, a cluster of settlements halfway between Jerusalem and Hebron, Dvir was not on a casual visit. His purpose was to consult Melamed on the same question that Melamed had posed to the forty sages. There was no dearth of eminent halachic scholars in Dvir's own yeshiva. But he had reason to expect that their response would be negative, because one of the deans of the yeshiva, Rabbi Yehudah Amital, was a founder of the politically moderate Meimad ("Dimension") movement. Dvir therefore sought counsel elsewhere. "He had an obsession about Rabin and went to consult with many rabbis," one of his students later reported.

Shmuel Dvir made little effort to hide his radical inclinations from either his colleagues in Gush Etzion or his neighbors in Carmei Tsur. He caught the attention of Yoel Bin-Nun's son, Eliad—another resident of Carmei Tsur, who studied in the Har Etzion Yeshiva—after the massacre in the Cave of the Patriarchs. Dvir was so delighted by the news of the slaughter that he broke out into a dance. Thereafter he caused a stir in the yeshiva by proposing that the prayer for the welfare of the government of Israel be dropped from the Sabbath service because it was inappropriate to pray for divine aid to a government that ceded territory to non-Jews. Nevertheless, the sharp intellect and excellent teaching abilities of the tall, round-faced father of six won him admiration among his colleagues and students. Seeing that his extreme political views did not prejudice his standing on Rabbi Amital's staff, he expressed them without misgivings. He seemed not to care that they sometimes made him the butt of mild ridicule. Behind his back, some of his students referred to Dvir as "the Shiite," because of his radicalism.

What few in the Har Etzion Yeshiva knew about Rabbi Dvir, however, was that he had gone beyond voicing the positions of such nationally known figures as Rabbis Shapira, Neria, Yisrael, and Druckman and commented freely on the delicate issue of *din rodef* and *din moser*. In talks with three of his students, he approached the subject with great confidence and ease, analyzing halachic injunctions and quoting from historical sources and commentators. Clearly he had given the subject much thought and had already reached his own conclusions, for two of his students subsequently reported that he told them it was definitely permissible to kill Rabin under the provision of *din rodef*. A third described Dvir's desire to execute the act personally. "If Rabin comes to visit Gush Etzion, I myself will climb on a roof and shoot him with a rifle," he boasted, though he subsequently backtracked by explaining that as a husband and father he was not required to put his own life on the line to honor the injunction, and it was preferable that a bachelor assume the task.

All three students shared the impression that Dvir's reflections on *din rodef* were not idle chatter. He told them that rabbis regarded as leading authorities on Jewish law had confirmed to him, in person, that *din rodef* was applicable to Rabin. He also claimed to have heard, second hand, that other illustrious rabbis had issued the same ruling. He did not mention Rabbi Melamed by name. But he did say that "one of the greats" he had consulted was Rabbi Nachum Rabinovitch, head of the Birkat Moshe ("Moshe's Blessing") Yeshiva in the large settlement Ma'aleh Adumim, and that Rabinovitch had pronounced—in the presence of two other witnesses—that Rabin was subject to *din rodef* "in the fullest sense."

Rabbi Nachum Rabinovitch is unquestionably one of the most respected halachic authorities in the territories. The sixty-four-year-old Canadian-born scholar holds a doctorate in mathematics, has served in rabbinical posts in Canada and the United States, and headed the Orthodox rabbinical seminary in London before immigrating to Israel. A man of keen intellectual prowess, he is also reputed to be the first figure of stature in Israel to have introduced parallels between the peace process and the Holocaust into the public debate. In an article published in the *Jerusalem Post* in July 1993, two months before the signing of the Oslo accord, Rabinovitch compared the positions of the Rabin government with those of the *Judenräte* in Nazi-occupied Europe. He also skillfully exploited the concept of *moser*, introducing it not as a direct charge against Rabin but as a warning to his government against trying to force the Israeli people into becoming collaborators in its designs. In a column entitled "Generals, Jews and Justice," published in the *Jerusalem Post* in December 1993, Rabinovitch quoted Maimonides's definition of a *moser* as "he who delivers his fellow into the hands of *goyim* [gentiles] to kill him or beat him; and he who delivers his fellow's property into the hands of *goyim* or into the hands of an oppressor like a *goy*," adding later in the piece: "Under the pressure of circumstances, even a legitimate government can be tempted to use the army against our own people in order to advance political ends. That spells the end of its legitimacy and it becomes thereby 'an oppressor like a *goy.*' . . . Perhaps our leaders should be reminded while there is yet time that not only soldiers but also ordinary citizens from all walks of life will not become '*mosrim.*'"

The warning was prompted by rumors that the government might evacuate Israeli settlements isolated within areas densely populated by Palestinians, particularly in the Gaza Strip. Both Rabin and Peres denied the government's intention to dismantle any settlement during the five-year interim period established in the Oslo accord. Nevertheless, in the spring of 1995, in a talk with other rabbis, Rabinovitch spelled out how "ordinary citizens from all walks of life" should respond to such a move. He recommended, for example, that settlers plant explosive devices along the paths of their communities to deter Israeli soldiers from entering them. Soon thereafter, in a taped dialogue with Yitzhak Frankenthal, leader of the small Orthodox peace movement Netivot Shalom ("Paths of Peace"), he justified the suggestion by comparing the Israeli government with the Nazis. When Frankenthal protested that if explosives were planted in settlements, Israeli soldiers would be killed, Rabinovitch reasoned: "IDF soldiers must know [the explosives will be there]. We will tell them: 'Don't dare enter [the settlements] under orders.'"

"IDF soldiers will continue to come in under orders. . . ."

"If they do so under orders, then they are truly evil."

"Why evil?"

"Because an order of that sort must not be obeyed, and I take full responsibility for saying that to you. Remember that German soldiers acted under the orders of a democratically elected government."

"Can you compare that catastrophe in any way with a Jewish government?"

"Yes, yes. In the beginning of the Nazi [period], we didn't know what would ultimately happen. . . . But the more they saw [their plan] was working, the worse things got."

A sophisticated as well as fervent opponent of the Oslo process, Rabbi Rabinovitch often delivered his messages in a kind of code based on allusions familiar only to those graced with halachic erudition. "Any action that diminishes our hold on the country or drives Jews out of the precincts of our land is definitely prohibited and is heresy against our sacred Torah," he wrote in *Issue*, the journal of the Rabbinical Council for the Land of Israel. While this statement may impress the uninitiated as no more than impassioned argument, students of the Talmud and the writings of Maimonides could be expected to know that persistent heresy against the Torah is one of the offenses for which the halacha warrants "justifiable" homicide. It would surely be difficult to prove that such allusions to recondite texts constitute incitement. Yet given an atmosphere in which some Israelis were actively seeking grounds for violent action against the government, such references played a role in spreading the belief in a halachic "case" against Rabin. In any event, Rabinovitch did not confine himself to subtleties. In a broadcast on the Voice of Israel in August 1995, he defined Rabin as a *moser*, "who, according to Maimonides, is liable to death," though he was quick to cover himself by adding, "I didn't say that it's permissible to harm him."

Shmuel Dvir placed great store in Rabinovitch's confirmation that Rabin was to be regarded as a *rodef* and repeated it to his students many times. The other rabbis he named as having pronounced the same ruling— or so he claimed—were equally eminent figures: former Sephardi Chief Rabbi Mordechai Eliyahu and Rabbi Dov Lior of Kiryat Arba (who had cosigned Melamed's query to the forty rabbis).

Rabbi Lior is probably best remembered for the controversy he sparked in 1992, when he was a candidate to become a judge of the Supreme Rabbinical Court, the highest legal institution with authority over religious affairs. Lior had the enthusiastic backing of both chief rabbis of the day, Avraham Shapira and Mordechai Eliyahu. What blocked him from receiving the coveted post was the unusual intervention of then Attorney General Yosef Harish, who moved to rule out Lior's candidacy on the ground that he had been known to make flagrantly racist statements. Ultimately the decision reached the High Court of Justice, which did not disqualify Lior outright but effectively derailed his appointment by declaring it "inappropriate."

Racist utterances, however, were far from the most serious offense of which the venerable rabbi was suspected. While under interrogation in 1984, two members of the Jewish Underground claimed that Rabbi Lior had provided halachic approval for the operation to assassinate three West Bank mayors (two of whom, Bassam Shaka of Nablus and Karim Khalaf of El Bireh, were severely maimed when bombs exploded in their cars). Lior was duly interrogated by the police, but no charges were brought against him, leaving him free to issue further rulings in a similar spirit. One such ruling was publicized early in 1994, after Lior had openly mourned Dr. Baruch Goldstein as a "martyr" who had been "killed by gentiles for being a Jew and thus joins the victims of the Nazi Holocaust." Angered by the damage that such perverse rhetoric posed to the repute of the Orthodox community as a whole, the late Avraham Stern, Knesset member from the National Religious Party, reminded the country of Lior's history by exposing one of his earlier rulings encouraging attacks on innocent Arabs. "Since the gentiles have harmed us," Stern quoted the ruling, "we are allowed to respond, if we can, with retaliatory actions—and there is no restriction [on taking measures against] innocent people, since this comes in response to an act of war, and it is beyond doubt that to take vengeance on gentiles is a [religious] duty." Rabbi Lior did not deny that he had authored the ruling, though he tried to defend it by arguing that "I never said everyone is personally entitled to commit such a deed, rather that it is a duty of the country's security forces." Thus, when Rabbi Dvir told his students that Lior was one of the "greats" who had categorized Rabin as *rodef*, they had little reason to doubt him.

It was from Shmuel Dvir's students that an account of his discussions on *din rodef* reached Yoel Bin-Nun after the assassination. This revelation placed him in a quandary, and he struggled hard to decide whether the information to which he had become privy merited a criminal investigation or whether he should make it public. Haunted by the implications of what he had learned, he decided to break his silence two days after Rabin had been laid to rest.

The setting he chose for doing so was both public and intimate: an open meeting in Jerusalem called by the Meimad movement and cosponsored by the Yesha Council. The purpose of the session was to explore to what extent the national religious community may have contributed to the atmosphere leading up to the assassination. The meeting drew a crowd of mostly modern Orthodox young men to hear leading rabbis and political figures debate the sensitive question, and there was considerable tension in the small auditorium. Meimad and the Yesha Council rarely saw eye to eye, and there were few opportunities to hear their leaders engage in a dialogue. What no one could possibly have expected, however, was that a longtime member of the Yesha Council, Rabbi Yoel Bin-Nun, would stand up and, in an explosion of anger, categorically demand that the leaders in the hall bring about the prompt resignation "from every post of rabbinical authority" of "certain people" who had ruled that Rabin was a *rodef* or a *moser*.

"If rabbis had not [sanctioned the murder], no youngster would have dared to do such a thing," he called out above the outraged cries from the audience. "If they do not stand up and resign from all their rabbinical posts by the end of the seven days of mourning—and this is an ultimatum—I will fight them before the entire Jewish people. I warn you: If these people whose rulings or words led to Rabin's death do not reveal themselves, take account of themselves, and resign from their positions, I myself will reveal their identity!"

Most of the people in the hall were stunned by the spectacle of a prominent settler-rabbi and Gush Emunim veteran threatening such a move. From the shouts and grumbling, it was clear that many would regard Bin-Nun himself as a *moser* if he followed through. Though the drama of the conclave was reported in the press, Bin-Nun's statement was at first treated more as a curiosity than a major news story. Most Israelis were preoccupied with more emotional aspects of the assassination's aftermath. Only within the national religious community did the mood grow increasingly tense as the mourning period drew to a close. Some rabbis feared that Bin-Nun's challenge referred to all of the forty scholars who had received Melamed's letter. Others feared it would spark a witch-hunt in which reputations would be ruined and spiritual leaders might be brought up on charges of sedition, or worse. No one in the religious establishment echoed his demand, and no one resigned in response to it.

Instead, the pressure on Bin-Nun to back down began almost as soon as he walked through the door of his home that night. In response to death threats he received by phone, the police recommended that he wear a bulletproof vest and provided him with bodyguards. A few rabbis threatened to excommunicate him if he carried out his ultimatum. His neighbors in Ofra let it be known that it would be best if he left the settlement. Rabbis closely associated with the National Religious Party quietly consulted on how to deal with the affair and turned to Rabbi Chaim Druckman, among the most respected and influential members of the national religious camp. Keenly aware of the weight of his views, the sixty-two-year-old educator and former NRP Knesset deputy proceeded cautiously. Having consulted with the party's leaders, Druckman decided that the best course was to deny flatly that any rabbi had issued a judgment on *din rodef* or *din moser*.

Thus Yoel Bin-Nun remained on his own, and when the week of mourning had ended he carried out his ultimatum—though not in the way most people had expected. Rather than go to the police or the press with the names of the suspected rabbis, Nun went straight to the top of the rabbinical establishment—Ashkenazi Chief Rabbi Yisrael Lau and Sephardi Chief Rabbi Eliyahu Bakshi-Doron—to propose that a committee of rabbis investigate the troubling testimony that had come to his attention. Persuaded by his arguments, the two chief rabbis agreed to the composition of a three-man panel. Only then did Bin-Nun reveal to them the names of seven rabbis he suspected of opening the way to Rabin's murder. The first, Shmuel Dvir, was virtually anonymous. But three others—Nachum Rabinovitch, Dov Lior, and former Chief Rabbi Mordechai Eliyahu—were so illustrious that Lau and Bakshi-Doron were astonished to hear their names. Bin-Nun left the meeting confident not only that he had taken the correct course but that the panel would handle the matter with the necessary firmness.

He was wrong. Word of the meeting spread quickly, the two chief rabbis quickly found themselves under pressure from their colleagues, and by the next morning the entire arrangement had collapsed. Tellingly, Bakshi-Doron's first conversation was with Rabbi Druckman, who conveyed the views of the NRP. Then both chief rabbis met with their immediate predecessors, Ovadiah Yosef and Avraham Shapira. Shapira's repeated defiance of Rabin left little doubt about his reluctance to take other rabbis to task for their imprudent use of the halacha.

Following these conversations, Bakshi-Doron was the first to retract his consent to an internal investigation. He summoned Rabbi Rabinovitch to a private meeting and accepted his denial that he had ever issued a ruling relating *din rodef* or *din moser* to Rabin. "Rabbi Bin-Nun is a liar, a cheat, and a gossip," Rabinovitch fumed during their talk. "I think he's insane." Bakshi-Doron then contacted a student of Rabbi Lior's, who likewise rejected the allegations against his mentor. Satisfied with the results of these two conversations, the following day Bakshi-Doron issued a communiqué stating: "If anyone has further anonymous information, let him go to the police. It is not the rabbinate's job to conduct investigations. I have met with two of the rabbis whose names were given to me by Rabbi Bin-Nun, and as far as I'm concerned, the matter is closed."

The previous evening Chief Rabbi Lau happened to meet Police Commissioner Assaf Hefetz and told him of the decision taken earlier that day. Hefetz suggested that the police handle the affair. Thus both chief rabbis were persuaded to remove themselves from the picture, though not before Bakshi-Doron had revealed to the media the names of two of the suspects confidentially cited by Bin-Nun: Nachum Rabinovitch and Dov Lior.

Yoel Bin-Nun was mortified by this indiscretion. "I almost fainted," he recalled many months later. "I had been done a terrible injustice. On the previous night the chief rabbis had agreed not to publish the names of the suspects without first obtaining my permission." For reasons known only to himself, Bakshi-Doron did not release the names of Shmuel Dvir or Mordechai Eliyahu. But an official of the chief rabbinate leaked Eliyahu's name to a local newspaper, and the revelation sparked a national uproar. Two days later Bin-Nun was summoned for a talk with Rabbi Eliyahu's secretary. Bin-Nun admitted that he did not have any direct evidence of wrongdoing on Eliyahu's part but noted that "people are naming him—not Shapira, not Druckman, but [Eliyahu]." When the aide demanded that he confirm, in writing, that he personally had no grounds to suspect Rabbi Eliyahu of having issued a ruling on *din rodef*, the embarrassed Bin-Nun complied. He was unaware that the Shabak had received an anonymous tip that a discussion of *din rodef* had taken place in the courtyard of Rabbi Eliyahu's Jerusalem home. In any event, Rabbi Mordechai Eliyahu's name was never again mentioned in connection with the matter.

With the option of a discreet internal inquiry scotched, Police Commissioner Hefetz went to the opposite extreme by assigning the investigation of the three remaining suspects to the high-profile National Unit for Serious Crimes Investigations. With considerable trepidation—and only after obtaining assurances that their identities would not be leaked—Bin-Nun confided the names of the three Har Etzion Yeshiva students who had brought Dvir's behavior to his attention. Only two of the students were called in to make statements; the third was doing reserve duty, and no effort was made to locate him. In fact, the third student—whose testimony would have held the most weight since he was the one to whom Dvir had made his threat against Rabin (and, after the murder, expressed his satisfaction over Yigal Amir's initiative)—has not been questioned to this day.

Rabbis Rabinovitch, Dvir, and Lior, however, were all summoned for interrogation at the National Unit for Serious Crimes headquarters, and all three flatly denied the allegations against them. When Rabbi Melamed of Bracha was called in for questioning, he admitted that Dvir had asked him whether Rabin was subject to *din rodef* but insisted that "I told him no one thinks so." The police duly recorded the denials of the four rabbis and sent them on their way. The crime squad was out of its depth in grappling with the complexities of the halacha, as is clearly indicated by the fact that the transcripts of the interrogations contain at least four different interpretations of *din rodef* and *din moser*. Ultimately the chief of the Investigations Division, Major General Yossi Levy, signed a recommendation to the State Attorney's Office that the files against the rabbis be closed. "I don't believe any rabbi explicitly ruled on *din moser* against Yitzhak Rabin for Yigal Amir," Levy told television reporters, and in the middle of March 1996 Attorney General Ben-Ya'ir adopted his recommendation in announcing his decision to close the files against the rabbis for lack of evidence.

Yoel Bin-Nun was not surprised by the results of the police investigation. "I never believed that the Israeli legal system had the proper tools to investigate and judge rabbis and their religious rulings. From the outset, I pressed not for a criminal investigation but for a public and religious clarification, so as to prevent the next murder," he wrote in *Yediot Ahronot* in March 1996, adding that he did not consider the attorney general's decision the final word on the matter. "The denials of the rabbis who pronounced sentence on Rabin closed the criminal case, but they are insufficient from the public and religious standpoint. The very fact that [*din rodef*] was a matter of discussion attests to the cavalier manner with which many religious people relate to bloodshed." To underscore the point, Bin-Nun cited the history of Jewish violence in the territories. "In a chain of very grave events, over many years, religious scholars who are meticulous in their observance of the commandments have behaved in a way that has inspired personal violence, including bloodshed—first against Arabs [and] later against [army] officers, policemen, and soldiers—until the tragedy reached the point of the murder of the prime minister."*

As he continued to speak out against the violence encouraged by some of his colleagues, Yoel Bin-Nun received anonymous threats and became practically a pariah within the national religious community. A kabbalistic mystic went so far as to place a curse on him. A handbill circulated in synagogues described Bin-Nun and Dvir's three students as "dupes, wicked and contemptible people who are exploited by the left," and the NRP weekly, *Shabbat be-Shabbato* ("Every Saturday")—distributed in some hundred thousand copies in Orthodox synagogues in Israel—broadly suggested that they should be punished as informers.

Still, the nagging questions would not go away. About half a year after the assassination two trusted leaders of the settler movement were appointed by a group of powerful rabbinical and political figures in the territories to conduct their own quiet inquiry. Their mandate was to work in secret, and it was understood that their findings would be kept "inside the family." The impulse behind the move was the same as Bin-Nun's: to ensure that if there were any truth to the rumors that four rabbis (three of whom were associated with yeshivas in the territories) had permitted themselves to judge Rabin a *rodef* or a *moser*, they would be removed from their posts.

As disciples of Rabbi Kook and founders of Gush Emunim, the two men chosen to conduct the inquiry could be trusted not to damage the national religious cause. Rabbi Chaim Druckman, dean of the Or Etzion Yeshiva, had been one of the signatories on Rabbi Shapira's halachic ruling against evacuating any army base in the territories. NRP Knesset member Hanan Porat was an equally outspoken crusader against the Oslo process. The two began their work by following the same course as the police— except this time all three of Dvir's students were asked to give their version of events (of which, incidentally, no record was made). Once again the

---

*In his book *Dear Brothers*, an account of the Jewish Underground, Haggai Segal wrote that Rabbis Dov Lior, Eliezer Waldman (also of Kiryat Arba), and Moshe Levinger (of Hebron) participated in planning the terror actions against the West Bank mayors. Menachem Livni, another member of the Underground, wrote an affidavit stating that Rabbi Waldman had asked to be included in the operation. Rabbi Levinger was said to have provided advice in the planning of the attack on the Islamic University in Hebron, which was carried out by his son-in-law, Uzi Sharbaf, and his neighbor Shaul Nir. Three students were killed in the action, and Nir subsequently testified that he had also received approval from rabbis in Jerusalem and Kiryat Arba for an operation to blow up Arab buses, which was foiled at the last moment by the Shabak.

students testified that they had heard Dvir say the halacha prescribed the killing of Rabin, and once again Dvir was confronted with their testimony. This time, however, reassured by the atmosphere of trust and camaraderie, Dvir did not deny it. Instead, he tried to make light of the matter by claiming that he had not discussed *din rodef* in any concrete context. He had "just been kidding," he said, when he had boasted that he would shoot Rabin if the prime minister visited Gush Etzion. Druckman and Porat were not appeased. "We had a sharp talk with him," Porat later revealed, "and found his views to be immature and distorted. . . . His halachic thinking lacks an understanding of the times and the situation, and he's likely to reach terribly twisted [conclusions]. . . . We scolded him, and he was frightened. We shouted at him: 'You can ruin yourself and lead to murder and the destruction of the [settlement] enterprise.' He was shocked and shaken."

Dismayed by his predicament, Dvir revealed the names of the rabbis who had told him, in private conversations, that Rabin was to be treated as a *rodef.* He also gave the names of other rabbis who, he had heard, had issued the same judgment. Druckman and Porat tried to corroborate his testimony, but had little success. Of the various rabbis named by Dvir, they interviewed only one, Nachum Rabinovitch. Under police interrogation, Rabinovitch denied that he had spoken with Dvir at all. But he admitted to Druckman and Porat that they had held an "off-the-cuff conversation" about "the halachic meaning"—rather than the practical one—"of who can be considered a *rodef.*" "I told Dvir the issue deserves to be discussed," he told them, "but that this is not the place to do so and that it must not be discussed in practical terms at all."

Porat and Druckman were now faced with conflicting accounts of the conversation between Dvir and Rabinovitch. Dvir claimed that Rabinovitch told him *din rodef* was applicable to Rabin "and all that this implies"; Rabinovitch insisted he had warned against discussing the injunction in any but theoretical terms. The two investigators chose to accept Rabinovitch's version, and that was as far as their inquiry went. In compliance with the rules set down for them, they did not bring their findings to the police and confined themselves to the "educational lesson" of rebuking Dvir and telling Rabinovitch that he should "publicly qualify" statements he had made prior to the murder (as he did by speaking in a number of yeshivas and by apologizing in a meeting with leftist intellectuals).

"I did not regard myself as an investigating magistrate," Porat explained their decision to the authors. "I saw the heart of the matter as an educational one. It was important for us to convey an emphatic message that these concepts of *rodef* and *moser* are irrelevant to our times, and anyone who toys with them is playing with fire."

Rabbi Dvir's "punishment" for what his neighbors apparently deemed a lack of mature judgment, but others might take as incitement to murder, was a banishment of sorts. Soon after the assassination he was asked to leave Carmei Tsur. Druckman and Porat would have preferred that he also be barred from holding any teaching post. "Dvir must not be allowed to educate a single young person," Porat said in an interview. But Dvir found a warm welcome in another educational institution in the territories: Rabbi Melamed's yeshiva in Bracha. His neighbors there describe him as an amiable man, and Rabbi Melamed is highly pleased with his acquisition. "We have taken in a rabbi who is extremely knowledgeable and can help the yeshiva," he replied when asked whether Dvir was a suitable choice as a teacher. "I am satisfied with his place on our staff."

The two perfunctory attempts to trace a connection between the invocation of *din rodef* and *din moser* and the assassination of Yitzhak Rabin produced little more than vague leads that are unlikely to be pursued any further. The highly pertinent question of whether Yitzhak Rabin's assassin received direct rabbinical sanction for his deed has been dropped completely from the national agenda. Since the assassination Yigal Amir has repeatedly claimed that as one who imperiled Jewish lives and turned parts of the Land of Israel over to foreign rule, Rabin deserved the fate of a *rodef* and a *moser*. More to the point, on a number of occasions he insisted that he had murdered the prime minister on the basis of rabbinical rulings. "Who am I to take such responsibility upon myself?" he protested to his interrogators.

In the course of his interrogation, however, Amir became evasive about the precise source of the halachic sanction. At first, when he was still confused and unsure of himself, he claimed to have received a rabbinical ruling on the issue. Later on, when he had recovered his self-confidence, he said he had deduced the obligation to act against Rabin from his own study of the Talmud, though he heard that various rabbis had come to the same conclusion. He also told his interrogators that his accomplice Dror Adani had consulted with a rabbi and obtained a ruling that supported his plan. But when asked to identify the rabbi in question, he pleaded ignorance.

The importance Amir ascribed to obtaining halachic approval is demonstrated by the fact that he tried to clarify the issue of *din rodef* with Rabbi Shmuel Kav, one of his teachers at the Kerem D'Yavneh Yeshiva (where he had studied while serving in the army). Summoned by the police for interrogation, Kav recalled the conversation distinctly enough to say that it had taken place when the two had met at a funeral. "I told him it is forbidden to even talk about that!" he recalled. Amir gave his interrogators a more equivocal version of Kav's response, claiming the rabbi had said: "According to the halacha, it is a duty to murder Rabin. But *you* are forbidden to kill him." Either way, the investigators placed little importance on the encounter.

Amir's brother and co-conspirator, Haggai, confirmed that Yigal had sought rabbinical approval. In March 1996, just before the holiday of Purim, when Jews traditionally dress in costume as part of the celebrations, word reached Haggai in his prison cell that Efraim Zalmanovich, the rabbi of the village of Mazkeret Batya, had expressly forbidden any member of his community to dress up as Yigal Amir. The reason he gave for this bizarre pronouncement was that "a Jew is not allowed to masquerade as someone evil."

Haggai promptly penned an outraged letter in defense of his brother's honor:

> Your Eminence attacks my brother and calls him wicked. Does Your Eminence know why he did what he did? My brother did what he did for the sake of the Lord, in the purest possible way. He received a halachic ruling from a rabbi, and he acted according to the halacha, and with sanctity, knowing that he was going to die for it. And the Almighty, blessed be He, performed a miracle for him, and he was not even scratched. . . . There is no doubt that to kill a Jew is a terrible thing, but Your Eminence knows that there were times when this was sometimes done for lack of choice, and it is necessary to do such things to save the people of Israel.

This letter merits mention not only because it confirms Amir's initial claim that he received rabbinical approval to murder Rabin but adds the detail that the murder was carried out "according to the halacha," suggesting that he had followed a direct prescription. The point becomes particularly intriguing when viewed in light of an anonymous tip received by the Shabak after the murder. The source described a curious scene in which not a word passed between Amir and the rabbi he had chosen to consult. But the latter must have known what Amir was going to ask him because as soon as Yigal entered his office, the rabbi exited through a second door. Left on a lectern in the middle of the room, however, was a copy of the Talmud open to the Sanhedrin Tractate, Chapter 49, in which the ancient sages discussed the biblical passage (II Samuel 2:12–28) from which *din rodef* derived. Amir understood the cue, read the page of the Talmud, and went on his way.

The historical setting of the incident described in the Talmud was the struggle for succession between King Ish-bosheth, the son of King Saul, and David, who had already been anointed as king of Judah but aspired to follow Saul as regent over all the tribes. The clash between the rivals began as a tournament between twelve men from each side that burgeoned into a full-fledged battle ending in the defeat of Ish-bosheth's men. As his fighters fled the scene, Asahel, one of David's captains, continued to pursue (*rodef,* in Hebrew) Abner, the commander of Ish-bosheth's army. The terse biblical account relates only that twice in the course of the pursuit, Abner turned to Asahel and implored him to stop. "Turn aside from following me; why should I smite you to the ground?" he called out to his assailant. But Asahel would not relent. Finally, Abner turned to face Asahel in combat and killed him with his spear. In discussing the incident, the talmudic sages repeated the detail that Abner's "spear smote [Asahel] under the fifth rib," precisely the spot at which Yigal Amir aimed his gun when he shot Yitzhak Rabin.

Thus all the evidence clearly suggests that Yigal Amir sought rabbinical confirmation that Rabin fell under the rubric of *din rodef.* Whether or not he obtained it, and from whom, was not discovered because the authorities were obviously loath to pursue the matter, even though they were in the ideal position of having the three co-conspirators—Yigal Amir, Haggai Amir, and Dror Adani—under detention simultaneously. The police questioned four rabbis as a result of Bin-Nun's allegations and a fifth (Rabbi Kav) as a consequence of Yigal Amir's interrogation but contented themselves with accepting their statements at face value. They did not arrange a confrontation between Dvir and his students, just as the Druckman-Porat team spared Rabinovitch a face-off with Dvir. Like the two chief rabbis and the two amateur sleuths, Israel's law enforcement agencies failed to investigate the problem adequately.

By now it may be impossible to do so. Yigal Amir told the authors, in an exclusive post-trial interview, only that "There were lots of rabbis who said *din rodef* applied to Rabin." Rabbis Dvir and Lior have made themselves inaccessible to the media. Only Rabbi Rabinovitch has willingly granted interviews to restate his opinion that Yoel Bin-Nun must have suffered a breakdown. "Perhaps he needs psychiatric care," he said. "He speaks slander. How can a man name names? I am convinced that no rabbi could say anything like [Rabin was subject to *din rodef* or *din moser*]. Anyone who knows anything about the Jewish way of thinking would find such a thing inconceivable."

A s we shall see, however, there were rabbis, albeit beyond the reach of the Israeli law, who publicly pronounced Rabin liable to *din rodef*. After the assassination, moreover, it was revealed that two of the rabbis who were interrogated about their handling of *din moser* had met with Rabin just five days before his murder. Advised by the Shabak that the intensity of anger among the settlers was rising dangerously, the prime minister had invited the Rabbinical Council for the Land of Israel for a meeting in his office, but only two of its members agreed to attend: Rabbi Rabinovitch and Rabbi Melamed.

"It was a polite meeting," Melamed recalled, "and Rabbi Rabinovitch, who is a professor, made a long and impassioned speech to Rabin. He spoke for about a quarter of an hour about Jewish history and the destiny of the Jewish people, while Rabin listened impassively."

The prime minister must have found the lecture trying, for when Rabin's chief of staff, Eitan Haber, commented afterward that Rabinovitch had said some "remarkable things," Rabin's response was a laugh. "And you still believe what they say?" he chided Haber. "How naive you are!"

CHAPTER 5

THE AMERICAN
CONNECTION

For all its crudeness and stridor, the incitement against Yitzhak Rabin in Israel seemed almost subdued compared with the parallel effort in a country where the general tone of political discourse is usually more civil: the United States. Soon after Oslo, Rabin's opponents in the American Jewish community began branding him a traitor and a *rodef*; it was not long before they had advanced to calling him a Nazi. By the summer of 1995 the invective showered on the prime minister and his government had become so savage that Israel's consul general in New York, Colette Avital, could restrain herself no longer. Avital knew that right-wing and Orthodox Jews were providing the extremists in Israel with inspiration and a great deal of money. She had accumulated on her desk stacks of Jewish newspapers, journals, pamphlets, flyers, cassettes of radio and television programs, printouts from the Internet, all of which were full of rumor, lies, fabrications, half-truths, and distortions directed against Yitzhak Rabin. She felt it was her duty to warn the prime minister of what was going on.

Avital had found that in the city boasting the largest Jewish community in the world, only one voice was being heard: that of a radical Orthodox minority that stood almost solidly against the Middle East peace process. Supporters of peace in New York seemed unable to utter more than a murmur of protest as Orthodox rabbis and right-wing radicals called for the disposal of the prime minister of Israel. Avital was appalled. Day by day she felt the wall of hostility between the Orthodox Jews of New York and the official envoys of the State of Israel grow higher. Never had whole Jewish neighborhoods in the United States—or anywhere else for that matter— been declared off limits to Israeli diplomats. Yet Avital had been warned that if she dared set foot in the bastions of Jewish Orthodoxy in New York, she would be met by bottles, bricks, and stones. The elders of the community told her that never before had they encountered such loathing for the elected government of Israel. Jewish fanatics were mounting a campaign of hatred against her country's government while the vast majority of American Jews stood idly by.

Colette Avital was the first female consul general to establish herself in Israel's diplomatic residence on Manhattan's Upper East Side. A cultured woman in her early fifties who carries herself with an air of muted elegance, she had been posted to New York in 1993 after serving as Israel's ambassador to Portugal. As a specialist in public affairs and press relations, as well as a famed workaholic, she was touted as someone the Labor Party might groom for a political post. But nothing in her distinguished thirty-year career prepared her to cope with the threats and abuse heaped upon her and her superiors in Israel.

The Orthodox Jewish community in New York was displeased by Avital's appointment from the start, convinced that a woman had no business in such a high-profile post. Various rabbis and communal leaders resolved to make her job as hard as possible by laying ambushes for her. Avital was invited to address the 1994 annual dinner of the Jerusalem Reclamation Project (JRP), a right-wing association that raises funds to settle Jews in Arab neighborhoods of Jerusalem, only to be whistled and booed down when she approached the microphone. Things deteriorated rapidly from there, so that when the *Jewish Press*—New York's most prominent Orthodox and radical right-wing weekly—invited its readers to participate in a poll on Avital's performance, the overwhelming majority called for her to be dismissed at once. She was also seen in the company of ABC News anchor Peter Jennings, who was reviled in right-wing circles as an "Israel-basher"—a fact that did nothing to endear her to her detractors.

Avital was essentially pitted against a united front of Orthodox and right-wing Jewish activists led by New York State Assemblyman Dov Hikind, Rabbis Abraham Hecht and Herbert Bomzer, and businessmen

Sam Domb and Jack Avital. Mayor Rudolph Giuliani, who was politically in their debt, lined up behind them. The thread connecting most of New York's opponents to the Middle East peace process was the late Rabbi Meir Kahane, whose associates and disciples had forged the alliance of Orthodox and right-wing forces and recruited the mayor to its cause.

When Avital composed her memorandum to Rabin, she began by listing the names of the organizations engaged in the anti-Oslo offensive. The group included Americans for a Safe Israel, the World Committee for Israel, American Friends of Hebron, Pro-Israel, Women in Green, the Zionist Organization of America (ZOA), the Jerusalem Reclamation Project (JRP), the Central Israel Fund-One Israel, Zo Artzenu, Yesha-One Israel Fund, Operation Kiryat Arba, Operation Chizuk ("Strengthening"), and the Committee for the Preservation of Eretz Hakodesh ("the Holy Land"). Perhaps the most troubling of them all, for its sheer size and influence, was the Orthodox Young Israel movement.

Young Israel is one of the most powerful forces in the Orthodox Jewish community in America, embracing some twenty thousand middle- and upper-middle-class families that maintain close ties with kindred circles in Israel. On September 19, 1993, just six days after the historic handshake on the South Lawn of the White House, the National Council of Young Israel gave the signal to launch the struggle against the Oslo accord. The decision was taken during an emergency meeting of East Coast rabbis in New York, with their Israeli colleagues participating by satellite hookup. Young Israel's call to "struggle for the cancellation of the Oslo Agreement" represented a departure from past practice, for whatever the disagreements between the rival political camps in Israel, the organizations representing American Jewry had long followed a tacit rule of supporting the country's elected government. The pledge to fight the Oslo Agreement also reflected the rift in American Jewry—between the Orthodox community, on one side, and the Conservative and Reform streams, on the other—that had been growing steadily deeper since the 1967 Six-Day War.

The war initially brought the American Jewish community together as never before. Thousands of volunteers signed up to fly to Israel and fill in for army reservists, whose call-up had left the economy in near paralysis. The America-Israel Public Affairs Committee (AIPAC), the chief pro-Israel lobby in Washington, worked to secure executive and congressional support for the beleaguered state and, for the first time, impressively proved its strength. At the end of the June blitzkrieg, when America's Jews grasped the magnitude of Israel's victory, they were as exhilarated as the Israelis themselves. Such feeling was powered by both a strong ethnic bond and a lingering guilt over the failure of American Jews to persuade their government to impede the slaughter during the Holocaust.

For American Orthodox Jews, however, the war also brought about a religious awakening. In an article published in the Winter 1993 issue of the Young Israel quarterly, *Viewpoint,* Rabbi Simcha Krauss of the Young Israel of Hillcrest, New York, described the victory's differing impact on Orthodox Jews in the United States and on secular Jews in Israel.

> In truth, for Rabin and other Israeli leaders who are insensitive to the spiritual dimensions of our heritage, the victory of the Six Day War was only military. The land which was liberated at the time had no special significance to them. For those of us who are *yirei shomayim* ["believers in God"], the unprecedented significance of the '67 war was overpowering, and the lands which it brought to us changed our lives. Not only did it renew our pride in being Jews, it inspired thousands of Jews to embark on a spiritual quest, energizing what we call today the *baal teshuva* ["return to religion"] movement.

Following the conquest (or "liberation," in Krauss's parlance) of the Greater Land of Israel, a rich symbiosis developed between the Orthodox camps on the two sides of the ocean. The number of Orthodox tourists to Israel soared, as did the volume of students who went there for a year or more to take part in special yeshiva programs. Thousands of young Orthodox Americans settled in the occupied territories, and funds created for specifically national religious projects—like the JRP, the Yesha Council, and the Hebron community—competed for Orthodox donors with the established United Jewish Appeal and Israel Bonds campaigns.

The flow of donations from the American Orthodox community to the Greater Land of Israel movement was further boosted by the visits of Israeli rabbis and right-wing leaders to the United States. Particularly in demand on the Orthodox lecture circuit in the early 1990s was Ariel Sharon. Sometimes he was accompanied by Yehiel Leiter of the Yesha Council, which moved its fund-raising apparatus to New York in 1992 and in December

1993 reported that the new branch had transferred $1.5 million to the settlements over the previous eighteen months. Rusty Moslow, the executive director of Pro-Israel, boasted that the response to a 160,000-letter post-Oslo solicitation was "off the charts." Other Likud luminaries, such as former Prime Minister Yitzhak Shamir, Jerusalem Mayor Ehud Olmert, and Likud Chairman Benjamin Netanyahu, also covered the circuit and were received enthusiastically.

So fierce was the competition over American funds for the settlements that it inevitably led to confrontations. In December 1993, for example, Jack Avital, vice-president of the World Committee for Israel, accused Netanyahu of using two hundred thousand dollars raised specifically for the Yesha Council to help cover the Likud's titanic debt. The Likud countered that the money had gone to pay for a large demonstration sponsored with other groups in the Joint Staff, thereby highlighting, perhaps unwittingly, that donations from the United States were helping to fund the incitement against Rabin.

The main difference between the Orthodox community in America and its Conservative, Reform, or secular counterparts was that only the Orthodox had built firm ideological and institutional ties with their comrades in Israel. The annual public opinion surveys conducted by the American Jewish Committee clearly reflect this gap. In the 1995 poll, for example, 72 percent of the Orthodox respondents said they felt "very close" to Israel, compared with 13 percent of Reform Jews. What's more, though Orthodox believers constitute only 10 percent of America's six million Jews, and their counterparts in Israel make up an estimated 20 percent of the population, the two communities enjoyed inordinate political influence. It was their passion, rather than their numbers, that gave the Orthodox communities their enviable clout.

If the conquest of the territories in 1967 was the first time the lives of Orthodox Jews in the United States were dramatically altered, the second time was on September 13, 1993, when the Oslo Agreement was signed by Israel and the PLO. As Ya'akov Kornreich, a journalist whose work appears in various Orthodox Jewish papers, wrote: "An agreement was publicly consummated which will eventually touch the life of every single Jew. We watched in shock and disbelief . . . stunned, speechless, looking on as helpless spectators as the homes of 130,000 Jews [in the territories] were, potentially, signed away with a stroke of a pen."

When they met in New York six days after that fateful stroke, the rabbis of the Young Israel movement decided to take action. There was no suggestion of pausing to give peace a chance. Veteran leaders like Rabbi Herbert Bomzer of Brooklyn (who had hosted Meir Kahane's funeral in his synagogue), Young Israel's president, Chaim S. Kaminetzki, and its executive director, Rabbi Pesach Lerner, led the movement rightward to bring it into line with the demands of members who had immigrated to Israel and opened dozens of branches in the territories. With Young Israel leading the way, other prominent Orthodox Jewish groups resolved to oppose the nascent Oslo Agreement by every means possible: prayers, rallies, demonstrations, newsletters, letters to the editor, radio and television broadcasts, and, above all, pressure on local and national officeholders.

On December 13, 1993, Colette Avital noted in her records the first demonstration by anti-Oslo activists. The demonstration was sponsored by the World Committee for Israel, led by Manfred Lehmann, who characterized it as a "non-partisan protest" organized because "the old-time established Jewish organizations are paralyzed." It was held in Times Square with three hundred protesters, most of them wearing yarmulkes, brandishing signs reading DON'T TURN ISRAEL INTO ANOTHER LEBANON and JEWISH BLOOD IS NOT CHEAP as they listened to speeches by Rabbi Abraham Hecht, Assemblyman Dov Hikind, City Councilman Anthony Wiener, and businessman Sam Domb. From time to time some of the demonstrators jostled their way into the road, blocking traffic on Broadway until the cordon of police around them could push them back. One young protester in a parka coat, New York Rangers cap, and sunglasses caught the attention of *Village Voice* reporter Robert Friedman. When asked what had brought him to the demo, the demonstrator replied: "Rabin is worse than Hitler. Hitler was a *goy* who killed Jews. Rabin is a Jew who kills Jews. Rabin should be killed."

At that time rabbis and other leaders of the Orthodox community still refrained from drawing such odious comparisons. Nevertheless, the demonstration was a milestone. For the first time shouts of "Rabin should be killed" and "Rabin is a traitor" were heard. Posters bearing the same message did not appear in Israel until four months later.

Incensed by the tolerance of such language, Colette Avital complained directly to Malcolm Hoenlein, director of the influential Council of Presidents of Major American Jewish Organizations, which represents fifty-two groups. She demanded that he publish a sharp denunciation of the chants and placards. Others contacted Hoenlein as well, but with a different message. The leaders of Young Israel and the ZOA pressured him to remain neutral. Even outspoken supporters of peace counseled restraint, lest issuing a protest give further publicity to the actions of a small minority. In the end Hoenlein published a statement of censure, to minimal effect.

After New York, Capitol Hill became the target of a two-pronged assault by Israeli and American Jewish opponents of the Oslo process. Through their direct connections with the Likud and the Yesha Council, Orthodox rabbis in America received a steady stream of reports on the Palestinian Authority's violations of the Oslo Agreement (as interpreted by the Israeli right). Many of them were written by three people: Yossi Ben-Aharon, the former director general of the Prime Minister's Office under Shamir; Yigal Carmon, who had been Shamir's adviser on counterterrorism; and Yoram Ettinger, a former attaché for congressional affairs in the Israeli Embassy in Washington. But the "Gang of Three," as Rabin had christened them, did not stop there. Much to the irritation of AIPAC and the Israeli Embassy, they set up their own operation in Washington to lobby Congress on three issues: transferring the American Embassy in Israel from Tel Aviv to Jerusalem; squelching the idea of stationing U.S. troops on the Golan Heights as part of the security arrangement in a future peace treaty between Israel and Syria; and especially withholding American aid to the cash-starved Palestinian Authority—a move that would have brought it, and the peace process, to the point of collapse.

They were joined in this enterprise by the Orthodox Jewish lobby, which invested an enormous effort in winning over two powerful Republican members of Congress: Jesse Helms of North Carolina, the chairman of the Senate Foreign Relations Committee, and Benjamin Gilman of New York, the chairman of the House Foreign Affairs Committee. New York Republican Senator Alfonse D'Amato and Representatives Michael Forbes, Charles Schumer, and Peter King had already been enlisted to spearhead the battle from inside Congress.

The climax of the crusade against the Palestinian Authority came on June 13, 1995, when a delegation of one hundred Orthodox rabbis descended on Capitol Hill to secure the delay of aid promised by the administration until the Palestinians had fulfilled the demands dictated by the Israeli right. Two weeks later Congress was to debate the administration's request to transfer another hundred million dollars to the Palestinians, out of a total package of five hundred million dollars in grants and loans to be disbursed over a period of five years. Washington's payments to the Palestinian account were already in arrears. Though two years had passed since the signing of the Oslo accord, the United States had transferred only eighty million dollars to the Palestinian Authority, through a special apparatus of donor countries known as the Holst Fund. Helms and Gilman were hoping further to complicate the process by proposing a bill that would make the continuation of the pledged aid conditional upon renewed congressional approval every six months. D'Amato had actually done them one better in proposing the cancellation of American aid to the Palestinian Authority altogether, channeling it instead to humanitarian projects administered by U.S. agencies.

Drumming up support for these bills was the purpose of the rabbis' crusade. It was launched on the initiative of Rabbi Sholom Gold, the past president of Young Israel, who told the press that until the PLO met the standards of compliance, accountability, and disclosure, it "is still to be regarded as a terrorist organization." Traveling to the capital on buses paid for by Young Israel, the Rabbinical Council of America, the Rabbinical Alliance of America, and non-Jewish groups such as Pro-Israel Christians and the Traditional Values Coalition (with which the Orthodox lobby had created an ad hoc alliance called the Coalition for Middle East Peace with Security), the rabbis fanned out into the offices of senators and representatives from the two foreign relations committees. They quoted from a sixteen-page ZOA report featuring a litany of Palestinian transgressions, from the failure to combat terrorism to the broadcast of anti-Israel propaganda on state-controlled media. But the real crux of their complaint was with the Oslo Agreement itself. "When you exchange land for promises and the promises are broken, they say, 'So sorry,' but the land is gone forever," Rabbi Moshe Portnoy told the senators. "Israel will never be able to go back and recapture the land."

Carefully sidestepped in these conversations was a State Department report, issued two weeks earlier, stating that the PLO had kept to the commitments laid down in the Declaration of Principles (Oslo Agreement) by taking key steps to prevent violence and punish those responsible for acts

of terrorism. Apprising Congress of these findings was left to Israeli officials, who did their utmost to counteract the Orthodox onslaught. Ambassador Itamar Rabinovich personally canvassed the Hill to warn that "a
small, well-organized, and effective group is operating with determination
in the United States against the Rabin government." His observation was
echoed inside Congress by men like Democratic Senator Joseph Lieberman
of Connecticut, himself an Orthodox Jew, who was relentlessly pursued
through the Senate's corridors by rabbis and other right-wing lobbyists but
refused to cave in to their demands. "Settlers are investing vast sums in propaganda," Lieberman complained. While conceding that the progress made
by the Palestinian Authority was less than he had hoped for, he strongly
questioned whether the appropriate response was to "cut off aid and therefore effectively stifle the peace process."

Other members of Congress were angered by the attempt to extend the
political battleground from Jerusalem to Washington. In one session of the
House Foreign Affairs Committee, Democrat Alcee Hastings of Florida
spoke his mind bluntly: "I believe that we are holding these hearings today
because partisan Israeli political pressures are spilling over into the U.S.
political agenda. And I believe that Israel's domestic politics have no place
in the U.S. Congress. . . . I am disgusted by the attempt by opposition parties in Israel to manipulate the sincere concerns of American Jews in order
to further their own political agenda." Equally trenchant was the criticism
voiced by Neal Sher, the executive director of AIPAC, who told an interviewer: "It's very problematic when there are efforts to lobby Congress
against the duly elected government of Israel. It is dangerous when domestic Israeli politics are imported into the halls of the U.S. Congress."

On the day the hundred rabbis scoured Capitol Hill, even Foreign Minister Peres threw himself into the fray by phoning Gilman and asking him
not to meet with the rabbinical delegation, lest such a meeting do harm
to the peace process. "Most American Jews support the Oslo Agreement,"
he reminded the congressman, "and the Orthodox are fringe elements."
But the rabbis prevailed. Gilman not only received them but appeared
alongside their leaders at a press conference in which he called the State
Department's report a "whitewash" and proclaimed his support for their
demands.

Buoyed by their success, the delegation then marched to the steps of
the Lincoln Memorial and offered their prayers for the Greater Land of

Israel. The venue had been chosen to jog Jewish memories of another delegation of rabbis, four hundred in number, who had demonstrated on the
same spot in the autumn of 1943 after imploring President Roosevelt to
save the Jews of Europe. The allusion was clear: The Jewish people were facing a calamity of Holocaust proportions. Still, the delegation avoided such
rhetoric in explaining its purpose to the press. "This is not a question of
being for the peace process or against the peace process. It does not even
involve directly the opinion of the Israeli government," Rabbi Steven
Pruzansky told reporters disingenuously. "This is purely an American tax-
payer issue."

In addressing their own constituencies, however, Orthodox and right-
wing leaders adopted a notably different tenor and tone. The World
Likud (an extension of the Israeli party) swamped Orthodox synagogues in
Brooklyn and Miami with leaflets assailing the Israeli government. Rabbi
Mordechai Friedman, head of the Orthodox American Board of Rabbis,
took up the banner by charging in radio and television interviews that
"Rabin's democracy is persecuting the settlers" and that "The Israeli Army
has been transformed into the ultra-radical left-wing Rabin/Peres militia."
When Rabbi Benjamin Sherfman of Cherry Hill, New Jersey, fulminated
from his pulpit that "Israel is no longer democratic but a dictatorship of
Rabin and Peres," his congregants accepted the dictum without protest—
and little wonder, for publications circulated in the Orthodox community
had already pronounced the Israeli government to be "the *Judenrat* police."
Other dignitaries spoke in more theoretical terms. Rabbi Moshe Tendler,
for example, a professor of biology at Yeshiva University and respected
authority on the halacha, patiently informed the media that according to
Jewish religious law, anyone perceived as a *rodef* should be killed.

While carrying their offensive forward, congregational rabbis also
barred the doors of their synagogues to IDF officers sent to the United
States to explain the workings of the Oslo accords. Noting that their congregants were unfriendly toward the present government of Israel, several
rabbis demurred that they could not be responsible for the officers' safety.
At least the military men were spared the mortification of their diplomatic
counterparts. Ambassador Rabinovich was pelted with tomatoes and eggs
in a Queens synagogue, and Talia Lador, the consul for public affairs in

New York, was greeted at the opening of a "Jerusalem Week" celebration with cries of "Traitor!" and "Nazi!"

Colette Avital was also the target of phone threats promising to "finish you off, Nazi!" Listeners calling in to Zev Brenner's radio show, *Talkline*, spoke of her as "an enemy of Israel" and "a traitor who should be put on trial." "We'll make sure she's placed before a firing squad," one caller growled. Brenner, who says he had never experienced such an outpouring of hatred, noted that the expressions of animosity for the Rabin government peaked twice: following the announcement of the Nobel Peace Prize in October 1994 and after the signing of the Oslo II Agreement in September 1995. "The Jews from Brooklyn who came on the air opened with a series of curses, calling Colette Avital and Rabin Nazis and traitors," he recalled. "I had to cut them off to maintain a minimum of decency." Avital fought back through channels that reached a far wider audience. She appeared on a Mike Wallace segment of *60 Minutes* to reply to threats made by Mike Gozovsky, the leader of Kahane Chai in New York, and warn against the verbal violence of Jewish fanatics. The appearance earned her another stream of maledictory calls.

Part of the incitement against the Rabin government was inspired by amateur "news items" transmitted by fax and E-mail or posted on Web pages and then spread by word of mouth or quoted in right-wing Jewish papers. "Once a rumor spread in the Orthodox community that Israeli soldiers who had been escorting settlers [in the West Bank] received an order to abandon them in the midst of an Arab area and thus jeopardize their lives," Avital recalled. "Many American Orthodox Jews have sons and daughters living in the territories, and they were enraged. But the report that had started the rumor was a canard."

In other instances, rumors were considered a legitimate means of substantiating slanderous accusations. Early in 1995, when Rabbi Sholom Gold addressed a convention of rabbis in New York, the *Algemeiner Journal* quoted his speech at length. After comparing the perils posed by Rabin's policies to the Holocaust, Gold justified his characterization of Rabin's ministers as "an immoral government" by citing a rumor that he had heard. According to the *Algemeiner Journal*, Gold "pointed out that two weeks ago on the night that a young Jewish taxi driver was killed on the road by terrorists, the Israeli Cabinet had a party. When asked about the appropriateness of continuing with plans for a party after a Jew had been killed by a terrorist, [Shimon] Peres answered: 'These things happen every day in Israel.' " The audience naturally responded with cries of outrage, whereupon Gold urged his listeners: "The time has passed for political politeness. Make life uncomfortable for any member of the government when they visit America."

One theme that circulated among Orthodox Jews in America was Rabin's supposed repression of Israeli citizens. During the summer of 1995, the opening pages of the *Jewish Press* featured giant photos of Israeli policemen dragging *haredi* demonstrators away from a protest action. The photos were accurate; the accompanying headlines, claiming that rabbis had been arrested at the demonstration, were a fabrication—one of many mendacious reports that the Israeli government was systematically arresting rabbis, then subjecting them to torture while in detention. Other reports insisted that the government was refusing permits for demonstrations, ordering the police to disperse protesters with brutal force, and especially encouraging them to beat women and children in the process. Claims that Yitzhak Rabin had turned his country into a "dictatorship" abounded in the Orthodox Jewish press. Somehow Israel's shocking decline from a "bastion of democracy in the Middle East" to a "police state" had escaped the notice of the major American news outlets, from *The New York Times* and *The Washington Post* to the national television networks. But for many Orthodox Jews that was no reason to question the findings of the *Algemeiner Journal* and the *Jewish Press*.

Even the flagrant bias of these papers did not undermine confidence in the accuracy of their reporting. The *Jewish Press* and its publisher-editor, Sholom Klass, had a rich history of affinity for Jewish fanatics. Rabbi Kahane and his son, Benyamin, once had regular columns in its pages, where the latter strove "to incite the apathetic Jewish people against the Israeli government that force-fed Israeli children drugs, AIDS, and other niceties of Western culture." The headline gracing the paper's report of the 1994 massacre of Palestinians in the Cave of the Patriarchs skipped past such details as the number of victims and identity of the murderer to get straight to the point: INSIDE STORY OF THE MASSACRE: RABIN GOVERNMENT BLAMED. Moreover, one of the pieces in that issue described Baruch Goldstein as "the saint of Kiryat Arba" and quoted from his admirers that "The Arabs who killed Goldstein were planning to kill Jews."

The prime minister was not the only object of journalistic invective. Shimon Peres was actually a more convenient target, having already endured a number of smear campaigns in Israel. The rumors floated about him during his long political career ranged from the patently absurd claim that his mother was an Arab (Peres was born in Belorussia and has an accent to prove it) to the gratuitously vicious one that his son was a draft dodger (he was, in fact, an air force pilot). In addition, Rabin's background made him a tougher adversary. His military record, from the days when he joined the Palmach underground as a youth to his tenure as IDF chief of staff during the Six-Day War, placed him solidly in the pantheon of Israeli heroes, particularly in nationalist circles. It also enhanced his image as the paragon of sabra earthiness and candor, even purity. Rabin had two enviable nicknames among Israelis: Mr. Security and Teflon, the latter earned for the great difficulty his political enemies had in making their accusations stick.

On the other side of the world, however, in quarters devoid of sentiment for the man who symbolized the best of his generation, attempts to portray Rabin as a villain were incredibly successful. His enemies depicted him as a man who had surrendered to alcoholism, abhorred religion, and was hostile to all Jewish values. Even his military record was assailed by claims that he had deserted his men on the field of battle during the 1948 War of Independence and suffered a nervous breakdown on the eve of the Six-Day War.

The February 1995 issue of the quarterly *Outpost*, published by Americans for a Safe Israel, is an illuminating example of how unsubstantiated charges are transmuted into hard facts that become an excuse for diatribe. It was devoted largely to articles that excoriated Rabin and his peace policy. The lead feature was a piece entitled "The Real Rabin," by Erich Isaac, a professor emeritus of geography at the City University of New York and a member of *Outpost*'s editorial board. At the start of his piece, Isaac ponders why "mainstream Jewish organizations and leaders in the United States" have placed their trust in Rabin, and he concludes:

> In good part the reason lies in trust in Yitzhak Rabin as a military leader. This attitude was typified in an advertisement published in a number of American Jewish papers in August 1994, with the

heading "When it Comes to Israel's Security, Nobody Knows More Than Yitzhak Rabin. *Nobody.*" The ad's theme was that Rabin, as the man who captured the territories won by Israel in 1967, would never make territorial concessions that would endanger the state.

For all those lulled by Rabin's supposed military distinction as intrepid battle leader in the pre-state days and victorious general in the defense of the Land, Dr. Uri Milstein's forthcoming book on Rabin, *The Rabin File,* should serve as a wake-up call. Perhaps the question "Suppose Milstein's book had appeared several years earlier; could that have swayed the small number of votes needed to prevent the Labor victory?" will one day join the "it might have been" scenarios that could have changed history.

Milstein's book, which accused Rabin of rank cowardice during the War of Independence, was received with utter scorn by his fellow historians in Israel for being short on facts and long on rhetoric. Nevertheless, Isaac concludes his article by quoting Milstein: "Rabin completely fails to grasp Middle Eastern and international developments. It is needless to point out what calamitous end this man can bring upon Israel on a day of wrath."

The same issue of *Outpost* contains an article by J. S. Sorkin, who further expounds on Rabin's purported cowardice. After deploring the "ghastly charade of the [Nobel Peace Prize] ceremony in Norway," he brands Rabin "a borderline alcoholic, known for a lifetime of psychological and military retreats."

> Whatever Rabin's personal fate, his legacy to date remains freighted with accusations of reluctance to engage the enemy in '48, his self-confessed psychological collapse in '67, his retreat in Lebanon in '85 [as defense minister in Israel's National Unity government in 1984–1988], his retreat from Gaza and Jericho in '94 and Heaven knows where else in the weeks ahead. . . .
>
> Much Jewish blood has already been spilled in the name of his peace, and although one has faith this madness can never succeed, the question remains how much more blood—half a century after the Holocaust—Jews must continue to spill until this pathetic man goes home.

These accusations bear close scrutiny. Rabin's "reluctance to engage the enemy in '48," which Sorkin took from Milstein, refers to a single incident when Rabin concluded that sending his men into a particular engagement would have accomplished little more than to decimate his already depleted units. Rabin's Harel Brigade repeatedly engaged the enemy in 1948 and in so doing opened and secured the road to Jerusalem. His "psychological collapse" two weeks before the outbreak of the Six-Day War, an episode related with rare and probably imprudent candor in Rabin's memoirs, was remedied by a sedative and a good night's sleep. His "retreat in Lebanon in '85" was merely a partial pullback ordered by the National Unity government, some of whose members were appalled that Israeli forces had penetrated so deeply into Lebanon in the first place. And his "retreat from Gaza and Jericho," in the first stage of the Oslo accords, was welcomed by the soldiers and reservists who were charged with keeping Israel's clamp on the million Palestinians living there. It was even supported by figures on the Israeli right. Informed Israelis were equipped to resist such tactics. But distant and uninitiated readers in the United States were more vulnerable to propaganda.

Manfred Lehmann, a Miami millionaire who chaired the right-wing World Committee for Israel, was particularly skilled in manipulating the media. An Orientalist by training, Lehmann did nothing to mask his contempt for Arabs and had been known to refer to Palestinians, collectively, as Nazis. In his contributions to Jewish papers he compared Rabin with Marshal Pétain and Deputy Foreign Minister Yossi Beilin with Hitler's propaganda minister, Joseph Goebbels.

Despite such invective Lehmann was present at a Friday night dinner hosted in October 1995 by two of Rabin's fondest friends, President and Mrs. Clinton. The White House had actually issued its invitation to Sam Domb, a contributor to Clinton's 1992 campaign fund. Domb had asked to bring Lehmann along, and the Clintons agreed. They soon had cause to regret their decision when Lehmann approached Mrs. Clinton in the course of the evening and informed her that the Rabin government was in the habit of brutally beating Jewish women who demonstrated against the Oslo process. Mrs. Clinton apparently extricated herself from the situation, but the next day a journalist phoned the White House asking for her response to what she had learned from Lehmann. Since it is not customary for presidential guests to share with the press the contents of conversations at a private event, the White House was furious. Sam Domb, having been rebuked for his friend's manipulative behavior, told the authors, "I'll never speak to him again!"

The gaffe, however, did not deter Lehmann. In February 1996 a number of American papers, including the *Wall Street Journal*, published an item that would prove highly controversial. It told of an address made by Yasser Arafat to a closed gathering of Arab ambassadors in Stockholm on January 30. The subject of the speech was quoted as "The Impending Total Collapse of Israel." In it, Arafat is reported to have told the diplomats that at least half the Russian immigrants to Israel are Christians or Muslims who, when the expected civil war breaks out there, would fight for a united Palestinian state. "We Palestinians will take over everything, including all of Jerusalem," he allegedly prophesied, adding that it would not be difficult since most of the Jews in Israel would immigrate to the United States. "You understand that we plan to eliminate the State of Israel and establish a purely Palestinian State. We will make life unbearable for Jews by psychological warfare and a population explosion; Jews will not want to live among us Arabs!" he supposedly added, ending his speech with the cry: "I have no use for Jews; they are and remain Jews! We now need all the help we can get through you in our battle for a united Palestine under total Arab-Moslem domination."

The speech, if true, had grossly violated both the spirit and the letter of the Oslo accords. The accounts of it generated such consternation that the American and Israeli embassies in Stockholm, along with the Mossad, investigated the matter. They found that there had indeed been a meeting of Arab ambassadors in Stockholm and that Arafat had addressed it. But there was no taped or written record of his remarks, and the most the investigators could obtain were vigorous denials of the accounts from the participants and from Arafat's office in Gaza.

In the United States the original report of the speech was credited to the Swedish daily *Dagen*. In fact it had appeared on February 16 in a Pentecostal paper of the same name published in Bergen, Norway. Intrigued by the source of the news, Akiva Eldar of *Ha'aretz* investigated further. The Norwegian *Dagen* was able to say only that the item had been passed on to one of its reporters by an anonymous Swedish journalist. The foreign editor of the Swedish *Dagen* recalled that she and some of her colleagues had also been approached with the item by a "pro-Jewish journalist" but had killed the piece when staffers were unable to corroborate the quotes from any other source.

Eventually Eldar discovered that the report had first been published not in Scandinavia at all but in New York, on February 9, in the *American Jewish Week*, by none other than Manfred Lehmann, a native of Stockholm who prided himself on maintaining close ties with his "sources" in Sweden. The anonymous "pro-Jewish journalist" had pitched Lehmann's piece to the Norwegian *Dagen*, and the American and Israeli papers had picked up *Dagen*'s item. The quotes from Arafat's speech given in the *Jerusalem Post*'s February 23 report, also credited to *Dagen*, follow Lehmann's English translation almost word for word. The *Post* added the even curiouser note that the substance of Arafat's talk had first been reported in Israel back on February 7 by "the off-shore radio station Arutz 7," which certainly hadn't taken it from the *Dagen* piece published nine days later.

How had Lehmann gotten his hands on the full text of Arafat's assumed address? He wouldn't say. The most he was willing to tell Eldar was that one of the ambassadors had passed his notes on the speech to "someone" in Stockholm, who translated them into French. The translator then gave his text to an unnamed Swedish Jewish journalist who rendered it into Swedish and gave it to the Norwegian *Dagen*. The quotes in Lehmann's New York article were thus translated into English from a Swedish translation of a French translation of the original Arabic. What's more, to this day there is no traceable proof that Arafat ever made the speech attributed to him by Lehmann, and the wily millionaire took the truth about his role in the affair to his grave.

By July 1995 Rabin-bashing had become so popular a pastime in Ortho-dox circles that the prime minister made a gruff reference to "a small group of rabbis in the United States for whom the name ayatollahs is more fitting than rabbis." The barb was provoked by a call to violent action by one of the most prominent members of New York's Orthodox rabbinical establishment, Rabbi Abraham Hecht.

At seventy-three Rabbi Hecht was a man of enviable influence. New York's John Cardinal O'Connor had thought enough of him to secure him an audience with the pope. Mayor Rudolph Giuliani had seated him on the dignitaries' platform at his December 1993 inauguration ceremony. While visiting New York in December 1994, Rabin himself had briefed Hecht on the Oslo process, as the rabbi listened in stoic silence. For more than fifty-two years Rabbi Hecht had been associated with the Shaare Zion Synagogue on Ocean Parkway in Brooklyn, whose congregants are mostly prosperous Jews from Syria. He was not revered as an authority on the halacha, but as the head of the 540-member Rabbinical Alliance of America he had excellent connections. He had been drawn to political activity early in his career, had supported Rabbi Kahane, and was a member of Dov Hikind's United Jewish Coalition. He was also a pillar of conservatism on issues exceeding the bounds of the halacha. While campaigning for Giuliani in 1989, Hecht ventured that his candidate would clean up a city corrupted by such evils as premarital sex, abortions, and homosexual crimes, and he supported a Texas judge's lenient sentence of a murderer because the victims were, in the judge's words, "queers."

On June 19, 1995, addressing a convention of the International Rabbinical Coalition for Israel, an organization of three thousand Orthodox rabbis dedicated to saving the occupied territories for Israel, Hecht made a harrowing statement. Surrendering any part of the biblical Land of Israel is a violation of Jewish religious law, he told his audience, and thus assassinating Rabin, and all who assist him, is both permissible and necessary.

Some of the rabbis supported Hecht and actually signed a statement that in their view Rabin was a *rodef*. Others were stunned by his pronouncement of such a dictum in public, visited him in his Brooklyn office, and implored him to retract the statement. But Hecht was adamant. "I do not represent myself but the Jewish law," he told them, "and the concession of territory is a grave crime in Judaism." In the months that followed Hecht sent letters to American Orthodox rabbis, with copies to their colleagues in Israel, reiterating his words. In August 1995 he used the platform of the *Jewish Press* to publish an open letter "to all the Rabbis in the U.S.A." confirming that "The Torah permits the most extreme action against those who would harm our fellow Jews." For good measure, he issued a declaration that the Israeli officers sent to the United States to explain the Oslo peace plan "are not wanted here and we must be prepared to expose them for what they are: enemies of the Jewish state and the Jewish people."

By October 9, 1995, Rabbi Hecht was quoted in *New York* magazine as

Yigal Amir at his trial for the assassination of Prime Minister Yitzhak Rabin.

Likud chairman Benjamin Netanyahu standing in front of a coffin painted with the words "Rabin is murdering Zionism," at the Ra'anana demonstration, March 4, 1994.

Baruch Marzel, Rabbi Meir Kahane's assistant and later head of the Kach movement.

Former Chief Rabbi Avraham Shapira, a leading halachic authority who issued rulings against withdrawal from the occupied territories.

Policemen carrying Yigal Amir from a Zo Artzenu demonstration in the territories, summer 1995.

Meeting of the Yesha Council showing Uri Ariel (center) and Aharon Domb (right).

Elyakim Ha'etzni (left) of Kiryat Arba, who branded Rabin a traitor.

Rabbi Abraham Hecht, who publicly regretted that he did not have the opportunity to carry out the sentence on a *rodef*.

Rabbi Shmuel Dvir, who threatened to shoot Rabin if the prime minister ever visited his settlement.

Placard calling Rabin a traitor.

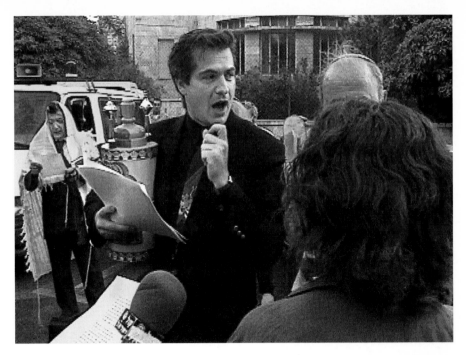

Avigdor Eskin chanting the *Pulsa da-Nura* curse in front of the prime minister's residence in Jerusalem.

Photomontage of Rabin dressed in an SS uniform that was distributed during the demonstration at Zion Square, October 5, 1995.

Benjamin Netanyahu addressing demonstrators at Zion Square, October 5, 1995.

Prime Minister Yitzhak Rabin (right) at the end of the November 4 rally, a few minutes before the assassination.

Yigal Amir reconstructing the murder for the police.

Shlomo and Geula Amir
on their way to visit Yigal in
prison.

Shabak informer
Avishai Raviv.

Ya'akov Novick, head of
the Action Headquarters.

Former Chief Rabbi Mordechai Eliyahu, Meir Kahane's mentor.

New York State Assemblyman Dov Hikind.

saying he felt "literally sick" over the peace process "because it eats me up alive." Asked how he would feel if someone were to conclude from his June statement that he was entitled to murder Rabin, Hecht replied, "I wouldn't feel [at all]. . . . Rabin is not a Jew any longer. This man has done so much harm. I can't forgive him for that." On the controversial statement itself, he elaborated:

> All I said was that according to Jewish law, any one person—you can apply it to whoever you want—who willfully, consciously, intentionally hands over human bodies or human property or the human wealth of the Jewish people to an alien people is guilty of the sin for which the penalty is death. And according to Maimonides—you can quote me—it says very clearly, *if a man kills him, he has done a good deed.*

How, his interviewer asked, could this principle be reconciled with the commandment "Thou shalt not kill"?

"[The] commandment says I 'shall not murder'; it does not say 'Thou shalt not kill,'" Hecht explained. "If it says 'shall not kill,' you can't go to war. And you can't slaughter chickens."

In the last week of October Hecht also gave an interview to Ya'akov Ahimeir, the correspondent of Israel television's Channel One, in which he repeated the assertion: "I said, according to Maimonides, of anyone who turns over land or bodies of Israel, that whoever is quick to kill him is privileged . . ."

"What's the conclusion to be drawn from this?" asked Ahimeir, astonished that anyone would make such a statement on camera. "That, heaven forbid, the prime minister of Israel should be harmed?"

"No, no—"

"You're saying that anyone who turns over—"

"Yes," Hecht confirmed. "But I wasn't privileged."

"What you do mean, 'I wasn't privileged'?"

"Simple. He's still alive," Hecht said with a laugh.

Ahimeir was so appalled by the material he had on tape that he decided not to air it, lest he or his station be accused of broadcasting incitement to murder. He released the interview only after the assassination.

Rabbi Hecht's harangues were the most explicit words of incitement publicly expressed against Rabin anywhere in the world. And they were voiced by a distinguished member of the Orthodox rabbinical establishment. Hundreds of rabbis had heard and read his screeds. Only a handful spoke out against them. "Hecht is not a voice of a lone, crazy extremist," *New York* magazine explained in printing its interview with him, "but that of one of a growing chorus of Jewish militants who have crossed the line of legitimate debate and dissent into calls for violence—and into violence itself."

As the campaign against the peace process spread beyond the Orthodox community into New York City politics, no figure was more crucial in orchestrating it than New York State Assemblyman Dov Hikind.

Born in 1950 in the Williamsburg section of Brooklyn, Hikind grew up in a self-imposed ghetto built by Orthodox Jews as a bulwark against assimilation. As the son of Holocaust survivors who had settled in New York in 1947, he was drawn to Meir Kahane's apocalyptic gospel on the future awaiting the Jews in America. In 1970, while studying at Queens College, he joined the Jewish Defense League (JDL) and took part in its patrols to "protect" the residents of Jewish neighborhoods from young blacks. Hikind immediately stood out among the young "militiamen" as a born leader who proved his valor in the JDL's protest actions. He was first arrested along with nine comrades when they stormed the offices of the Soviet Mission to the United Nations and handcuffed themselves to the gate. On another occasion, together with a comrade, he charged into the Egyptian Mission and set off a brawl in which three of the staffers were injured.

Hikind entered the state assembly on the Democratic ticket in 1982 and harbored hopes of moving on to Washington. While his behavior may not have augured well for a successful career in politics, it did help Hikind to become Rabbi Kahane's right hand in the JDL. Then he formally resigned from his JDL leadership post in 1973 to accept an appointment as the head of SOIL (Save Our Israeli Homeland), a new organization founded by Kahane to enlist, by guile, Jews who were put off by the belligerence of the JDL. Kahane had by then relocated his headquarters to

Jerusalem but was still commanding his New York operations from afar. A letter he wrote to a JDL board member (republished in the *Village Voice*) is instructive of how the new front operated:

> SOIL under Dov H. is a good example of what can be done. I think Dov should be invited to the next board meeting [of the JDL] to explain what has been done and what is being done. All SOIL names should be discreetly funneled to JDL, which in turn should be careful to contact these people only many weeks later and without saying that they were gotten from SOIL. Work closely with Dov. I told him to listen.

Twenty years later Hikind was still using the name of the ostensibly moderate SOIL, now to draw people to demonstrations against the Oslo Agreement.

Hikind's assistant in SOIL was Victor Vancier, a pugnacious young man who specialized in preparing explosive devices and whose involvement in dozens of violent attacks against blacks, personnel of Soviet institutions, and Arabs earned him a place on the FBI's list of terrorists. He was eventually caught, tried, and convicted of a bomb attack against a Soviet diplomatic residence in New York and, in a separate incident, of tossing a canister of tear gas into the Metropolitan Opera House during a performance of the Moiseyev Dance Company. In October 1987 Vancier was sentenced to ten years in a federal prison but was released after serving half his term. On Zev Brenner's Saturday night cable show, *Talkline*, Vancier praised Baruch Goldstein as a *tzaddik* ("holy man") and pronounced Rabin a "traitor and murderer of Jews." Hired to host two cable television programs, *Positively Jewish* and *Jewish Task Force*, Vancier used them to broadcast diatribes against blacks, Arabs, and non-Jews in general.

Somehow the infamy of Vancier's crimes never rubbed off on his boss at SOIL, though Hikind himself had been suspected of similar activities. In 1976 Hikind was arraigned in federal court for throwing a smoke bomb into the Ugandan Mission to the UN after Israel's rescue of an Air France plane hijacked to Entebbe. A decade later the FBI suspected him of involvement in planning a string of six bombings against Arab targets in New York, Massachusetts, and California—in which one man was killed and seven were injured—but no evidence was found against him. At least five other suspects in those attacks, all Kahane people, fled to Israel and settled in Hebron, one of the West Bank settlements, or Jerusalem. Two of them had been connected to Hikind in a separate campaign, against the Reverend Jesse Jackson when he ran in the 1984 Democratic presidential primaries.

Jackson had angered many Jews by his embrace of Yasser Arafat in Lebanon in 1979 and by his 1984 crack calling New York "Hymietown." Because of the complex relations between the black and Jewish communities, the Jewish leadership chose to protest the insult quietly with their black counterparts. But Hikind went after Jackson with a vengeance. When the latter ran again in 1988 and 1992, Hikind resumed his attacks, working through two organizations: Jews Against Jackson and the more euphemistically titled Coalition for a Positive America. He spared no effort or nasty epithet, smearing Jackson as "anti-American." Various Jewish leaders fretted that Hikind's rabid assaults—he once reportedly told a Borough Park fund-raising dinner for primary rival Al Gore that "I have a dream that Jesse Jackson would disappear from American politics"—were doing irreparable damage to black-Jewish relations. But they brought Hikind great political benefit by spreading his name far beyond the Orthodox Jewish precincts of New York.

Hikind's Borough Park assembly district is the seat of the largest Orthodox Jewish community in the United States. The lifestyle of its residents, from religious practice to mode of dress, has changed little from that of their forebears in the ghettos of Eastern Europe in centuries past. And in all matters of import, from birth to death, the *haredim* of Borough Park and nearby Flatbush rigorously obey the dictates of their rabbis. Hikind stands out among his ultra-Orthodox constituents. He wears a business suit rather than the black frock coat still preferred by members of the Hassidic sects, dons a crocheted yarmulke rather than the black hat that is the community's sartorial hallmark, and keeps his beard trimmed short. But he holds to the *haredi* code of boundless loyalty to the rebbes and serves their interests by securing public funds for the needs of their community. These efforts, in addition to advancing their political aspirations for the United States and Israel, have won him their trust.

Under Hikind's guidance, in 1993 the ultra-Orthodox Jews of Brooklyn discovered that they possessed a hitherto unsuspected power: Under certain conditions, if they cast their vote en bloc, they were capable of decid-ing the outcome of a municipal election. In a break with a half-century-old tradition, they voted for a Republican candidate for mayor, Rudolph Giu-liani. Hikind explained his boldness in engineering this switch as follows:

> The Orthodox community is ready to cross lines and support Re-publicans. Even though we are Democrats, we supported [Repub-lican Senator] D'Amato, and he won. . . . And we supported [gubernatorial candidate] George Pataki, who is a Republican, and he won. And we supported Mayor Giuliani and he won. In politics the worst crime you can commit is to cross lines. If you are a Democrat and you support Republicans, forget it—you're finished. They will look out to get you and hurt you. But I have done it because I understood that for Jews, to be loyal to any party is stupid. I have learned that when Jews were being slaughtered in Auschwitz during the Holocaust and we had a wonderful presi-dent, FDR, the great president for the American people was the worst tragedy for the Jewish people.

Hikind first tried his hand at this strategy in 1989, when Giuliani was running against the black Democratic candidate David Dinkins. To pave his candidate's way to City Hall, he created the United Jewish Coalition, an umbrella body for seventy Orthodox organizations that was Giuliani's most important base of Jewish support. It helped Hikind deliver 70 percent of the votes from his district to Guiliani. But in 1989 that did not suffice, and Dinkins won the election. The next time around, in 1993, Hikind tried harder. He assisted Giuliani in strengthening his ties with prominent Orthodox leaders in Brooklyn like Rabbi Hecht and Rabbi Bomzer and in securing the financial backing of right-wing Jewish figures like Sam Domb. Domb, in turn, brought Jack Avital (vice-president of Lehmann's World Committee for Israel) into the Giuliani campaign. The coterie was rounded out by Dr. Joseph Frager, a friend of Hikind's who was president of the Jew-ish Reclamation Project; Charles Posner, who in the following year would accompany Hikind to Oslo to demonstrate against Rabin as he was receiv-ing the Nobel Peace Prize; and Sholom Klass of the *Jewish Press*, whose paper endorsed Giuliani with alacrity.

All this help was undoubtedly efficacious. But what clinched the massive Orthodox turnout for Giuliani was Hikind's skillful exploitation of a double tragedy that had occurred in the Crown Heights section of Brooklyn two years earlier. In August 1991 Yankel Rosenbaum, a yeshiva student from Australia, was stabbed to death during a riot by blacks. The outburst had been sparked by the death of a black youngster accidentally hit by one of the cars in the Lubavitcher rebbe's cavalcade. Three days of mayhem ensued in Crown Heights, the Jewish community of New York was badly shaken, and Hikind aggravated the mood on both sides by accusing Mayor Dinkins of forcing the police to exercise restraint in quelling the violence. Two years later he was still pummeling Dinkins with that charge. He also targeted his electioneering on behalf of Dinkins's rival at the rabbinical leaders of the ultra-Orthodox districts, confident that their followers would obey whatever they decided.

"The concept is a very simply one: a bloc vote," he explained. "You know, sometimes I have to go out and convince you to vote for me. Then I have to convince your wife, then your son. But in this community, when I get the rebbe, then probably I'll get the whole community. Once there is the sense that Giuliani is good, or Pataki is good . . . you don't get that individual, you get the whole community."

He was right. In 1993, when Orthodox Jews constituted 8 percent of New York's population and 2.8 percent of its electorate, 95 percent of them voted for Giuliani. Hikind failed to make his charges against Dinkins stick with the broader Jewish population of New York, for the incumbent received only 3 percent less of the overall Jewish vote than he had in 1989. But the Orthodox vote was the decisive one because the 1993 election was close, with Giuliani besting Dinkins by just 2 percent. It would have been very difficult for Giuliani to win had the Orthodox community not voted for him en masse.

Delighted by the triumph of his method, Hikind then worked to replicate it in Israel. The strategy had already proved successful in Jerusalem in 1993, when the solid vote of *haredi* citizens for Likud candidate Ehud Olmert toppled the twenty-eight-year incumbent, Teddy Kollek. The practice had also been followed by the *haredim* in national elections in Israel. But these elections had been conducted according to the parliamentary system, whereby the party with the largest number of votes got a chance to form a coalition and, if successful, appointed its leader as prime minister. In 1996 this system changed, and Israel held its first direct vote for prime minister (simultaneous with the Knesset elections), so that the effect of en bloc polling operated differently. Once again it clinched an election: this time for Benjamin Netanyahu, who defeated Shimon Peres by a hair-thin margin of less than 1 percent of the vote.

Hikind was particularly proud of his contribution to Netanyahu's victory using the same method employed in Brooklyn three years earlier. "There were people involved from America in the Israeli campaign," he reported unabashedly.

> I was in Israel during the [1996] election, and it was a remarkable thing to watch in the community of the observant and the Hassidic community. An incredible effort was made to get the Orthodox community to be unified, every single one of them. I sat with the Belzer Rebbe* and had a long talk with him a few days before the election. I didn't tell him what to do, but he knew where I stood. And I met with the Gerre Rebbe, and I met with the Vizhnitzer Rebbe, and I met with many others in the last four, five days before the elections.

Hikind did not have to expend his energies on the followers of the late Lubavitcher rebbe,† for that would have been preaching to the converted. The Lubavitchers' Habad movement, an empire with two hundred branches throughout the world, a quarter of a million members, and disbursements of hundreds of millions of dollars a year, was already running a crusade of its own to defeat Peres. Its rationale was spelled out with striking simplicity and conviction by Rabbi Shmuel Butman, the director of Lubavitcher Youth International in Crown Heights. "The rebbe said very clearly: The prime minister has no right to give away [the Land of] Israel because it does not belong to him," Butman explained. "The Arabs hate the Jews. The Jews are afraid from the Arabs," besides which, "God said—this is God's ruling—you can't give away any territory to the enemy because the enemy cannot be trusted!"

For years Habad had been given access to Israeli schools and army camps as an apolitical movement interested only in exposing secular

---

*Head of a large Hassidic following, as are the other rebbes mentioned hereafter.
†Rabbi Menachem Mendel Schneerson died in June 1994 and has not been succeeded because his disciples believe he is the messiah and will himself return to lead them.

youth to religious practices and values. Then, prominently in the last days before the May 1996 election, it revealed its true colors by decorating the country with banners reading BIBI IS GOOD FOR THE JEWS. Its status has been a matter of sharp controversy ever since.

Back in New York, meanwhile, Mayor Giuliani repaid his debt to his right-wing and Orthodox patrons by seating Hecht, Bomzer, Domb, and Jack Avital on the stage at his inaugural ceremony; accompanying Domb and Klass to Jewish events; appointing Posner to a civil court judgeship in Queens; celebrating Jewish holidays and family events with Hikind at home and calling him "a role model for all New Yorkers"; and finding City Hall jobs for Hikind's brother, Pinchus, and wife, Shoshana (who spent her free time managing the Jerusalem Reclamation Project). Giuliani also coolly told Rabin, a few weeks after the signing of the Oslo Agreement, "I am hopeful it will work. Sometimes things like that work, sometimes they don't." The mayor made time to address the JRP's annual dinner in 1994, emceed by Hikind, and told the audience that Israel would be best off not relinquishing the occupied territories. On that same occasion he also heard the advice of guest speaker Mayor Ehud Olmert, who suggested that he bar Yasser Arafat from entering New York.

The JRP's next annual fund-raising dinner, again attended by Giuliani, would prove less auspicious for the Hikind family. The master of ceremonies was Sam Domb, who earlier that year had described Rabin in the *Jewish Press* as "a man seemingly devoid of honor, self-respect, compassion, common sense and a sense of history" who was "spiritually destroying the Jewish people." Domb invited to the rostrum Shoshana Hikind, by then an aide to Republican Governor George Pataki (who had similarly benefited from Dov Hikind's influence with his constituency). She called for the prompt removal of the Rabin government. Upon learning of her speech, Colette Avital picked up the phone to the governor to object to a state civil servant's use of a public platform to meddle in Israel's internal affairs. Pataki was evidently embarrassed, and Mrs. Hikind soon found herself out of a job.

Dov Hikind found himself in even less clement circumstances two years later, in the summer of 1997. Not only had his relations with Giuliani turned sour, but he was indicted by a federal grand jury on thirty-four counts of embezzlement for allegedly taking some forty thousand dollars of federal and municipal funds allocated to the Council of Jewish Organizations of Borough Park and putting them to personal use. In July 1998 he was acquitted of these charges, although Rabbi Elimelech Naiman, a former official of the council, was convicted of making bribery payments to Hikind.

Hikind and his network received scant coverage in Israel until two events in 1995 put their names into the headlines. The first was an incident that took place before New York's annual Israel Day Parade. Israel Day had always been synonymous with Jewish unity. The parade's participants—schoolchildren, representatives of Zionist organizations, and members of Jewish youth movements—put on a colorful display as they sing, dance, and march their way up Fifth Avenue before an audience of thousands of people carrying flags and banners. In May 1995, however, the celebration was marred when the Jewish right took over the event. Domb had offered to fund the parade and saw to the appointment of his friend Jack Avital as its honorary chairman. Mayor Giuliani was honored with the post of grand marshal. Israel's contribution to the occasion was to send one of its ministers to salute the marchers from the reviewing stand.

The government chose Minister of Communications, Culture, and Science Shulamit Aloni, the head of the Meretz Party and a frontline fighter for civil rights and against religious coercion. Anticipating tension with the march's right-wing sponsors, Colette Avital recommended that the choice be reconsidered, but Aloni was adamant. Most New York Jews were not Orthodox, she argued, so there was no reason to discriminate against a liberal figure. When Domb discovered that Aloni would be representing the State of Israel, however, he threatened to withdraw his backing for the parade. Still Aloni would not be deterred.

At a breakfast hosted by Domb on the morning of the parade in a New York hotel, many in the audience jeered each time Aloni's name was mentioned and again when she stood up to give her address. Then, suddenly, Jack Avital rushed to the stage and punched Aloni, who had recently undergone abdominal surgery and was still suffering from a liver ailment, in the stomach. He later contested the reports of the assault by claiming that he had "intervened to control the state of chaos. My intention was to keep the breakfast schedule on time and move on to the next speaker." Aloni collapsed onstage and withdrew from the celebrations.

As the Jewish right explained it, Jack Avital's conduct was, like all the other outbursts of right-wing violence since the reascendance of the Labor Party in 1992, the fault of the Israeli government. On the following day Joseph Frager assailed Aloni as a symbol of the "anti-God, anti-Torah, anti-settler mentality" and called her appearance in New York a deliberate "provocation." In a letter to the editor of the *Jerusalem Post*, Lehmann denounced her "unscheduled" appearance at the breakfast, which, he wrote, "now appears to have been part of a deliberate, well-orchestrated plan to discredit the traditional leadership of the Salute-to-Israel Parade and replace it with bodies controlled by the leftists in the government of Israel." Kach's spokesman in New York simply praised Avital's attack in the pages of the *Jewish Press*.

The second incident occurred at the end of October 1995. Unable to take Olmert's advice and actually ban Yasser Arafat from entering New York, Giuliani had him ejected from a gala city-sponsored concert at Lincoln Center to mark the fiftieth anniversary of the United Nations. The mayor justified his move by saying that Arafat had been responsible for acts of brutality. The State Department, UN Secretary General Boutros Boutros-Ghali, former Mayor David Dinkins, and his Jewish predecessor, Ed Koch, all deplored the expulsion, with Koch crediting the mayor's conduct to "behavioral problems." But the quarters to which Giuliani was politically obliged were delighted. Congressman Charles Schumer of Brooklyn published a letter commending the mayor for doing "the right thing," while the *Jewish Press* editorialized that "The Mayor simply refused to build upon the pact they made with the devil." One expression of praise came out in a doggerel: "Rudy Giuliani! Congratulations for showing Arafat the gate! / Using your mayoral power against the one we truly hate."

Humiliating Arafat at Lincoln Center was the most spectacular example of Giuliani's dubious judgment on matters relating to Israel. Some New Yorkers questioned the seemliness of an alliance between the former U.S. attorney, who had run for mayor on a law and order platform, and a Brooklyn assemblyman with a history of scrapes with the law as a member of what the FBI had defined as a "domestic terror organization." (As late as

1991 and 1992 Hikind was still making donations to the American branch of Kahane Chai.)

In trying to fathom Giuliani's choice of allies, Israeli diplomats were bewildered because they knew that men like Hikind, Hecht, Bomzer, Klass, Domb, and Avital represented only a small minority of American Jewry. The American Jewish Committee's 1993 *Annual Survey of American Jewish Opinion*, the most respected barometer in this field, revealed that 84 percent of the Jewish community backed the Oslo Agreement and the policy behind it. The AJC's *Survey of American Jewish Attitudes Toward Israel and the Peace Process*, done two years later in August 1995, after a number of shattering Hamas terror actions, still showed that 75 percent of American Jews backed the Oslo process. And its survey done in January 1996, after the signing of the Oslo II Agreement and the Israeli redeployment in the West Bank, showed that figure unchanged. Rarely, however, was this firm majority a vocal one, for its leaders preferred to keep the political differences within the Jewish community as muted as possible.

The Israeli government also bore responsibility for the lopsided expression of American Jewish opinion on its policy. "Since the Labor government was formed in 1992, there has been a vacuum here, and people feel they're being ignored," said David Pollak of the Jewish Community Relations Council of Greater New York. "During the days of the Likud government, that wouldn't have happened. There are Jews here in a state of chagrin." Colette Avital too admitted that "The public relations effort of the Israeli government failed in the United States" because "the Labor Party neglected the arena of progressive Jewry." She had tried to warn Peres and Beilin that anti-Oslo incitement in the United States was spinning out of control. Before writing her detailed memo to Rabin, she had also mentioned the problem in a talk with him during one of his visits to New York. But Rabin brushed off her warning with a typical wave of the hand.

Unfortunately, Rabin's understanding of American Jewry was woefully out-of-date. He had served in Washington as Israel's ambassador in the late 1960s and early 1970s, a time of cohesive support for the Israeli government. Since then the picture had changed, but Rabin had paid little attention to the small but vociferous minority that opposed his policies. In a certain sense he had even opened the door to dissent. Peeved over the alacrity with which the American Jewish leadership had defended Likud's policy on the occupied territories, just after his election Rabin bluntly told AIPAC leaders in Washington that from then on Israel would conduct its affairs with the United States without American Jewish intermediaries. Then he proceeded to shock a meeting of the Conference of Presidents by announcing that as far as his government was concerned, American Jews could say what they liked about Israel's policies, since their opinion didn't count anyway. By September 1995 he had come to see things differently, however, and during his visit to Washington to sign the Oslo II Agreement sharply told a gathering of American Jewish leaders, "Never before have we witnessed an attempt by U.S. Jews to pressure Congress against the policies of a legitimate, democratically elected government." Blasting these efforts as "loathsome," he warned his listeners that they were causing severe damage to Israel's relations with the Diaspora. The Orthodox lobby ridiculed his belated offensive. His sympathizers among the Jewish leadership applauded, but they did not press the issue.

November 5, 1994, the day after Yitzhak Rabin's murder, happened to be the fifth anniversary of another assassination. In Brooklyn the usually somber memorial ceremonies for Rabbi Meir Kahane turned into a celebration as men embraced one another over the news from Israel. In the days that followed, funds were established in Flatbush for the defense of Yigal Amir. In Borough Park ultra-Orthodox Jews congratulated one another and began appending to Rabin's name the curse "May his name and memory be blotted out" (a malediction usually reserved for anti-Semitic tyrants of the caliber of Hitler and Stalin). Rabbi Mordechai Friedman extolled Amir, and Rabbi Kahane's successors appeared on cable television to salute him. The World Likud distributed leaflets in synagogues decrying the "misleading" data published in Israel about the number of mourners who had filed past Rabin's coffin. And although most of the letters to the editor in the *New York Post* condemned the assassination, many asserted that the prime minister was killed because he had acted like "Chamberlain at Munich" and because he had slandered the rabbis in America.

The *Jewish Press* published a special "mourning issue" in which Klass declared the "shock and anguish of our people over the death of Prime Minister Yitzhak Rabin" and in almost the same breath recited the threnody:

Because of the effort to hasten the implementation of the Oslo Accords prior to the next election, and in order to weaken the opposition, Israel was turned into a virtual police state, peaceful demonstrations were banned, freedom of speech was sharply curtailed, police brutality against men, women and children was rampant and dissidents were targeted for harassment and worse. In the name of Peace, many deaths of Israelis and hundreds of incidents of Arab brutality against Jews were simply ignored. . . . But most of all the Peace Process violates the commandments of our Holy Torah. G-d promised our ancestors that the entire land of Biblical Israel was to be an inheritance for the Children of Israel in perpetuity. When confronted by the Rabbis of today, the Peace Process proponents answered as did Pharaoh of ancient Egypt: "Who is your G-d that I should listen to him!"

In the same issue Professor Paul Eidelberg, formerly a lecturer at Bar-Ilan University, wrote a piece excoriating Rabin and his government, the Israeli legal system and High Court of Justice, and particularly the supporters of the peace process. "It is not easy for me to say, but it must be said even now," he intoned, "that Yitzhak Rabin and his cohorts created the emotional climate that led to his assassination."

Other mourners received the news with dismay. Rabbi Hecht, who was in Florida at the time of the assassination, fretted to his associates that Peres might send Mossad agents to kill him. A few weeks before the murder he had sent Rabin an apology and later claimed to have heard that it had been accepted. But Eitan Haber, Rabin's chief of staff, recalls the situation differently. The apology was so weakly worded, he said, that the prime minister spurned it.

In December 1995 Israel's Interior Ministry banned Hecht and six other American Jews from entering the country by classifying them as security risks.* Rabbi Hecht had proved no more welcome in his own synagogue. In mid-November the president of Shaare Zion, Morris J. Franco, told *The New York Times* that the rabbi had been asked to remain in Florida

---

*On March 22, 1998, Israeli Minister of Interior Eli Suissa of the ultra-Orthodox Shas Party lifted the ban on Hecht's entry to Israel, saying that since the rabbi had apologized for his remarks against Rabin, he should be treated with grace. Suissa added that should Hecht come to Israel, he would be prepared to shake his hand.

until his congregants could decide on whether to request his resignation. When they chose to suspend him for six months, Hecht protested the "defamation on my character by the State of Israel." His friend Dov Hikind rushed to his defense and told an interviewer, "For fifty years Hecht contributed to Israel. Can you judge a man on the basis of the ten seconds in which he said a terrible thing?" By October 25, 1996, Rabbi Hecht was back on the battlements of the *Jewish Week*, now denouncing Peres for having the "maddening gall to parade around in the Arab capitals of the world and here in America," making remarks "geared to create an atmosphere of distrust and doubt. In a true democracy," Hecht thundered, "Peres would have been put on trial for sedition and treason. . . ."

Those words were written a year after the assassination. It took far less time for other purveyors of incitement to get their second wind. They inspired Colette Avital to organize a memorial service for Yitzhak Rabin in Madison Square Garden. The Council of Presidents of Major American Jewish Organizations supported the idea, but not all its members were prepared to exert themselves to help organize it. The suggestion made the Foreign Ministry in Jerusalem downright nervous. No large Jewish assembly had been convened in New York for years, and given the sharp division among American Jews, Jerusalem was wary of risking one now. There are 15,000 seats in Madison Square Garden, and if many of them remained empty, the skeptics argued, the Jewish community would be disgraced.

Edgar Bronfman, the president of the World Jewish Congress, had agreed to underwrite the event with a $250,000 contribution but withdrew the offer after sensing qualms in Jerusalem. Avital asked Prime Minister Peres to intervene with him, but on hearing of Bronfman's misgivings, Peres waffled and suggested dropping the idea. Finally Avital persuaded the prime minister to back the memorial assembly unequivocally. She then worked day and night, urging the leaders of Jewish communities throughout the United States to pitch in. The American Jewish Committee helped enormously, as did the Israeli ambassador in Washington, the consul general in Philadelphia, and senior aides in the White House. The date was set for December 10, and the Council of Presidents promoted the theme of the assembly as one of Jewish unity. But then two of its members—the National Council of Young Israel and the Zionist Organization of America—not only withdrew from the roster of sponsors but took out a full-page ad in *The New York Times* deploring the "partisan politics" of the event, which was to be addressed by, among others, Vice President Gore, Prime Minister Peres, Mrs. Rabin, and Israel's Chief Rabbi Lau.

The advertisement, which earned its signatories an official letter of censure from the Council of Presidents, may have kept some people away. Yet not a seat in Madison Square Garden remained empty, and hundreds of people were left stranded outside the gate for lack of room, including groups that had come from out of town. Yet even on that solemn occasion, a note of enmity was struck. For camped opposite the Garden in the remains of the previous day's snow, a contingent from Kahane Chai stood behind the police cordon tirelessly waving placards reading PERES IS A TRAITOR!

CHAPTER 6

THE LOVER

On the morning of Saturday, November 4, 1995, Yigal Amir had, as usual, prayed before the Holy Ark in his neighborhood synagogue. As the service drew to a close, his brother Haggai, standing beside him, heard him murmur: "Lord, give me the strength to shoot Rabin and come out of it alive." Haggai said nothing. He knew it was pointless to waste words on Yigal. Haggai recalled how Dror Adani had been dispatched to obtain a halachic ruling, for all three of the conspirators knew that without rabbinical approval, they were not entitled to act. Yigal's face had glowed when Dror returned with the answer. The rabbi's decision was clear: "The moment a Jew turns over his people and land to enemies, he must be killed for endangering the lives of Jews." Yigal was satisfied. The ruling meant that whoever murdered Rabin would save the Land of Israel and be considered a saint.

Yigal feared nothing—not arrest, interrogation, or even death. His only concern was that he would fail to kill Rabin but be killed by his bodyguards in the attempt—and he did not want to die for naught. After they left the synagogue, Haggai offered his brother one piece of advice. "I know you're going to try this evening," he said. "Rabin has many more bodyguards now, and your chances of getting him with a pistol are close to zero. Wait until we can get you a sniper's rifle."

"Don't worry, Haggai," Yigal responded after a few seconds. "When the time comes, I'll decide as I must."

In the evening, when darkness fell and three stars could be seen in the firmament, as the law prescribed, Shlomo Amir gathered his family for the Havdalah ceremony marking the end of the Sabbath. Yigal stood in a corner of the living room and seemed unusually withdrawn. Haggai gave him a long, penetrating look, but Yigal's eyes were blank. A few years earlier, when Haggai had been steeped in doubt about his faith, he confided in Yigal. "I have too many questions," he said, "and very few answers." Haggai removed his yarmulke, but Yigal easily persuaded him to put it back on. Haggai adored his brother. A clear division of labor existed between them: Yigal did the thinking and made the decisions; Haggai carried them out.

As Shlomo Amir chanted the blessing for "He who distinguishes between sacred and profane," Geula Amir eyed Yigal pensively. She and her husband knew that Yitzhak Rabin would be speaking that night at an open-air rally in Tel Aviv. A few hours earlier, at Sabbath lunch, their son had again called Rabin a traitor. "He must be eliminated! He's the one responsible for the phony peace," Yigal cried. His parents heard the oft-repeated statement and let it pass.

Every Saturday evening the Amir house was abuzz with people. The front door lay open to the neighbors and guests filing in and out as children played noisily in the yard. "What are you doing tonight?" Geula asked her son, and Yigal replied that he was going out to meet friends. He intended to leave for the university early the next morning and wanted to gather together his books and papers before he left that night. There was nothing unusual about that plan. Geula also planned to spend the evening out with some women friends.

It was just after seven when Yigal went up to his room. Locking the door, he pulled open his desk drawer, removed his nine-millimeter Beretta, held the cartridge clip in one hand, and arranged the bullets in two neat rows on the desk: one row of hollow-point bullets, with etched casings; the second of regular, unmarked bullets. Haggai had etched the hollow-point bullets and explained that their effect was devastating. If Rabin were wearing a bulletproof vest, they would penetrate it, and inside his body they would expand and shred the organs and tissues. Slowly, systematically, Yigal loaded the cartridges into the clip: first an etched one, then a regular one. Three times he alternated them until six bullets were inside. Then he finished loading the clip with four regular cartridges, slid it into its carrier, and punched its base with the heel of his hand—twice, for good measure, he later recalled. Satisfied that the magazine was in place, he moved to the window, raised his arm out straight, and aimed just below eye level. He was pleased that his hand was steady. Then he drew the gun up to his chest and loaded a bullet into the barrel, removed it, and loaded it again, to be sure that the gun would not jam when he opened fire.

"I'd been thinking about this for two years," Yigal would tell his interrogators two days later. "I'd always been afraid that [the gun] would jam. What I feared most was that when I pulled the trigger, nothing would happen and I would be caught and sit in jail like a jerk for the rest of my life. . . . I also took into account that I would shoot and they would kill me. But I was prepared for that."

Setting the readied weapon on the desk, Yigal tended to his disguise. Removing his white Sabbath shirt and tzitzit, he slipped into a dark blue T-shirt. Then he pulled off his good pants and put on dark jeans. After reaching for the gun again, he checked that the clip was properly fastened, moved the catch to lock, and stuffed the Beretta between his waistband and his left hip. He packed his backpack just in case he received a sign not to act that night and would be going to the university the next day. Then, right before leaving the room, he picked up the phone and dialed Margalit Har-Shefi's number in Beit El, a settlement just north of Ramallah in the West Bank. Her father answered and said that she would be back in a little while. Yigal was disappointed but did not take her absence as an omen.

At a quarter to eight Yigal stood at the bus stop near his house. The weather was unusual; it was November yet still warm. He could see the No. 247 bus approaching and boarded it when it stopped in front of him. The road to Tel Aviv was clear, and he quickly reached the stop near the corner of Arlozorov and Ibn Gvirol Street, a few blocks from the Kings of Israel Square. He stood up, walked to the back door, surveyed the street, descended a step, removed his yarmulke, and slipped it into his pocket. His disguise was complete. *Now I look just like the leftists in the square,* he thought. Then he stepped down into the empty street and began walking southward past the shuttered shops. A police car drove quickly by, and in the distance he heard the dull ring of applause. When he entered the dim parking area in the tunnel under the Municipality Building, he immediately identified Rabin's car. He nonchalantly strolled past the steps leading up to the square. The stage was directly above him, and in the plaza a hundred thousand joyous citizens were applauding the prime minister.

"This rally must send forth a clear message in favor of peace and against violence," Yitzhak Rabin's voice boomed over the loudspeakers. The crowd cheered again. *Rabin is speaking right above me,* he thought. *If my bullets could penetrate concrete, I'd only have to shoot straight over my head.* Yigal looked up as if to double-check the possibility and then began planning his movements. He felt safe in the darkened parking area. Had the area been lit, he noted, he might have had to call off his plan. Like a coach before a game, he repeated the moves in his mind. He told himself to focus, to approach Rabin from behind and draw quickly before the bodyguards could react. He would aim for the spinal cord, the lower back by the fifth rib.

Yigal smiled at the thought that this time he would act. In a little while the rally would draw to a close. He noted to himself where the VIPs would walk. Glancing over at the prime minister's car, he noticed that the guard was lax. Then his thoughts jumped from one notion to another: from Haggai's warning that the guard had been doubled around Rabin to the possibility that he might be wearing a bulletproof vest. Suddenly, he later told his interrogators, he thought of Margalit walking quickly down the path in front of him, her heavy braid bouncing on her back.

The clash between religious conviction and sexual desire had caused Yigal Amir considerable distress. As a youth he had tried to repress the forbidden thoughts and feelings welling up in him. As a soldier studying at the Kerem D'Yavneh Yeshiva he asked his mentor, Rabbi Kav, how to overcome desire. The rabbi told him to study—pore over another page of the Talmud, and another, and another, and the feeling would vanish. But the stirrings continued. Sometimes he felt them so strongly that he punished himself by taking on onerous tasks as repentance: studying for hours at a time and doing volunteer work. Once he sent himself to wash tombstones in the cemetery; then he volunteered to work with autistic children. "Life is a constant struggle between reason and desire," Yigal said at his trial. "My worldview is that of the Torah, [to obey] the 613 commandments, to keep desire under total control . . . to overcome bodily pleasures and emotional needs."

Amir seemed always to be found in the company of attractive, strong-willed Ashkenazi young women. His first girlfriend was Navah Holtzman, a twenty-two-year-old student at Bar-Ilan. She came from an Ashkenazi background and was the daughter of a wealthy, established Tel Aviv family. Amir was from a large Yemenite family that lived in a lower-middle-class neighborhood. He hosted Navah in his home; she preferred that he not visit hers. His parents were sure that their relationship would lead to marriage; her parents were intent on separating them.

After the murder, when he was questioned by the police, Shlomo Amir said that he had urged Yigal to become engaged to his girlfriend. He clung to the belief that if Yigal got married and started a family, he would become more mature and established and would abandon his callow ideas about redeeming the nation by disposing of Rabin. But Navah was a subject that Yigal would not discuss with his father. He was even insolent to Shlomo for prying. In January 1995 the subject at any rate became irrelevant. Navah's parents, say some of Yigal's friends, demanded that she end her relationship with Yigal, and she capitulated. All in all, the two had gone steady for six months but, according to Yigal's friends, had never had sex.

"As far as I can tell, Yigal is still a virgin," says Shlomi Halevy. "I'm not sure that she left him and not vice versa. He always took the lead in his relations with women; he was the one who would say what to do. I don't think that when he told girls he was going to murder Rabin, it was to make an impression on them. He had an amazing degree of self-confidence with girls, even though he's no Robert Redford. He never felt dwarfed by them, and he usually gave off an air of superiority. He would start up with a girl by testing her, to see how susceptible she was to his rhetoric. If she was someone with right-wing views but was flighty, she didn't interest him."

After ending his relationship with Navah, Yigal threw himself into his political mission by lecturing his fellow students on his beliefs. Most of them heard him out politely. Some brushed him off in annoyance. Yet it was always women who were especially taken by him. He would sit with them on the campus lawn, gaze deeply into their eyes, and imagine himself to be a biblical prophet. Yigal had a standard spiel in these "talks": the radical left had taken control of the prime minister; the press was inciting against the right, gagging it and mocking its desperation and protests; the country was at war—a civil war—because a small minority of atheists—the military establishment, the legal establishment, the media—had wrested control of power and were imposing their views and distorting the concept of peace. In the name of peace, they were causing the murder of Jews; closing Jews up in ghettos surrounded by Arabs; creating an army for the Arabs; supplying it with weapons.

A month after Yigal broke up with Navah, a new woman entered his life. Margalit Har-Shefi was a twenty-year-old law student at Bar-Ilan when Amir met her at the end of February 1995, on the anniversary of the Goldstein massacre in Hebron. He was sitting on the grass with his friend Hila Frank, reciting his litany of Goldstein's virtues, when Margalit passed by. Hila knew Margalit, and Yigal had seen her on campus but had never spoken to her. When Margalit asked if she could join them, Yigal promptly began wooing her.

"I don't take up with girls just like that," he later told one of his interrogators. "First I discuss ideology with them. I'm a great admirer of Goldstein, so to get to know a girl I ask her one question: 'What do you think of Goldstein?' The answer will tell me whether she's shallow or has substance, that is, whether she's attractive."

Yigal told Margalit that Baruch Goldstein was a saint, and she instantly rebuked him. "What do you mean?" she snapped. "Goldstein is a murderer, a butcher."

"I talked about Rabin, saying he had to be killed, and she said to me: 'What, are you crazy? I'll turn you in.' And from the moment she said [that], she'd won me. I had a challenge: to break her resistance," he later told his interrogator. "I explained my view [on *din rodef*], and she said: 'Maybe you're making it up. How do you know that? You have to ask a rabbi.' 'Go [ask], if you want,' I said to her, and she went to see a rabbi and returned to me shamefacedly."

A month before the murder Margalit approached Shlomo Aviner, the rabbi of her settlement, Beit El, and asked about the matter. "Half of Bar-Ilan thinks Rabin is a *rodef*," she told him.

"That's right, Rabin is subject to *din rodef*. But killing him is forbidden," said Aviner, according to Yigal's version of the conversation. When Margalit returned to Yigal, "she told me the rabbi had tried to duck the issue," he told his interrogator.

Amir threw himself into winning the tall, haughty Margalit. She devoted most of her time to her studies, sitting in the library for hours on end. One of her fellow students described her as intelligent and a plugger, but not brilliant. A friend of Yigal's portrayed her as the sort of religious young woman who strains so hard to accentuate her modesty that she draws attention to herself. Another friend defined her as "a spoiled child."

Margalit Har-Shefi came from a prominent family whose members included supporters of the right and the left. Her father, Dov, held radical right-wing views. One of her grandfathers, Pinchas Peli, lectured on Judaism at Ben-Gurion University in Beersheba and did not count himself among the nationalist camp. Her aunt Emuna and uncle Benny Elon were settlers who were then gaining increasing political prominence. Rabbi Benny Elon, a radical right-wing messianist who was to found Zo Artzenu, had first earned Yigal's admiration for his belief that the Redemption will not come on its own, so that "we must learn to fathom God's Will and 'come to the help of the Lord.'" He was another figure that Yigal recruited to speak at his weekend seminars.

Sensing that Margalit was a young woman of "substance," Yigal turned the full force of his persuasive powers on her. In Margalit's eyes, Yigal was the master of all worlds: *haredi*, national religious, and secular. He knew how to read between the lines of the secular press and explain what was *really* happening in the country. Margalit was impressed that he had organized seminars and galvanized hundreds of students at them.

"Rabin is the key," Yigal told Margalit over and over again. "He must be brought down." She listened intently and promised to help him obtain weapons. He asked her to check out the arrangements for guarding the local arsenal in Beit El; perhaps it would be possible to steal a rifle from there. When Margalit consented, their relationship grew closer, and he told her about Haggai's cache of explosives. She knew Yigal had a plan to kill Rabin. Before he left for the ceremony dedicating an underpass near Kfar Shmaryahu on April 23, 1995, Yigal had told Margalit that he was going to shoot Rabin. He had even showed her his Beretta and said: "You see, this is the gun I'm going to kill Rabin with." And Margalit encouraged him by saying, "I'll be glad if Rabin dies."

In Yigal's eyes Margalit became his comrade, confidante, partner. He came to adore the comely young woman who sat patiently with him for hours, gazing into his eyes and drinking in his flow of fantasies. He wanted her desperately, but although she expressed warm feelings for him, when he drew closer, she pulled back. When he became romantic, she signaled that she wasn't ready. When he talked about marriage, she grew evasive. After the murder some of their friends wondered whether Yigal hadn't gone through with his plan to prove that he was ready to sacrifice everything for her. He wanted her as a mate; she wanted him as a mentor.

The assassination was planned in the small storage shack behind Geula's kindergarten. At first there were just three of them—Yigal, Haggai, and Dror Adani—who met once or twice a month. Yigal was the decision maker. Haggai was the weapons expert. Dror was the "idea man" with a rich imagination that generated a steady flow of suggestions. Yigal had first brought Dror home not to help plan the demise of Yitzhak Rabin but to meet his sister Hadas. The suggestion came from his father.

Yigal liked the idea. The Adani family was much like his own, large and of Yemenite origin. Dror's father worked in a gas station, and some of his extended family lived in the Amirs' neighborhood. Yet what excited Yigal most about Dror was that beyond being a pious Jew and a settler, he was a man with backbone, and Yigal believed that his headstrong sister needed a husband like that.

When Hadas had volunteered for National Service,* Yigal feared that out on her own, far from the family, his sister would lose her innocence. Worse yet, she was assigned to tend the children of drug addicts in the Red Sea resort town of Eilat, which Yigal imagined as a den of iniquity. Only a successful match, Yigal thought, would save her from ruin and the family from indelible shame. So he arranged for Dror to visit their home.

No match ensued from that meeting. But from then on Dror became a permanent guest in the shack behind the kindergarten. He quickly found a common cause with the Amir brothers: to fight the betrayal of the Land of Israel. They discussed ways of intimidating Palestinians and contemplated volunteering to defend the threatened settlers. But their first preference, they decided, was to take action against the government. Since it had signed the agreement of betrayal, it had to be brought down. Dror proved himself a loyal and discreet partner. He had no doubt that Rabin deserved to die.

It was Yigal who chaired the sessions in the storage shack. The three men had two handguns—one licensed to Yigal, the other to Haggai—plus

---

*Alternative service for young men and women exempted from the army on religious or medical grounds.

ammunition and explosives that Haggai had stolen from the army. Hidden in the attic were ten fragmentation and phosphorus grenades and seven bricks of dynamite. For hours they planned how to take vengeance on Palestinians. They devised ways to attack Faisal Husseini, who was responsible for Jerusalem affairs on behalf of the Palestinian Authority. They toyed with the idea of killing Yasser Arafat by firing a shoulder-launched missile at his helicopter as it flew over the Gaza Strip. They planned to set up roadblocks in the West Bank, stop Palestinian cars, and arrest men on the official, or their private, "wanted list." Hours were spent critiquing the negative stereotypes with which the press had branded the settlers. Yigal sought pragmatic ways to protect the settlers, whom he called "warm, wonderful, and sensitive." He proposed knocking down Palestinian power lines and burning their fields. But the discussion invariably circled back to the need to eliminate the prime minister. Fretting that it would be a difficult task to accomplish with a handgun, Haggai suggested obtaining a rifle and fitting it with a silencer.

Yigal quickly realized they needed reinforcements. Dror was against the idea; he feared the Shabak would learn of the plan and infiltrate the group of conspirators. But Yigal pressed ahead.

Margalit joined the "inner circle" in the middle of 1995. She helped organize the weekend seminars. When the Amir brothers were planning to use explosives, she volunteered to purchase the timers. When Yigal wanted to learn more about dynamite, she gave him the name of a chemist from Beit El who would be willing to guide him. "You could say that Margalit was like us," Yigal later told his interrogators. "In the business about planning to attack Arabs, she was number three."

Another source of reinforcements, Yigal decided, would be the kolel at Bar-Ilan. He had a talk there with Avshalom Weinberg and asked him to recruit ten young men for the covert cells that would attack Palestinians who had been released from Israeli prisons under the terms of the Oslo agreements. Explosives would be supplied by Aryeh Schwartz, a soldier who had studied with Yigal in the Kerem D'Yavneh Yeshiva and was serving in Yigal's old unit, the Golani Brigade. (No fewer than twenty-four thousand bullets, detonators, bricks of explosives, and grenades were found in Schwartz's house after the assassination.) Also recruited was Ohad Skornik, a twenty-three-year-old law student who had studied with Yigal in Kerem D'Yavneh and came from a prominent right-wing family (his father was a surgeon in Tel Aviv's largest hospital). Before the November 4 rally the Amir brothers visited Skornik's apartment, near the Kings of Israel Square, to check whether there was a direct line of fire between its windows and the stage on which Rabin would be standing.

Yigal was heartened by the cell's progress and believed that soon he would be ready for his big move. He hadn't yet told Dror and Haggai that he was planning to act alone. But the two had agreed to obtain a rifle and silencer. Haggai had submitted a request to the army for a personal weapon. "I live in a settlement in the territories," he lied on the application, "and need an effective weapon for self-defense." The army turned him down. In place of a rifle, Dror offered his Uzi submachine gun. The brothers took it out for a trial only to discover that an Uzi is not designed for long-range fire. Then Haggai met Michael Epstein, a settler who agreed to lend them his personal rifle. The three agreed that it was suitable for the job and searched for a spot from which they could fire at Rabin from a distance.

The planning and fantasizing must have been gratifying in themselves, because even after they had secured Epstein's rifle, Dror kept coming up with alternatives. He suggested booby-trapping Rabin's car. The brothers packed some dynamite and drove to Rabin's neighborhood in Tel Aviv. But when they approached the prime minister's car, they saw that it was guarded and left. Dror then suggested parking a booby-trapped car along Rabin's regular route to Jerusalem, but Yigal rejected the idea for fear of harming innocent bystanders. Haggai also proposed acquiring a shoulder-launched antitank missile and firing it from a distance at Rabin's moving vehicle. He was sure there would be no difficulty obtaining the missile, observing that reservists sometimes bring them home. Yigal accepted the task of finding out how to get a missile. In the meanwhile, he asked Haggai to find a silencer for Epstein's rifle. He gave his brother a hundred shekels and suggested that he find a soldier to lend them one.

Dror continued to generate ideas. He suggested booby-trapping a microphone and having Yigal, masquerading as a reporter, thrust it into Rabin's face and set it off. Talk of explosives inspired Haggai to think of slipping a bomb into Rabin's apartment though the water pipes. Yigal thought it would be better to poison the water, but Haggai objected that such a plan might kill someone other than Rabin. Dror favored the idea of a bomb, but he questioned whether it was possible to float one through the pipes. So Yigal and Haggai took a second journey to Rabin's neighborhood of Ramat Aviv. After parking near the local shopping center, they walked the few blocks to Rabin's apartment building. Yigal entered the lobby alone. If asked to identify himself, he planned to say he was a plumber. No one stopped him; no one asked. As he checked out the water system, he realized that projecting a bomb up to the fifth-floor penthouse was a complex affair requiring the installation of a pressure pump specifically for that purpose. The brothers proceeded to Peres's apartment building nearby and then returned to the shack in Herzliya for a long discussion on whether to center on Rabin or Peres. "Perhaps both of them at once?" Haggai mused. But Yigal believed that without Rabin, Peres was nothing, and they agreed to focus on the prime minister.

The next suggestion—Yigal's—was even more fantastic: landing a drone on the roof of Rabin's moving car. Haggai vetoed it because they didn't know enough about drones. It was better, he said, to shoot Rabin with a rifle.

On Fridays Yigal took to joining the raucous demonstrations outside Rabin's Ramat Aviv house to study the building from all sides and memorize a view of the penthouse. After two weeks he reached the conclusion that it would be difficult to shoot Rabin there. "It's complicated because of the neighbors and the guards," he told his co-conspirators. Haggai suggested shooting Rabin with a sniper's rifle as he left the building, but Yigal countered that there were no escape routes from the area, and the idea was dropped.

A s Yigal Amir stood in the dimly lit parking area under the square, he checked his watch and sensed that the rally was soon to end. About half an hour earlier a policeman had walked up to him and scrutinized him, trying to decide whether to question the slim young man. At just that moment, the teen idol Aviv Gefen walked past them and began walking up the steps to the square.

"Hey, did you see that joker?" Amir asked the policeman, pointing at the rock star.

The policeman nodded.

"He ducked out of the army," Amir sneered.

"The son of a bitch is a draft dodger," the policeman echoed.

After that bonding exchange, the two stood talking for a while, and at one point the policeman pointed to another figure standing not far away.

"Who's that?" he asked.

Amir hadn't the vaguest notion but replied, "It's all right. He's one of us."

The man was in fact Rabin's driver Menachem Damti. His identity was irrelevant, however, for Yigal had achieved his goal of convincing the policeman that he himself was "one of us."

A few minutes after the policeman had walked off, another officer walked up to Amir and said roughly: "Hey, driver, where's your car?"

"Here," Yigal replied, making no effort to identify it.

"Fine," barked the policeman, "go stand next to it."

"Okay," Yigal said obligingly, and the policeman walked on.

A few minutes later two policemen came close enough for Amir to hear their conversation. One of them pointed to him and asked the other: "Who's that?"

"It's okay," his colleague said reassuringly. "He's under cover."

Yigal read his success at casting off suspicion as a sign from God that he was meant to act that night. He seated himself nonchalantly at the edge of a large concrete flower pot, about ten meters away from Rabin's car, and waited.

In the square above him, the prime minister's deep bass voice boomed out of the loudspeakers as the crowd listened intently. Among the people who had gathered that evening were many who knew well the ravages of war, as well as the price of peace. Following the disastrous 1973 Yom Kippur War, they had surrounded Golda Meir's office and protested for weeks until she and her government resigned. In 1982, when Israel had hurled itself arrogantly into a war in Lebanon and its Christian allies had massacred Palestinian refugees in the Sabra and Shatilla refugee camps in Beirut, they had come here, to this very square, to demand an accounting of the atrocity. That was the largest demonstration of all: four hundred thousand people, according to the police estimate.

On the night of November 4 they had returned to the square for a very different cause: to thank the peacemaker, bolster his resolve, raise his spirits in light of the ugly campaign of incitement against him. Yitzhak Rabin looked out on a hundred thousand of his cheering countrymen. It had been quite a while since secular Israel had mounted such a display of tribute. They proudly waved their banners, and some wept with emotion. They hadn't felt such collective joy since the night of Rabin's election three years earlier. Even the Oslo Agreement, the coveted start of reconciliation with their Palestinian neighbors, had not brought them out into the streets like this. For fifteen years, from the time of Menachem Begin's 1977 electoral upset until Rabin had returned to power, many secular Israelis had felt that their country had been wrested from their hands and entrusted to warmongering nationalists and *haredi* draft dodgers who huddled in their yeshivas whenever the firing started. Now, finally, history was changing course. And there, in the heart of Tel Aviv, their rough, guarded prime minister was holding an intimate conversation with tens of thousands of his grateful admirers.

"Allow me to tell you that I am touched," he said, his voice cracking with emotion.

Yigal Amir was not listening to Rabin's speech. He concentrated only on himself, blocking out policemen, bodyguards, and the huge crowd singing the "Song of Peace." He began to focus on the arcane art of gematria, a product of the mysticism to which Yigal and his mother Geula were both drawn. Gematria involved manipulating the letters of biblical verses to predict the future. Yigal envisioned various verses, remembering the passage in which God made his Holy Covenant with his people: "When the sun had gone down and it was dark, behold, a smoking fire pot and a flaming torch passed between these pieces. And that day the Lord made a covenant with Abram, saying: 'To your descendants I give this land, from the river of Egypt to the great river, the river of Euphrates'" [Genesis 16: 17–18]. In his mind, Amir moved one letter of each word forward to join the next and discovered Rabin's name hidden there in the story of the Covenant. The Hebrew words אש אשר עבר בין ("a flaming torch passed between") became אש אש רע ברבין ("fire, fire, [there is] evil in Rabin"). He took it as a sign that today his fire, gunfire, would hit the prime minister.

Above him Yitzhak Rabin was singing the "Song of Peace," and the crowd was ecstatic. In his dull baritone, endearingly off-key, Mr. Security stood belting out the anthem of the peace movement that he had so often mocked in the past. The lyrics had been printed for him on a piece of paper that he folded, when the song had ended, and slipped into his jacket pocket. Then his hand warmly clamped Shimon Peres's shoulder. Yitzhak Rabin was pleased. He hadn't been so visibly moved by a public display of support since a joint session of the U.S. Congress had given him a standing ovation more than a year before. His face flushed with emotion, Rabin thanked the organizers, even the television crews, and embraced Aviv Gefen, the flamboyant rebel bard who was in every way his opposite.

As Leah Rabin stood at the edge of the stage, gazing at her husband and smiling, a journalist turned to her and asked if Rabin was wearing a bullet-proof vest.

"What kind of a question is that?" she snapped. "What does he need a vest for? Are we living in a banana republic? I don't understand the kind of ideas you journalists have!"

Standing next to her was B.L., the head of the Shabak's VIP Protection Unit.

"Thank God everything has gone peacefully," she said to him.

"For the moment," he replied.

When the rally ended, as Yigal Amir sat on the concrete flower pot in the parking area, Shimon Peres descended the steps beside him. Amir noticed that there was only one bodyguard with him and no policemen. Yigal's arm moved to act, but he held back. Peres's bodyguard cast a suspicious glance at him.

"For God's sake, what's that dark guy doing down there? Is he one of us?" the bodyguard whispered into his tiny microphone.

But the bodyguard did not stop, and Peres came immediately behind him, walking toward his car. "Bravo, Shimon!" someone shouted from the side, and Peres's head turned toward the cry. At the end of the sidewalk stood a small group of his supporters. As he strode vigorously toward them and extended his hand, his bodyguard stood tensely at the ready. "Bravo, Shimon! Bravo! It was great tonight!" they called.

Then Rabin appeared at the top of the steps to the parking area. Yigal stood up. From the corner of his eye he could see that the door to the prime minister's car was being opened. Suddenly Rabin was striding quickly past him. Less than five meters separated them. As Rabin thrust out his arm to grasp the door, Yigal's hand reached for his gun.

Yigal Amir fired three shots. Two of the hollow-point bullets hit Rabin, rupturing his spleen, severing major arteries in his chest, and shattering his spinal cord. The third bullet wounded his bodyguard, Yoram Rubin, in his left arm. As he fired, Amir shouted: "It's nothing! It's nothing! It's just a joke." One witness heard him shout: "Blanks, blanks." Rabin clutched his stomach and fell forward. His wounded bodyguard grabbed him and thrust him into the car. The driver, Damti, accelerated and drove to Ichilov Hospital, a few blocks away.

When the shots rang out, a few of the people standing near the car instinctively hit the ground, but policemen and Shabak agents jumped on Amir and wrested the gun from his hand. Then the policemen rushed the assassin over to the wall of the nearby shopping center, where dozens of police quickly surrounded him to create a human wall between Amir and the crowd. About an hour and a half later, a few minutes before 11:00 P.M., Yitzhak Rabin died on the operating table. His chief of staff, Eitan Haber, walked out to the waiting reporters and, in a voice choked with tears, read out the statement: "The government of Israel announces with shock, great regret, and profound grief the death of Yitzhak Rabin, who was murdered by an assassin. . . ."

Close to midnight the police told Amir that Rabin had died. "Do your work," he told them, "I've done mine." Then he turned to one of the policemen and said with a smile: "Get some wine and cakes. Let's have a toast."

An hour after the murder, Margalit Har-Shefi called Yigal Amir's home. Haggai answered, and the conversation was brief.

"Is it him?" she asked.

"I don't know anything," Haggai said.

"Just tell Yigal I called," she said, and hung up the receiver.

Two days later Margalit was arrested and held by the Shabak in Jerusalem. For two weeks she invoked her right to remain silent, unaware that most of the details of her involvement were already known to her interrogators. In their first two days under arrest both Amir brothers had willingly confessed their crimes and given a list of the inner and second circles. On only one point were they not forthcoming: the names of the rabbis who had ruled that the halacha permitted the murder of the prime minister of Israel.

Within two days all of the other "fellow travelers"—Dror Adani, Ohad Skornik, Aryeh Schwartz, Avshalom Weinberg, and Michael Epstein—were arrested and cooperated with their interrogators. Only Har-Shefi would not talk—except to demand that she be allowed to pray, light Sabbath candles, and fulfill all the other religious injunctions in her cell. She impressed her interrogators as being stunningly arrogant. Lacking permission to use "special methods" to break her silence, they were in need of Amir's help. The Shabak knew of the relationship between the two. Amir's friends had been questioned at length about his relations with women, and they all spoke of his special bond with Har-Shefi.

On November 8, four days after the assassination, the Shabak interrogator known to Amir as "Gonen" asked him for his help. Margalit is needlessly tormenting herself, he told Amir. She refuses to talk with us, and unless she gives us her version, we won't release her. Who appreciates better than you that we already know everything about her? If you want her freed, Gonen stressed to Amir, you must persuade her to talk.

Amir promptly agreed. In his mind there was no reason for Har-Shefi to be in torment; all her actions had been innocent. Gonen gave him a ballpoint pen and a sheet of paper, and Amir quickly scrawled a few lines. Throughout the interrogation he had been calm, almost aloof. Now his handwriting betrayed great stress. The lines of his note were crooked, the letters uneven, with basic punctuation missing. Here is what Yigal Amir wrote to the woman he loved:

Margalit

I know what you're thinking, I thought about everything before I did it.

I don't regret a thing and if I could do it again I would. It's just a pity that the family isn't strong and doesn't believe in me They're not helping me that way.

Tell [your interrogators] everything I ever said to you and don't be afraid and don't try to be a heroine They know everything anyway Nothing will happen to you.

See you in better times.

Yigal Amir

P.S.

I told them that you knew, after the fact, about Yad Vashem and Kfar Shmaryahu, so that you can rest easy.

Regards to my parents and all the friends, especially Hila and Nili and Ohad. [Indecipherable line] that the gang should help my family by visiting [them] and talking about me because my family doesn't know me as you do.

Everything is from <u>Heaven</u>.

See you. The interrogator I'm sending this letter with is Gonen. You have nothing to fear.

Har-Shefi received the letter that same day. She read it a few times and decided to give a partial version of events but still refused to answer most of the interrogators' questions. Eleven days passed, "Gonen" asked Amir to try again, and he wrote a second letter. By this time he had recovered his self-confidence and discovered that interrogation was not a nightmare. No one was pressuring or abusing him; on the contrary, he had the interrogators wrapped around his finger. They were virtually ignorant about halacha. Sometimes Yigal had the feeling that he was dominating the interrogation, dictating the subjects and the pace.

This time he wrote an orderly letter in which the lines were straight, the margins equal, the handwriting perfectly clear. Two weeks had passed since the murder, and Amir knew that his plan had succeeded in full. Rabin was gone, he himself had survived, and the campaign against the peace process went on. The government was still in a state of confusion, but Yigal was already at the next stage, planning moves and issuing directives. He even allowed himself to tease Margalit. He believed she would reveal only what he allowed her to. He was sure she would support his deed by proudly stating that the murder was justified. After all, he assumed with only rudimentary knowledge of the law, such a declaration was not a crime; she could not be charged with conspiracy or abetting a crime just for endorsing it after the fact. He wrote her on November 19:

Dear Margalit,

I am still cut off from the papers and the news, but some items do reach me. It seems to me that Peres has learned some lessons, but this is still not enough. The weekends must continue. When my interrogation is over the lists can be taken and the activity continued. Nothing is over. I am fine and doing everything I thought I would. My parents must be shored up and the gang [must] go to talk to them about me, because they don't understand very well what's happened here. They live in a secular environment, which likewise has no idea what's going on in the country, and they're in total shock.

Gonen is coming to you in Jerusalem today and he's a great and genuine guy. Believe what he says to you and tell the <u>whole</u> truth. You have nothing to lose. On the contrary, if you don't tell the truth you can only be harmed. Don't try to be a heroine when it's not necessary. I need you on the outside to continue the work, so don't do anything stupid.

I miss all the gang, especially Nili and Hila. Give them my warm regards. You are my voice on the outside. Only you know exactly what I did and only you can get the message across, so don't screw up. No one is beating me during the interrogations and all the information they know about you is not from me. I've just tried to help and lessen the damage, so I told them about the weapons' store, what really happened, and about your [unintelligible word]. What really happened, and not as they've tried to frame you. You have nothing to fear from this. You didn't do anything. By the way, one of the interrogators here talks about you all the time. What have you done to him? Good luck on the outside and see you in the next life.

Yigal Amir

This second letter shows that Yigal still trusted Margalit. He obviously had no way of knowing that she was about to break free of his grip. For Margalit read his second letter, immediately relented, and gave her version of events. Rather than endorse his act, as Yigal believed she would, she utterly dissociated herself from it—and from him. Yes, Amir had boasted to her that he would murder Rabin, she told her interrogators, but she didn't believe he had it in him. She thought he was merely a braggart. She didn't take him seriously.

Had Margalit Har-Shefi been a party to the murder conspiracy? The results of her interrogation were inconclusive, and prosecuting attorneys were uncertain. A few days later she was released on bail, returned to Beit El, and received a heroine's welcome. Hundreds of settlers wildly cheered her. Rabbi Aviner made a speech in her honor. Neighbors lifted her on a chair, like a joyous bride, singing and dancing their way to her home. That evening, when clips of the reception were shown on the news, a still-mourning Israel was stunned. Unknown to the public then was that two weeks earlier, when the seven-day mourning period had ended and air-raid sirens were sounded in memorial to the slain prime minister, Har-Shefi had violated a sacred national tradition. When everything stopped and Israel stood at attention, she was seated in an interrogation room and chose to remain that way.

"You can start the questions," she said to the officers, who were already on their feet. "I don't intend to stand at attention for Rabin's memory anyway."

At that same moment Yigal Amir, who was likewise in an interrogation room, silently rose and patiently waited for the siren's wail to end.

In June 1996, after Amir had been tried and convicted of premeditated murder, his second trial opened in Tel Aviv. In the dock with him now were his brother Haggai and his friend Dror Adani. The charges against them were conspiring to murder Yitzhak Rabin, illegal possession of arms, and conspiring to assault Arabs and damage their property. Absent from the dock was Margalit Har-Shefi. The State Attorney's Office had hesitated to bring any charges against her. But a year and a half after the assassination, the state attorney finally decided to try her. In June 1998 Margalit Har-Shefi was convicted of failing to prevent a crime. As of this writing she is awaiting sentencing and is still studying law at Bar-Ilan University.

Between the assassination and her trial, one journalist reported that he had seen Margalit dancing at a wedding in Jerusalem. When the groom's uncle spotted her, he shouted, "Get out of here! You murdered my prime minister. You have no reason to be here!" Some of the guests hustled him out of the hall, while Har-Shefi continued dancing. Another journalist reported that he had seen her in the Kings of Israel Square (now renamed Rabin Square) one evening during an open-air book fair. She was strolling among the stands with a girlfriend.

"I was close to the two all the time," he wrote. "They didn't look at me, and passersby didn't look at Margalit. . . . She led her friend to the side of the square. . . . On the way they passed by the low concrete [flower pot] that Yigal Amir had sat on while waiting for his victim. After they had passed by the memorial to Rabin, they sat and waited for the bus that would return them home to Beit El."

On July 16, 1996, Yigal laid eyes on Margalit for the first time since the murder. The encounter in the Tel Aviv courtroom was extremely tense. Margalit had come to testify against the Amir brothers and Dror Adani. Yigal's glance kept locking on her, searching for a sign, waiting for a gesture, but she turned away. Margalit looked calm; Yigal seemed distraught. He was expecting her to repeat to the court what she had said in their long, intimate conversations: that she believed Rabin must be eliminated. He saw her as a political partner and wanted her to justify the murder before the country and the world. In any case, he believed, the state lacked hard evidence against her. After all, Margalit was a free woman. And if she were safe against prosecution, why shouldn't she support him?

Har-Shefi's lawyer had prevailed upon her to distance herself from Yigal Amir. He persuaded her to portray the Amir she knew as a childish blowhard, and she followed his advice. Margalit testified to hearing Yigal say that it was necessary to dispose of Rabin but added that she didn't believe he would do it. It never even occurred to her, she said, that Amir truly intended to murder the prime minister.

"I didn't realize that Yigal Amir was serious," she said on the witness stand, and Yigal could not contain his rage.

"Liar! You're lying!" he growled from the bench while pointing his hand upward, as if to say: See, she's betraying me, and God will be her judge.

On March 27, 1996, at the end of his first trial, Yigal Amir was convicted of murdering Yitzhak Rabin and was sentenced to life imprisonment plus another six years for injuring Rabin's bodyguard. On September 11, 1996, at the end of his second trial, he was sentenced to another five years' imprisonment for conspiring to harm Arabs. Haggai Amir was sentenced to twelve years' imprisonment, and Dror Adani to seven, both for conspiring to murder Yitzhak Rabin and to cause harm to

Arabs. Yigal is incarcerated in the south, in Beersheba Prison, where he is kept in solitary confinement. Haggai is imprisoned in the north, in Shata Prison on Mount Carmel.

Once every other week Geula Amir goes to see Yigal in the south; once every week she travels to visit Haggai in the north. After the murder Geula was at first overwhelmed. "I didn't want to get out of bed," she recalls. "How could he do such a thing to us? . . . I joined those who condemned the murder." But her anger was short-lived. Right-wing Israelis made hundreds of phone calls and sent stacks of letters in support of Yigal, an outpouring that persuaded Geula to think better of her son. A year after the assassination she still maintained that Yitzhak Rabin's murder was a despicable act but then immediately qualified that it was not Yigal who was responsible for the deed but "forces stronger than he."

"Who were these forces?" she was asked.

"I don't know," Geula said. "Yigal was moved by strong forces. It's true that he shot Rabin, but the work of 'finishing him off,' as they say around here, was done by somebody else. They knew he was going to do it and they didn't stop him."

She meant the Shabak, for Geula Amir had convinced herself that her son was the victim of a plot against Rabin hatched at the highest levels of government.

CHAPTER 7

DENIAL

The consequences of the assassination were felt not only in the political realm; they also left a deep impression on the personal lives of ordinary Israelis. When interviewed by the authors months after the killing, Daniel,* a Jerusalem physician, recalled a conversation he had had with his ten-year-old son, Aaron, on the afternoon of November 5. The child had returned from his liberal Orthodox school with the startling news that several of his teachers had expressed approval of the previous night's events.

"Aaron told me that his teacher insisted Rabin was punished because he had sinned, because he had given part of the Land of Israel to foreigners," Daniel recalled. Aaron also said that the children had argued among themselves about whether Rabin had deserved his fate.

"I was appalled," Daniel said. "I shouted at Aaron that he must never say such things, that Rabin's death was a despicable crime."

Like many Israelis, Daniel had not been raised in Yitzhak Rabin's secularized Israel. He had been born in France forty years earlier into a practicing family that had settled there during the Middle Ages. But Daniel

---

*The names of Daniel and his son have been changed in deference to their privacy.

considered himself a man of science, as well as an observant Jew. He wore a crocheted yarmulke and defined himself as modern and liberal. When he finished his medical degree ten years earlier, he had come to Israel in fulfillment of a lifelong dream.

After speaking with his son that night, Daniel announced to his wife that he intended to meet with Aaron's principal and strenuously protest the teacher's remark. "I told her that the school must know we will not abide this sort of education. That teacher must be dismissed," he said. Daniel had no doubt that his wife would support him in his crusade.

To his amazement, however, his wife told him firmly, "Don't go to the principal. It won't go down well with our friends." That evening, her brothers came to talk with him. "'The child is being educated properly,' they told me. 'It's best that you stay out of it.'" For fear of damaging his marriage, Daniel did nothing. But in the days that followed, he knew no peace. He told his wife that he wanted to transfer Aaron to another school, but she vigorously protested the idea. A year later Daniel sensed that his relationship with his wife was still severely strained.

Reactions similar to those in Aaron's school were voiced all over Israel in the weeks and months following the murder. Judgments that "Rabin was responsible for his death" or that "Rabin brought his demise upon himself" were heard in *haredi* neighborhoods, Jewish settlements, yeshivas, religious grade schools, and meetings of religious organizations. A few voices unabashedly lauded Yigal Amir. Far more common, however, was the failure to condemn the murder unequivocally, to praise it by faint censure, or to express understanding for a young man like Amir who was so devoted to the Land of Israel. Only a handful of people publicly pronounced Amir a hero, but many dwelled on the theme of his self-sacrifice to foil the Oslo Agreements.

The extent of this response was initially hidden from the public at large. Immediately after the assassination the media were preoccupied with covering Rabin's funeral, the many memorial ceremonies, and especially the remarkable phenomenon of the "candle children" in the square where Rabin had been shot. Masses of children and teenagers gathered in the square to light candles, sing songs, and grieve together by weeping in one another's arms. Many wrote poems and letters to Rabin's family. Some sprayed graffiti at the site of the murder. Almost all these youngsters came from secular homes. Their rite bore no resemblance to traditional Jewish mourning rituals and went on day and night for almost two weeks. Children of the rich and the poor, from established kibbutzim and struggling development towns, schoolchildren, university students, and soldiers on leave all flocked to the square. Teenagers who were totally alienated from politics, children who were barely acquainted with Rabin's life and had only a tenuous grasp of his political doctrines were suddenly speaking of the slain prime minister as their father. The phenomenon was unprecedented in Israeli life, and commentators wondered where this flood of grief was coming from. Was it genuine bereavement, they asked, or merely a fad picked up from imported television programs?

As the children sat in small circles, singing the "Song of Peace" and "Forever, my brother, I'll remember you"—the poignant lyrics of Aviv Gefen—networks shifted from coverage of the formal ceremonies in Jerusalem to shots of the weeping "orphans." Leah Rabin thanked and chided the youngsters. Where were these thousands of supporters, she asked, when it had been necessary to protect her husband against the viciousness of his opponents? Her listeners vowed to honor Rabin's memory and legacy. Some of them even founded a new political movement called "A Whole Generation Demands Peace." They chose Rabin's son, Yuval, to be its leader.

For two weeks the cameras focused on Rabin Square because the candle children photographed so well. Appearances can be deceiving, however. For in concentrating so sharply on Rabin Square, the media failed to capture the fact that two sectors of Israeli society did not share in the public mourning: the *haredi* and national religious communities. In Israel's divided society the secular, mainstream media had difficulty penetrating the world of Orthodox and ultra-Orthodox Jews. Most of the country's religious citizens reside in relatively closed communities—whether separate neighborhoods or settlements over the Green Line—where the synagogue is the center of their lives. They have built autonomous social and political networks presided over by rabbis or party officials who honor the rabbis' directives. The religious sector has its own schools and trains its own teachers. Over the years the opportunities for its members to encounter nonreligious Jews have grown more and more restricted, as communities have opened their own supermarkets (run strictly according to religious dietary laws), expanded their internal social welfare systems, and even established their own medical clinics.

The more inner-directed the religious community grew, the more hostile it became to the secular mass media. The Gush Emunim settlers in the territories were angered by the press's refusal to portray them as innocent victims of Palestinian violence. Thus the past two decades had been marked by a growing desire to keep the media at bay, with the result that various trends developing in the religious community did not reach the attention of the secular public until they were already well advanced. Few secular Israelis appreciated that hundreds of thousands of religious Jews had internalized the doctrine of messianic Redemption and consequently transferred their political allegiance to the right. The recruitment of religion to serve a right-wing ideology was not a wholly new development. But it took a while for the extent of its influence to sink in. Only after the assassination did secularists realize that a broad theocratic subculture was operating in their midst.

Reports on expressions of support for Yigal Amir within the religious community slowly leaked out. A resident of the *haredi* stronghold of Bnei Brak stood before television cameras and declared: "There is no mourning here. Yitzhak Rabin was not one of us." In the Jerusalem neighborhood of Ramat Polin, *haredim* raised glasses of wine and gleefully toasted the murder. Others thanked God for allowing them to live to see this day. In Tapuach and Yizhar, two West Bank settlements inhabited by Kahanist extremists, pictures of Amir were hung on the walls at parties celebrating the "miracle." When word of the assassination reached the large West Bank settlement of Ariel, participants at a political assembly stood up and applauded; no one in the hall tried to silence them. In the Kahane-inspired Yeshiva of the Jewish Idea in Jerusalem, young men embraced one another on hearing the news. In the kolel study group at Bar-Ilan University, students called Yigal Amir a "saint." Avigdor Eskin, who had conducted the *Pulsa da-Nura* ceremony against Rabin, boasted on television that the curse had succeeded.

No real effort was made to stifle these responses. In the first days after the assassination, a few secular Israelis had reacted by indiscriminately abusing or attacking men wearing yarmulkes. But upon being firmly condemned by public figures, such behavior promptly ended. A fleeting debate on the expressions of support for the assassin erupted only months later, in August 1996, after Israel television's Channel One showed a news feature on girls studying in a state religious high school who had formed a Yigal Amir Fan Club. Their main activity was to collect photos of Amir and quotes from his court appearances. But they also sent him adoring letters. Three of these members had no compunction about being interviewed on national television. "Somebody had to do it," said one, who also characterized Rabin as a murderer, "and he was the only one with the courage."

These sentiments were also expressed in the unlikeliest of venues. A question on the 1996 high school matriculation examination in citizenship prompted a substantial number of essays indicating support for Yigal Amir and his motives. Two of the teachers grading these exams spoke out about the answers of students from religious high schools and sought to publish them. But the Ministry of Education and Culture—by then headed by Minister Zevulun Hammer of the National Religious Party—forbade them to do so.

Meanwhile, in settlements, yeshivas, and synagogues dominated by advocates of the Greater Land of Israel movement, many spoke of divine intervention. "There's a feeling among the religious public that Rabin's death was a miracle," Bar-Ilan sociologist Professor Nissan Rubin, a man of moderate political views, reported six months after the assassination. Citing ancient Jewish myths of miraculous rescue, Rubin wrote in *Ha'aretz*: "Just as the Jews were always saved from destruction at the last minute"— an allusion to the parting of the Red Sea during the Exodus and to the eleventh-hour rescue of the Jews of Persia from the wicked Haman—"so now [people are saying] a miracle has occurred."

Secular Israelis had heard these views, in one form or another, before. What appalled them now, however, was their magnitude. Yigal Amir, it turned out, represented not a "lunatic fringe" of the right but a large contingent of Israelis that comprised three ideological camps: secular nationalists, religious nationalists, and *haredim*. Sociologists who examined levels of support for the assassination found that many of Amir's admirers would not admit their feelings to strangers. But surveys done by means of indirect questions showed that one out of every six Jewish Israelis condoned the murder or at least did not condemn it. In one such survey, conducted in the middle of 1996, about one-quarter of the respondents in religious high schools failed to condemn the murder, compared with one-tenth of their counterparts in secular schools.

Hebrew University Professor Moshe Lissak, one of Israel's most prominent sociologists, states bluntly that "Yigal Amir grew out of the mainstream, not the margins. What is referred to as the 'ideological fringe' is actually very broad. We're speaking of a variety of groups—social networks—some of which speak and write on a high level. They share a good degree of common ground, and they live and act in contiguous circles. These are not isolated or reclusive elements, and there is a big difference between them and the Kahanist thugs." Yet most of the Israeli public was oblivious of their ideologies, Lissak explains, because they did not see the material being distributed in yeshivas and synagogues.

At the same time, various right-wing politicians tried to play down the national tragedy. Like Amir, they were careful never to use the word "murder" in referring to the assassination, saying only that "Rabin was killed" or "Rabin died," as though he were the victim of an accident. A few tried to ward off blame by simply denying that the right-wing incitement was in any way connected to the assassination.

Member of the Knesset Uzi Landau, one of the more radical members of the Likud, charged the government with trying to make political capital out of the tragedy, using the term "dancing on Rabin's [spilt] blood." Former Defense Minister Ariel Sharon openly scoffed at warnings that another assassination might follow, adding cynically after the outpouring of grief for Rabin, "There are ministers in Israel who are waiting in line to be threatened."

Before the murder retired General Rehavam Ze'evi, the leader of the radical right-wing Moledet Party, had incited against the prime minister by writing that "Rabin is pushing us to the borders of Auschwitz" and calling for him to be put on trial. After the assassination he gave a mawkish eulogy of his old "comrade-in-arms." Similarly, before the murder Sharon had called Rabin a "pimp of blood" and likened his government to the *Judenräte* during the Holocaust in saying: "During the Shoah, the Jews were forced to collaborate; here the government is doing everything of its own volition." Two months before the assassination, writing in the mass-circulation daily *Yediot Ahronot*, Sharon had called Rabin a despot and accused his government of spreading fears of a political murder as a way of discrediting the opposition, just as Stalin had done. But after the murder he self-righteously called for the incitement to stop. In an article published in the same newspaper under the title "Stop Inciting and Unite," he too eulogized Rabin, extolling his achievements as a "great commander." "To me Yitzhak Rabin was a political rival, but I regarded him as the prime minister of us all," he wrote. "He was an adversary, but he was a friend."

On September 6, 1997, Sharon gave an interview to Israel's Channel One. Since the Oslo Agreement was the subject of controversy, he said, Rabin should not have signed it against the will of a large portion of the population. Had Rabin heeded his call to form a unity government with the right, he would probably not have been killed. The statement was not a slip of the tongue. Thus almost two years after the murder, Sharon, then a senior minister in Netanyahu's government, essentially echoed the claim of the radical right and extremist rabbis that, by his own obstinacy, Yitzhak Rabin had brought his death upon himself.

The most sustained and brazen effort at denial, however, was mounted by Benjamin Netanyahu. In the first hours after the assassination, the leader of the opposition was frantic. He phoned the head of the Action Headquarters, Ya'akov Novick, in fear that Peres would have Novick arrested and that, as a result of Novick's interrogation, Netanyahu himself would be charged with complicity in the incitement. He worried that he would be compelled to explain his participation in meetings at which the leaders of the Action Headquarters were told to organize mass demonstrations at which placards reading RABIN IS A TRAITOR were displayed. It would also be difficult to rationalize his continued cooperation with the Action Headquarters even after he had seen that it was escalating the incitement to violence. Novick suggested they consult a judge he knew who held right-wing views. Netanyahu agreed, and the two met with the judge to work out a line of defense.

Over the following days Netanyahu also realized that he was being singled out for blame by leading members of his own party. Member of the Knesset Dan Meridor, a former justice minister, noted that Netanyahu had never dissociated himself from the extremists. Meridor and his close friend Knesset member Benny Begin, perhaps the Likud's most outspoken critic of the Oslo Agreements, had both walked out of mass demonstrations organized by the Political Guidance Headquarters and Novick's Action Headquarters. "I saw the signs reading RABIN IS A TRAITOR and RABIN IS A MURDERER, and I fled," said Meridor of the July 1994 demonstration in

Jerusalem's Zion Square. "I saw how they were delegitimizing Rabin and the government on the ground that they lacked a Jewish majority. . . . I understood that grave things were happening at these demonstrations [and] said to myself: 'I'm not coming anymore.'"

"Netanyahu feels comfortable with extremists," Likud Knesset member David Levy told *Ha'aretz* journalist Daniel Ben-Simon. "He whips them up and incites them. I know clearly that he was behind the defamation, curses, and vituperation voiced against me at the violent demonstration in Zion Square a month before the murder. I've checked this out thoroughly. Netanyahu and his people are the ones who turned the event into a dangerous fascist extravaganza."

Knesset member Shaul Amor, a Likud representative from a constituency of development towns and poor neighborhoods, put his complaint against Netanyahu in even sharper terms. "I loved Rabin deeply, and I can't forgive myself for remaining silent when a few disturbed members of my party engaged in perilous demagoguery against him."

Knesset member Michael Eitan revealed that before two major right-wing demonstrations he had warned Netanyahu they might spin out of control. Eitan had feared that a fanatic might open fire on the police and that responsibility for the carnage would be placed on the Political Guidance Headquarters, of which he was a member. "I told him that people are walking around [at the demonstrations] with weapons—some of them mentally disturbed, some of them political elements interested in escalation—and that . . . there were organizations with radical, revolutionary thoughts, terrorist organizations acting quasi-overtly. . . . I was very fearful that in the course of an event like that, carried out under the auspices and appearance of a decent and legitimate parliamentary [protest], they might lead us into a dreadful crisis," he said in an interview late in 1996. "How did we turn the Likud into the operational headquarters of a group of crazies?" he added. "I recall telling Bibi a few times: 'Listen, the people who are rioting and inciting don't belong to us. They will cause us damage.' I told him that my foot would not tread into any demonstration [organized] by the right. Unfortunately, Bibi paid no attention. He saw only the electoral gain."

"[Netanyahu's] ambition to become prime minister at any price drove him out of his senses," echoed Likud Knesset member Meir Sheetrit in a 1995 interview. "I believe this will lead people to have second thoughts about him. Given the situation, I doubt whether Netanyahu will be the Likud's candidate for prime minister."

Netanyahu remained the Likud's candidate, of course, and all these men subsequently backed him in the May 1996 elections. But following the assassination, many of his colleagues intimated that it would be best if he resigned to spare the party an ignominious whipping at the polls. Thus, desperately in need of moral and political rehabilitation, on the fourth day after the murder Netanyahu asked to meet with Shimon Peres. He reasoned that if Rabin's political partner and successor accepted his explanations, the attacks on him within his own party would cease. Peres's advisers strenuously argued that such a meeting would vindicate Netanyahu's dubious behavior. But Peres believed that the public would reward a gesture of reconciliation in an hour of national crisis and agreed to receive Netanyahu in his office.

"Shimon, they're perpetrating character assassination against me without any cause," Netanyahu told the prime minister. "The debate between us has been businesslike and will always be. I wasn't the one who kindled the fire. I always drove the Kahanist inciters away from the events . . . and I don't have control over every Kahanist who hitches a ride on our [backs]."

Peres responded by preaching a bit to Netanyahu, suggesting that he "lower the tone." He then shook his hand.

Three days later, on November 13, 1995, the Knesset convened to mark the end of the week of mourning. In the first row of the balcony sat Rabin's widow with her children and grandchildren around her. Netanyahu was invited to speak on behalf of the opposition. Five weeks earlier he had stood above Zion Square facing placards that read RABIN IS A TRAITOR. Now, standing on the Knesset rostrum, Netanyahu looked up into the eyes of Rabin's widow, who conspicuously avoided his gaze. When Rabin's body was lying in state, Netanyahu had tried to shake her hand, and she had refused the gesture. At the graveside after the funeral she had also ignored his words of condolence. "Mr. Netanyahu incited against my husband and led the savage demonstrations against him," she told the press on November 6. Now, standing beside Rabin's portrait, Netanyahu used the memorial session to pronounce his own absolution. "We never imagined that a terrible thing like this would happen in our generation," he said. "A minister and a great man has fallen this week at the hands of the wicked."

Netanyahu chose a strategy of blanket denial of association with the incitement. Three weeks before the assassination, he had responded to Labor Party charges about his involvement in the abusive campaign against Rabin by saying: "These are groundless claims that are the opposite of reality. I denounce, publicly and privately, every expression of violence in general, and against ministers of the Israeli government in particular, as well as the shouts of a certain nature that have no place in Israeli politics. There are always a few oddballs on the fringe of any very large [political] camp." And on the day after the assassination, at a special meeting of Likud Knesset members, he lashed out at critics in warning: "Let no one dare accuse the Likud of [the incitement that preceded the murder]. This is a false charge. The incitement began ten minutes after Rabin's assassination . . . [when] people began blaming the Likud, as though it stood behind [the incitement]. The wild things being said by people are vile."

From the start, however, evidence to the contrary eroded these claims. A few days after the murder, Israel's two television networks showed clips of a small procession that right-wing activists had held in March 1994 at the Ra'anana junction near Tel Aviv. Crews from two foreign networks—ABC and WTN—plus the still photographer Ben Shlomo had photographed the demonstration. The video clips showed Netanyahu marching in front of a black coffin painted with the words "Rabin is murdering Zionism." Next to the coffin marched a demonstrator carrying a pole inscribed "Oslo Agreement" with a noose hanging from it. Asked to explain how he had dared march before a coffin bearing Rabin's name, Netanyahu protested that he had come upon the demonstration by chance and not seen any coffin. From the brief clips aired at the time, it was impossible to refute this statement, and he was given the benefit of the doubt.

Then, before the May 1996 elections, Rabin's friend Jean Friedman gathered video clips of the incitement campaign from TV networks around the world. Among them was the unedited version of the Ra'anana demonstration. He gave a cassette of the clips to the Labor Party, but its contents were not broadcast during the campaign. A year after the elections, in May 1997, a longer clip of the Ra'anana demonstration was included in the film *The Road to Rabin Square*, produced by Rabin's friend David Mosevics and directed by Michael Karpin. A shortened version of Mosevics's film was aired on the television documentary program *Fact*. However, a few days before the *Fact* broadcast, the uncut film was shown to an audience of eight hundred people in the Tel Aviv Museum. When the clip of the Ra'anana procession came on-screen, a gasp echoed through the hall, and some of the viewers called out, "He saw it!" The coffin and noose were such prominent features of the small demonstration that it seemed impossible they had gone unnoticed. Prime Minister Netanyahu's spokesman reiterated the original denial.

Three months later, in August 1997, Yaron London, one of Israel's most respected journalists, published Ben Shlomo's still shot of the Ra'anana demonstration in *Yediot Ahronot*. This time there could be no doubt: The photograph clearly showed Netanyahu standing facing the noose and coffin, although the prime minister's spokesman repeated his denial that Netanyahu had seen the coffin. Netanyahu also claimed he had never seen the photomontage of Rabin dressed in an SS uniform, or the signs reading RABIN IS A TRAITOR facing the balcony in Zion Square. The chant "Rabin is a traitor" had been drowned out by the wind, he insisted. On many occasions Rabin's followers have asked Netanyahu to apologize, at the very least for his acquiescence in the incitement. Each time he has indignantly refused.

F our days after the assassination, rabbis and other leaders of the religious community spoke out for the first time at a meeting of scores of men wearing crocheted yarmulkes, as well as a few *haredi* yeshiva students, held in Jerusalem. The meeting was sponsored by Meimad, a small movement of politically moderate religious nationalists. The leaders of the Yesha Council also attended. The front row of the auditorium was occupied by leaders of the National Religious Party, originally a centrist group that had steadily changed its allegiances after the Six-Day War and now formed the strongest bloc of the radical right.

Rabbi Yehudah Amital, the founder of Meimad, spoke first. He had established the movement four years earlier as an alternative to the messianic brand of nationalism sweeping through the religious community and as a counterweight to the Yesha Council, which had led the religious settlers far to the right. Amital firmly held that Judaism placed the sanctity of life above the integrity of the Greater Land of Israel. He too lived in a settlement in the West Bank, and he too believed that all of the ancient homeland was the patrimony of the Jewish people. But unlike the leaders of the Yesha Council, he was above all a confirmed democrat and held that a government supported by a parliamentary majority was entitled to cede territory. He had planned to set the tone of the conclave so that the next day's headlines would report the start of introspection by Israel's religious community.

"We are stunned, depressed, shocked, pained, grieved, offended, mortified, and shamed in the face of the murder of the prime minister of Israel," he began, pausing for the words to sink in. "Maimonides says: 'If one is chosen by the people, it is a sign from above that he has [been chosen to] be a king and leader.' [What has happened] is an offense against the kingdom of Israel in the age of the return to Zion and the first budding of the Redemption. Gentlemen, we must truly prostrate ourselves for this terrible desecration of God's Name."

Heads bowed in the ensuing silence. Amital knew that many of the messianist settlers viewed him with suspicion. Behind his back some of them called him a "collaborator" with the "traitors to the Land of Israel." But that night Amital's message remained firm. "The murderer came from among us, out of religious Zionism and Judaism, and we cannot say that 'our hands have not shed this blood.' Rather than be a tempering influence, many of [our] rabbis have been a radicalizing one, creating a political dogma and public mood that made the murder possible," he intoned. "Political extremism has been dressed up as religion. Not only did the prime minister's murderer come from among us, [but Baruch] Goldstein, the murderer in the Cave of the Patriarchs, did too. That the religious community brushed off [that] slaughter . . . shows that its moral sensibility is flawed. . . . The decline began when the rabbis chose to turn a blind eye to the attacks on Arabs that eventually led to acts of murder. We have been taught by our revered sages: 'He who robs a gentile is ultimately destined to rob a Jew. He who lies to a gentile will ultimately lie to a Jew. He who sheds the blood of a gentile will ultimately shed the blood of a Jew.' "

The audience received the rebuke in silence. Rabbi Amital was followed by Shalom Rosenberg, a scholar of Jewish philosophy at the Hebrew University and another founder of Meimad, whose remarks were no less pointed: "Rabin's murder is graver than were the fanatic actions of the Jewish Underground and Goldstein's massacre. A line has been crossed [here] that means destruction."

Rosenberg was alluding to one of the most traumatic chapters in

Jewish history, the destruction of the Second Temple in C.E. 70. His listeners knew that he meant not just the ravage of Jerusalem by the Romans but the internal political context of the disaster. For the assault on Jerusalem was prompted by a revolt against the emperor, led by the messianic Zealots of the day, and the fall of the city was hastened by internecine strife among the defenders themselves. There were many conclusions to be drawn from the fanatical mood of that age. Yet the one retained in the national memory for two millennia was that Jerusalem was destroyed because of "needless hatred" among Jews. Now Rosenberg explicitly invoked that lesson. "If we're going to have a civil war," he told his listeners, "it's better to return to exile."

The most forceful accusation, however, came from Rabbi Yoel Bin-Nun. He railed against the rabbis who had pronounced Rabin subject to *din rodef*, referring to them as "revolutionary courts, like a Jewish Hezbollah." When he demanded that by the end of the week of mourning they either resign or be dismissed from their posts, some of the young men in the audience shouted, "Shut your mouth! Don't you dare threaten anyone! If you have proof, give it now."

"The worse has not yet [happened]," Bin-Nun shouted above the uproar, "and if this dreadful thing is not expunged, we will all bear responsibility. Because if, heaven forbid, another political murder occurs, it's doubtful whether there will be a Jewish state; it's doubtful whether we will endure."

At this, the hall dissolved into bedlam. Cries of "Leftist!" and "Shame on you!" were hurled at Bin-Nun. The tumult subsided only when Knesset member Zevulun Hammer stood up and signaled the audience to quiet down.

Hammer had led the National Religious Party for about twenty years. Although he himself had not settled in the territories, he backed the settlers enthusiastically, while drawing his party from the pragmatic center to the radical right. In the early 1980s Hammer had helped a number of rabbis associated with Gush Emunim avoid a legal investigation of suspicions that they had sanctioned the terrorist activities of the Jewish Underground. The auditorium now fell silent as Hammer introduced a very different theme. "We reject with revulsion the vicious charge [being laid against us] collectively [and] those who point an accusing finger at us all." At this point a yeshiva student shouted: "Don't be so self-righteous! You yourself spoke of

Rabin's policy as anti-Jewish and anti-Zionist! You yourself took part in demonstrations at which people shouted, 'Rabin is a traitor!'" An uproar again broke out in the audience, but it hardly mattered by then. Hammer had already made his point: There was no need for the national religious community to examine its thoughts, beliefs, or behavior.

Then came Hammer's fellow Knesset member Hanan Porat, who represented the more extreme settlers. Not long before the assassination, Porat had called Rabin's government "illegitimate" and its decision to sign the Oslo II accord "treason" because the Knesset had ratified it with the votes of what he called "anti-Semitic Arab deputies." At the meeting that night, Porat did not actually commend Yigal Amir's crime. But he tried to balance out its gravity by speaking of the heinous deeds of Rabin's government in forfeiting hallowed territory.

"I admired [Rabin] as prime minister," he said. "Nevertheless, . . . when I pass by Rachel's Tomb [in] Bethlehem, and I know that the city is about to be abandoned to foreigners . . . I know that whoever raises a hand to uproot Jewish communities from their land is lifting a hand against the Word of God. . . . Whoever walks in this abyss and thinks that the fate of the Jewish people can be solved this way is simply stupid and wicked."

The brief conclave on November 8, 1995, was the only attempt of its kind at self-examination. No others were necessary; there was nothing more to discuss. Prominent rabbis and political leaders had declared themselves free of blemish. Neither did the government challenge them to face squarely up to the role they had played in the incitement. In fact, no serious investigation of the incitement campaign was ever undertaken. Instead, Peres made do with halfhearted and qualified condemnations of the murder, for he had a more pressing agenda.

Seven months after the assassination the Labor Party lost the elections. The winner of the 1996 race for prime minister was not Shimon Peres, Rabin's partner in the peace initiative, but Benjamin Netanyahu, the leader of the opposition to the Oslo process. The "assassination factor," it seemed, had little impact on the electorate. The same forces that had conducted the incitement against Rabin were the most energetic campaigners for Netanyahu. Religious Israelis followed directives of their spiritual leaders, voting en masse for the Likud candidate. They helped Netanyahu score an extraordinary triumph, besting an incumbent whose victory was practically assured by all the polls and most of the experts. The goal of their struggle, first against Rabin and then against Peres, was identical: to thwart the territorial compromise with the Palestinians.

On strictly religious grounds, Netanyahu had no more to commend him to Israel's religious Jews than did his rival. Like Peres, he was at heart a secular Jew. He desecrated the Sabbath; he ate nonkosher food; and, perhaps most offensive of all in the eyes of Israel's Orthodox and *haredi* communities, he had married his second wife, Fleur, in a Conservative synagogue. (The practice of Conservative and Reform Judaism is deemed, by these two communities, as far more reprehensible than not practicing Judaism at all.) The common ground the religious right shared with Netanyahu lay elsewhere, and they made it clear—especially after he spoke of being constrained to honor the Oslo agreements—that he was but a tool in their hands, a leader on probation. If he did what they expected of him and sabotaged the Oslo process, they would continue to back him. If he compromised the integrity of the Land of Israel, they would bring him down.

Very soon after the assassination Prime Minister Peres was encouraged by colleagues and advisers to call new elections immediately. The polls, they argued, promised him a smashing victory and a fresh mandate to pursue the peace policy he had shared with Rabin. The surveys conducted immediately after the assassination showed a marked rise in support for the Labor Party. Even opponents of the Oslo process were loath to assail it now for fear of further aggravating political divisions. At the same time, considering all the attention focused on the subject of *din rodef,* there was also a clamor in the secular community to reinforce the principle that leaders are removed from power by the ballot, not by the gun.

Peres was urged to act swiftly. But he hesitated, fearing that if he called a quick election, he would be accused of exploiting a national tragedy for political gain. There was no need for unseemly haste, he thought. The majority of the electorate favored the peace process—or so the polls had consistently shown—so that the Labor Party enjoyed a marked advantage. Peres was also confident that the impact of the assassination would last for a long time to come, at least a number of years.

Within three months it was clear that the pollsters, pundits, and Peres all had erred. Had the new prime minister called an election at the end of

1995, he almost certainly would have won it. By the end of January 1996, however, the post-assassination rise in backing for the peace process had withered, and the polls showed a steep slide in support for the Oslo agreements, the Labor Party, and Shimon Peres personally. Labor's leaders were slow to take note of this reversal. They placed their faith in the polls commissioned by the party itself and ignored the data published by objective academic institutions. One of the most important of the latter was the Peace Index, a monthly survey that had been conducted consistently since the summer of 1994 by Tel Aviv University's Tami Steinmetz Center for Peace Research, directed by Professor Ephraim Ya'ar. Considered the most reliable gauge of public opinion on the peace process and attendant issues, the Peace Index initially confirmed Labor's expectations. Its poll conducted in November 1995, directly after the assassination, showed a peak of 73.1 percent of Israelis in favor of the Oslo process. But by the end of January 1996 this figure had slipped by over twelve points to 60.3 percent.

Over the same period the Peace Index also showed that support for Peres was shrinking. The November 1995 index reported that 57.3 percent of the public preferred Peres as prime minister, against 24.5 percent for Netanyahu. In December Peres's support slipped to 53 percent, while that for Netanyahu rose to 30.4. By the end of January 1996 Peres's support had dropped to 46 percent, while Netanyahu's was up to 35.2. Thus in the course of those three months, Peres's advantage had shrunk from almost thirty-three points to less than eleven. And by February, when Peres called an early election for May, the Peace Index showed that Netanyahu had practically closed the gap.

Perhaps the most noteworthy aspect of this process was that the greater part of Peres's slide in the polls occurred before the end of February 1996, when Israel was rocked by an unprecedented wave of terrorism from the fundamentalist Hamas movement. The attacks came as revenge for the liquidation of "the Engineer," the twenty-nine-year-old Yihye Ayyash, who headed the military wing of Hamas. Ayyash had been responsible for the previous wave of terror bombings, from the summer of 1994 through the winter of 1995, to avenge Goldstein's massacre in Hebron. He had earned his epithet by constructing explosive devices, choosing suicide bombers, and dispatching them—with bombs strapped to their bodies or packed in briefcases—to wreak havoc on the streets of Israel. For two years the

Shabak had hunted him down in vain. The Palestinian Authority was asked to arrest Ayyash and extradite him to Israel but claimed that he was not in Gaza or Jericho, the two areas then under Palestinian control. In January 1996 his hideout was discovered in Gaza City, and he met the same gruesome end he had inflicted upon his victims. Ayyash was killed by a bomb inserted into a cellular phone, which detonated in his hand. No one claimed responsibility for the action, but in Israel the news of his demise was received with satisfaction. The Palestinians reacted with fury, and tens of thousands of them—followers of Hamas and the PLO alike—poured into the streets to vent their anger. Over one hundred thousand people attended Ayyash's funeral. Again the cycle of violence had been fueled; again there was a score to be settled.

Less than two months later, at the end of February 1996, Hamas began avenging Ayyash's death through a series of suicide bombings carried out over the course of nine days. The first blast was in Jerusalem, on a No. 18 bus, followed almost immediately by a second bombing at a hitchhiking stand for soldiers outside the city of Ashkelon, just north of the Gaza Strip. A week later a third suicide bomber blew himself up in Jerusalem, again on a No. 18 bus, and the following day a fourth detonated a double bomb outside the Dizengoff Center shopping mall in downtown Tel Aviv. The toll was harrowing. Between February 25 and March 4 sixty people were killed and hundreds were injured, some to remain maimed for life. Broadcasting live from the scenes of the atrocities, the television networks dwelled on the blackened skeletons of destroyed buses, the burned corpses strewn on the streets, the agony of the wounded. Israelis were in the grip of near hysteria, afraid to board a bus or enter a shopping center, and wherever they went, their eyes ranged nervously to identify dark, bulky figures or otherwise suspicious characters. Through it all Peres was helpless, just as Rabin had been in the face of the earlier bombings.

The opposition took full advantage of Peres's plight, charging that Hamas's ability to mount these attacks followed directly from the Oslo process. Had the government not withdrawn Israeli troops from the Gaza Strip and the cities of the West Bank, critics charged, they would not have become havens for terrorists. The one voice conspicuously absent from this chorus was Netanyahu's. Experience had taught him circumspection. In October 1994 he had rushed to the site of the bus blown up on Dizengoff Street in Tel Aviv and, while the wounded were still being evacuated, stood by the mangled remains of the vehicle and accused Rabin of preferring "Arafat and the welfare of the residents of Gaza over the security of the residents of Israel."

In so doing, Netanyahu inaugurated a style of political conduct unprecedented in Israel or any democracy victimized by terrorism. The Republicans in the United States had not blamed President Clinton for the bombing of the World Trade Center or the Murrah Federal Building in Oklahoma City. The opposition in Britain did not blame the government for the terror actions of the IRA. So too had it been in Israel, where coping with terrorism had almost become a way of life. At the very least, the opposition had withheld its criticism of the government after terror actions until the seven days of mourning were over. When Netanyahu swerved from this norm he was met with savage scorn. Never again did he show up at the scene of a suicide bombing.

Peres did not benefit from Netanyahu's restraint. By mid-March he had lost his advantage in the polls, which showed the two candidates tied, or Netanyahu with a slight lead. Labor leaders would ultimately blame Peres's defeat on Hamas. But this conclusion was belied by the fact that once Peres had forced Arafat to take firm measures against Hamas, had postponed the IDF's redeployment in Hebron, and had slapped a closure on the territories, he surged ahead in the polls. By May he was leading Netanyahu by some five points. From then on it was no longer possible to blame the Palestinian fundamentalists for his predicament. His resultant defeat was Labor's very own handiwork.

In retrospect, it is not difficult to discern the party's mistakes. Two stemmed from Labor's basic campaign strategy and are related to Rabin's assassination. The first was Peres's decision to woo the country's religious parties into forming a united front with Labor. The second was effectively to banish all reference to the murder from Labor's election campaign. Both attest that Peres had missed, or chosen to ignore, the primary political lesson of the assassination: that a strong bond had been cemented in Israel between religion and nationalism. Peres conducted a campaign in 1996 that was suited to the Israel of 1974. He failed to heed the transformation in Israeli society, and his lagging perceptions cost him heavily.

The courting of the religious parties was a pathetic spectacle. Peres entreated the NRP to restore its historical alliance with Labor and, as a tacit gesture to it, he forfeited the option of prosecuting the rabbinical figures who had placed themselves above the rule of civil law. Rather than investigate the incitement campaign against Rabin, he moved to open a dialogue with the rabbis, politicians, and radical settlers, though his chances of succeeding were negligible. In the hope of receiving their endorsements, he waited humbly to meet with the few rabbis who begrudgingly deigned to receive him. In striving to win over the pragmatic core of the NRP, he failed to notice that it had long since been superseded by a cadre of diehard messianists. Some of his associates were revolted by these overtures. "It's the religious [elements] that led the fascist stream in Israeli society," said Knesset Speaker Shevach Weiss. "How is it possible to hold a dialogue with them now, as though the assassination had never happened?" In the end Peres's gestures proved futile. The religious community voted for Netanyahu.

Labor also adopted a strategy of self-denial. Perhaps the oddest feature of the election campaign was that the two key rivals, Labor and the Likud, worked hard to trade identities. Each masqueraded as what it was not in order to win the votes of the nebulous "center." This may have been a prudent tactic for Netanyahu, who took great pains to obscure his basic extremism, for he was a political parvenu whose image was still malleable. But when Peres tried to conceal his moderation, he failed miserably at this game. His image as a seeker of peace—distorted by his opponents to mean peace at any price—could not be erased overnight. Labor chose as its campaign slogan "Israel Is Strong with Peres." The word "peace" had vanished from its PR lexicon and miraculously emerged in the Likud's campaign slogan, "A Secure Peace with Netanyahu."

The masquerade tactic proved so appealing that the NRP adopted it too. The radical line its leaders had pursued against Rabin was erased from its campaign. The Yesha Council dropped out of sight. Nationalist slogans were all but expunged from the party's propaganda. The NRP reinvented itself as a party whose only interest was in preserving tradition and cultivating strong family values. And in his desire to draw it into his next coalition, Peres shrank from exposing this ruse.

Labor also refrained from attacking the right for its role in the incitement against Rabin. This was a colossal mistake on its part, and some of Peres's most trusted advisers strongly protested it. One of them was Jean Friedman, who, along with Shlomo Lahat, had organized the November 4 rally. Friedman was one of the people who had pressed Peres to call a quick election. He had also invested thirty thousand dollars in producing the collection of incriminating video clips, which he was sure would be shown during the campaign. Labor never used the cassette and later claimed that it had been lost.

Labor's worst blunder, however, was alienating its most natural electoral ally: the Arab citizens of Israel. The cause of that alienation was a military operation mounted just a month before the elections. Operation Grapes of Wrath came in retaliation for an extended rocket barrage by Lebanese Hezbollah guerrillas, which caused heavy damage in the Galilee panhandle. Peres had hoped to get through the elections without a military confrontation in the north. As pressure from local residents mounted on him, he sought a political solution through the mediation of the United States. When these efforts failed, however, he decided to take action by shelling and bombing the Hezbollah's positions.

Matters quickly got out of control. The "surgical strike" planned by the General Staff dragged on into a war of attrition. Israel warned the residents of south Lebanon that it intended to shell the guerrillas operating out of their villages and advised them to leave the area. About half a million refugees began streaming northward, just as Israel had planned. The scenario was to create a domino effect in which the refugees would exert pressure on Beirut, the Lebanese government would in turn pressure Syria, and the Syrian government—a tacit patron of the Hezbollah—would force the guerrillas to halt their rocket fire. It was a cruel strategy that punished Lebanese civilians, but it had worked for Israel before and was expected to succeed again. Israel's message to its neighbors was plain: As long as life on its northern border was disrupted, the same would hold true in south Lebanon.

On the seventh day of the operation tragedy struck when Israeli artillery shelled a UN camp near the Lebanese village of Kafr Kana. Hundreds of villagers had taken refuge there, and one hundred of them were killed in the incident. World public opinion was outraged, and Israel was expected to cease its shelling and take responsibility for the disaster. But Peres chose to do the opposite. He dug in his heels, blamed the guerrillas for the calamity, and ordered the shelling to continue. He expected that his firmness would help him during the sensitive period before the elections. Certainly he never imagined that it would bring about his downfall.

For of all the protests to the slaughter, the most strident came from Israel's Arabs. In calculating its election strategy, Labor had left them out. It was taken for granted that they would vote for Peres, the moving spirit of the Oslo process and the visionary of a "new Middle East" in which Jews and Arabs would thrive through cooperation. But his benign image could not survive such a brutal military blunder. Arab Knesset members called him a "murderer of children." Other community leaders pointedly snubbed him and urged their followers to express their disgust by placing a blank ballot in the box when voting directly for the prime minister. On election night some thirty thousand white slips were counted among the ballots, almost all of them cast by Arab citizens. It was this protest vote that decided the election. Peres would have won it if he had garnered fifteen thousand additional votes.

CHAPTER 8

CONSPIRACY

Rumors about an informer working for the security services had been rife in the occupied territories even before Amnon Abramovich sat down before the cameras in Channel One's studio on Friday night, November 17, 1995, and plunged the country into turmoil for the second time in less than two weeks. "A radical right-wing activist, Avishai Raviv, is a Shabak agent whose code name is Champagne," he announced. The repercussions of that statement would buffet the State of Israel for years to come.

A seasoned journalist with the mass-circulation daily *Ma'ariv* before joining Channel One, Abramovich was known to have impeccable sources in the political and security establishments. Only recently had Avishai Raviv's name become a household word in Israel. The stocky twenty-eight-year-old student had had a minor reputation as a right-wing agitator even before he was arrested, two days after the assassination, on suspicion of collaborating with Yigal Amir.* His name was associated with Kach and a

---

*Abramovich was not the first to suggest publicly that Raviv was working for the Shabak. The day before he made his disclosure, Rabbi Benny Elon of Zo Artzenu had called a press conference to announce his own suspicions about the young man's ties with the security organs. Raviv had in fact been released from police custody that same day and, upon hearing Elon's accusations, called his Shabak handler for instructions. He was told to issue a sharp denial and declare that he

small, shadowy group called Eyal that specialized in attacking Palestinians. But for the most part, only those who followed the radical right had any more than a passing familiarity with his exploits.

Now he was to become the chief protagonist of a far more tantalizing tale. If Channel One's scoop were true, people speculated, was it possible that Eyal had engaged in its exploits on orders from the state's security organs? Had Raviv been used as an agent provocateur to discredit the political right? Had Raviv told his handlers about Yigal Amir's intention to murder the prime minister and had they done nothing about it? Or had someone within the Shabak even used Raviv to prod Amir into action? Was the murder of Yitzhak Rabin, in short, the fruit of a conspiracy hatched within the Shabak?

Before the evening was out, many Israelis understood that Abramovich's revelation would forever taint Yitzhak Rabin's memory with questions about a conspiracy. Prime Minister Peres immediately demanded all the details on Raviv from Shabak chief Carmi Gillon. The Prime Minister's Bureau remained silent even after Internal Security Minister Moshe Shahal had issued his statement. "We do not believe the Shabak had any connection with the assassination," he said. "I believe in the loyalty and probity of the members of the Security Service, and anything else is speculation." Noting that Shahal had not denied Abramovich's report outright, the press nagged the Prime Minister's Bureau for an elaboration. But Peres's spokeswoman remained mute. Peres even refused to comment on the issue to his cabinet when it met on November 19. All he did was admonish his ministers to stop discussing rumors related to the Shabak. "If you're asked about Avishai Raviv, say that the matter will be clarified by the state inquiry commission.† An investigation is taking place, and it will clear everything up," he said.

While the government preferred silence, however, the opposition pounced on Abramovich's revelation. During the two weeks that had passed since the assassination, details about the incitement campaign had featured prominently in the press, forcing the entire political right on the defensive. The public mood had also altered radically from the days before

---

intended to sue Elon for slander. The media believed Raviv. They knew he was far from a sterling character, but Elon's allegations sounded politically motivated. The next day, when Abramovich reported the same information, it was accepted at face value.

†The Shamgar State Commission of Inquiry, appointed by the government on November 5, 1995.

November 4. One poll showed that support for the peace process had reached an all-time high, soaring from 54.9 percent on October 29 to 73.1 percent on November 8. But word of Raviv's ties with the Shabak now restored the self-confidence of the beleaguered right.

"I am concerned," Netanyahu told his colleagues at a meeting of the Likud Bureau on November 22. "Even if only a portion of the things that have emerged is correct, there is a grave danger here for our democracy. We demand a full investigation. We will not agree to any cover-up here."

Revived by the response of the opposition's leadership, other interested parties joined the fray. Activists from Zo Artzenu were the first to link the assassination with "a leftist conspiracy." Writing in the Yesha Council monthly, *Nekudah* ("Point"), Shlomo Filber, a right-wing lawyer, insisted that the murder was a "work accident in the Shabak, which knew everything in advance—who would commit the assassination, when, and where." Arutz 7 typically served as a prime conduit for the conspiracy theories. Most of all, however, the fantastic stories were passed by word of mouth, as well as by acquiescent media.

One rumor claimed that immediately after the murder one of Rabin's bodyguards plunged into a depression and committed suicide. He was supposedly depressed because it had been discovered that he had deliberately lagged behind Rabin for a few seconds to allow Amir a clear shot. Like any promising rumor, this one was embellished as it went along. The government was putatively able to suppress word of the suicide by having an autopsy quietly performed on the bodyguard at Ichilov Hospital (where Rabin himself had died), rather than at the National Institute for Forensic Medicine. Another rumor circulated widely in religious and settler circles held that a member of the Burial Society who had attended the bodyguard's covert funeral died mysteriously and that his terrified colleagues were sworn to secrecy. A year after the assassination it was repeated by Ya'akov Novick of the Action Headquarters, who vouched for its veracity. A second variation of the tale asserted that the agent who had taken his own life was Yoram Rubin, the bodyguard wounded in the arm during the shooting. This version spread so quickly and gained such credence that the Shabak was forced to produce Rubin for the press, inviting photographers to immortalize him in his hospital bed.

A more elaborate conspiracy theory thrives to this day. It holds that the

Shabak had learned about Yigal Amir's plan from Raviv. Seeking both to foil the assassination and to exploit the sympathy factor for Rabin, its agents arranged to have blanks loaded into Amir's revolver. The plot thickened, however, when Foreign Minister Peres—Rabin's longtime political rival and natural successor—learned of the ruse and ordered one of the agents to replace the blanks with live ammunition.

What made this account particularly marketable was that elements of it were borrowed from two disparate stories widely reported in the press. The first was an incident that occurred over a year before the assassination and accounted, however vaguely, for the Shabak's mysterious access to Amir's revolver. In the summer of 1994 the Shabak received a tip (apparently from Raviv) that two brothers from Kiryat Arba, Eitan and Yehodaya Kahalani, were planning to murder a Palestinian as an act of gratuitous revenge. A Shabak agent managed to get hold of their gun and remove the firing pin, so that when the trigger was pulled, the weapon failed to fire. The two brothers were tried and found guilty of attempted murder, and the Israeli public learned that the Shabak was able to tamper with the weapons of Jewish fanatics.

The second component of this theory drew upon testimony given to the police that as Amir was shooting at Rabin, shouts of "Blanks, blanks" were heard at the scene. Three witnesses thought Amir had been the one shouting, but a rumor had it that the cries had come from the side, perhaps from an accomplice. The Shamgar Commission delved into this intriguing detail but failed to ascertain whether the shouts were heard at all and, if so, who had uttered them. "There is no reason to rule out the version of [Rabin's] driver, Damti, and [police officer] Superintendent Youlzary, who attributed the shout to Yigal Amir," the panel stated in its report. "It is also possible that he [Amir] was not aware of issuing the cry at the time of the [shooting], perhaps as an act of defense and camouflage, and later refused to admit it."

When the inquiry commission failed to solve the mystery, the conspiracy buffs ascribed the shout to a bodyguard who had not been informed of the double cross and, believing that the assassin was shooting blanks, instinctively reminded his colleagues that it was all a charade. In March 1996 a simpler version of this story found its way into the pages of the London weekly *Observer*. It too set out from the premise that the

Shabak had concocted a plan to fake an attempt on Rabin's life in order to turn public feeling against the right. In this rendition, however, it was Raviv who double-crossed the Shabak by telling Yigal Amir that blanks were being put in his gun. Amir then replaced the blanks with live ammunition and shouted, "Blanks, blanks," at the scene to ensure that bodyguards would not shoot him.

In the summer of 1996 two Israeli journalists, Uri Dan and Dennis Eisenberg, pieced all these themes together into a comprehensive conspiracy theory and published it in a book entitled *Crimes d'État* ("Crimes of State"). They argued that the Shabak had intended to foil Amir's assassination attempt by tipping off the police and having him arrested, thus making political capital for Rabin without endangering his life. The scheme went awry when Amir chose to act alone and did not let Raviv in on the details of his plan. No proof was offered for any of the elements of this theory, and the book's explanations were so implausible that no Israeli publisher was willing to bring it out.

The oddest case of all was that of Barry Chamish, a Canadian-born journalist living in Israel. Chamish courted the press, lectured before right-wing audiences, posted convoluted theories and testimonies on the Internet—about the angle of trajectory, the composition of the explosives in the bullets, and the paths they took after entering Rabin's body—and ultimately summed up his conclusions in a book entitled *Who Killed Yitzhak Rabin?* Unlike other conspiracy theorists, Chamish holds that there was a conspiracy within the Shabak to assassinate the prime minister. He claims that Rabin could not have been killed by Amir's shots and was actually murdered by the Shabak after being pushed into his car.

At the beginning of December 1997, however, Chamish, by then emotionally devastated by the toll of his lonely campaign, sent selected recipients an E-mail message entitled "I Quit." In an outpouring of self-pity, he lamented his treatment at the hands of the media (which largely ignored him) and the Israeli left (which, he complained, stereotyped him as a right-wing fanatic). Fearing "to be arrested at any time for a variety of trumped up charges" and even for his life (an "invaluable source," he claimed, warned him that "at a closed meeting of Meretz leaders, a plan was hatched to eliminate me"), Chamish moaned that he didn't "want to be at risk anymore" and would therefore "contribute no more original research."

For all this theorizing, however, no evidence direct or circumstantial, was ever presented that anyone in the political establishment or the security services had been involved in plotting foul play. As a result, the conspiracy fever died down. Then, on May 13, 1997, Israel television's commercial Channel Two broadcast selections from *The Road to Rabin Square*, the documentary on the incitement campaign against Rabin. A few days before the broadcast, the film had been previewed in Tel Aviv and received coverage in the press, eliciting outrage from the right. Justice Minister Tsachi Hanegbi threatened to sue the film's producer and director for its portrayal of his role in the campaign. The Action Headquarters and its supporters lodged appeals with the High Court of Justice to block the broadcast, all of which were rejected.

One of the sharpest critics of the incitement machine interviewed in the documentary was Likud Knesset member Michael Eitan, who confessed that not everyone in his party had taken adequate steps to ensure that extremists were kept away from the rallies it sponsored. He conceded that the October 5 demonstration in Zion Square had been conducted in what he delicately called "an unlawful manner" with "the tacit agreement of some of the organizers." He also noted that although Hanegbi surely regretted his "very bad mistake" in cutting off Rabin's microphone at a public event, "it was definitely possible people concluded that [if this] is permissible to us, politicians, it was permissible for them to go two or three steps further." Eitan spoke in even stronger language about the Likud's allies, charging that "Within the Action Headquarters and under the control of Uri Ariel [of the Yesha Council] were some forces that indulged and perhaps lent tacit support to people prepared to preach violence as one of the expressions of protest."

Eitan's candor infuriated party colleagues, who demanded that he take measures to mitigate the impression he had made in the film. He promptly complied, not by retracting anything he had said on camera but by appearing on television to pronounce the documentary "one-sided" because it had failed to address the issue of the agent provocateur Avishai Raviv. Eitan then held a press conference to announce that he was investigating the ties between the Shabak and Raviv, whom he categorized as "responsible for more threats, acts of violence, and incitement of a political nature than any other person in the history of the state." Promising to demand that the

State Attorney's Office place Raviv on trial, he began interviewing witnesses and collecting testimonies.

One of Eitan's primary sources was Barry Chamish. He also cited a pamphlet entitled *The Champagne File*, compiled by Emuna Elon, Prime Minister Netanyahu's adviser on the status of women and the wife of Rabbi Benny Elon. A third source was Sarah Eliash, a school principal from the settlement of Kedumim who had already testified before the Shamgar Commission. Eliash said that at a demonstration attended by two of her daughter's friends, Raviv had told the girls, "The leftists and the prime minister must be killed." They met Raviv again at another protest action, in the Palestinian-controlled town of Jericho, where he was wearing a yellow Kach T-shirt and advised his fellow demonstrators to shoot at any Israeli soldiers who might try to remove them. Raviv had harsh words for Rabin there too. He preached that it was permissible to murder the prime minister under the terms of *din rodef*. A fourth source was Raviv's deputy in Eyal, Benny Aharoni, who testified in a sworn affidavit that Raviv had incited to murder Rabin in saying to him: "Benny, Yitzhak Rabin must be eliminated."

Eitan composed a long letter based on these testimonies, which he addressed to State Attorney Edna Arbel. When members of her staff noted that it contained no new evidence, he insisted that he possessed "surprising information" showing that the police had received "orders from above" not to investigate Raviv. "I will not relax the pressure until Raviv is brought to trial," he declared. Four months later Eitan sent the state attorney a pointed reminder about prosecuting Raviv. "We're talking about the greatest provocateur in the history of the State of Israel," he wrote, accusing the Shabak and State Attorney's Office of "working together to mislead the public about the immunity given to Raviv's provocations. Raviv is responsible for hundreds of criminal acts of incitement and violence, many more than the State Attorney's Office attributes to him."

As the second anniversary of the assassination grew near, the right had still not succeeded in getting its version of events across to the wider public. Eitan's barrage failed to revive popular interest in Raviv, though the conspiracy theories continued to circulate among right-wing groups. Although the Shamgar Commission Report had categorically stated that "no basis has been found for the claims of an alleged conspiracy," the opponents of the Oslo process were not appeased. In some corners of the right the Shabak was pilloried as a "branch of the Labor Party" and Carmi Gillon was branded as a "stooge" who had ordered the service to help the government realize its plan to "sell the Land of Israel to the Arabs." But most Israelis had accepted the Shamgar Commission's conclusion and were now bored by the subject.

Then, just before the second anniversary of the assassination, the whole issue erupted again.

On Friday, October 30, 1997, *Hatsofeh* ("The Spectator"), the daily of the National Religious Party, led its weekend edition with a piece entitled "Who Killed Yitzhak Rabin?" The feature quoted material from a Web site that contained the text of a book called *Srak* ("Blank"). The book was written by Uri Barkan (a pen name), who had posted his material on the Web because he failed to find a publisher for it. In an interview found on a linked site, Barkan stated that the book was a novel, not an exposé. Nevertheless, Barkan gave his characters the names of real people, including Peres and Justice Shamgar. He also admitted that Chamish was one of the sources for the book's plot. The novel implies that the Shamgar Commission Report was a whitewash and that its members knew that Peres had arranged for Rabin's murder. Barkan cited the head of the Jewish Division of the Shabak, Avri Zamir, as Peres's co-conspirator. Basing itself on Barkan, *Hatsofeh* wrote that after Raviv had told his Shabak handler of Amir's design, Rabin himself suggested that instead of arresting the would-be assassin, the bullets in his gun be replaced by blanks. Avri Zamir, then approached Peres with the idea of restoring the live ammunition. Peres not only agreed but promised to appoint Zamir head of the Shabak if the assassination succeeded. In a separate article the paper also quoted a young settler saying that she had overheard Raviv tell Amir that Rabin must be killed.

The right-wing establishment seized on these "revelations" in *Hatsofeh*. Environment Minister Rafael Eitan of the Tsomet Party demanded an immediate investigation of both "the provocation" engineered by the Shabak and Avishai Raviv. Adir Zik of Arutz 7 read out a litany of fifty-eight unanswered questions he had about the conspiracy. On Saturday night, October 31, an unnamed caller phoned Finance Minister Ya'akov Ne'eman to bring the article to his attention. "I was shocked by what I read," Ne'eman professed, "and have sent a letter to the prime minister and head of the Shabak [asking them] to immediately check [the allegation], which is very grave. There's no need to fear another examination of the theory of a conspiracy against Rabin."

Peres was enraged. Barely hiding his fury as he sat for an interview on the prime-time news, he said: "This is truly a blood libel by the government against the Shabak. If something like that had been published by *Pravda* in Moscow, or in Germany, they would be howling in the streets about anti-Semitism."

The next day the government prudently changed course. Ne'eman apologized for his behavior, saying that he had never intended to cast aspersions on Peres. Netanyahu pronounced, "There [was] no conspiracy," and Attorney General Elyakim Rubinstein echoed that judgment in a statement reminding the public that "The Shamgar Commission did its work and determined that there was no [conspiracy]. Anyone with eyes in his head must let this issue go." Justice Minister Hanegbi went so far as to aver that "The conspiracy theory is the fruit of a sick and loathsome imagination. The slander that a conspiracy led to the assassination is akin to the denial of the Holocaust."

Even Justice Meir Shamgar felt obliged to intervene. It is highly unusual for members of an inquiry commission to speak out after they have issued their conclusions. But Shamgar, whose reputation for impartiality and integrity have kept him above controversy, issued a statement that said:

> The various claims were examined by the inquiry commission and witnesses were summoned on the subject. In the evidence brought before us, no basis was found for the claim that [anyone in] the Shabak conspired to murder Rabin. . . . The rumors were based on interpretations of factual data related to the circumstances of the assassination [that were] augmented by assumptions and speculation.

Yet even this recap of the commission's findings failed to quell the demands for another inquiry into the matter. What piqued the public's curiosity most were the findings detailed in the secret appendix to the commission's report, which was purported to deal specifically with the Shabak's connections with Raviv. The contents of the appendix had been read by only a few officials before being locked in a safe in the Prime Minister's Office. Now a new government was in power—with presumably different interests to protect—and it had the power to decide whether to make the contents public. A team of three jurists was appointed to read the 118-page appendix and make its recommendations to the prime minister. When it counseled that parts of the document be published, the government accepted its judgment but prudently decided to postpone the release of the material until the day after the official memorial ceremonies for Rabin. Thus the second anniversary passed in an atmosphere of dignity and restraint.

B orn a year after the Six-Day War, Avishai Raviv grew up in Holon, a drab, lower-middle-class suburb of Tel Aviv, in a secular family that reflexively voted Labor. Teachers and classmates remember the young Avishai as an average student with a slight stutter, a talent for sports, and a penchant for practical jokes. He seemed to take a greater interest in political affairs than other children his age. But until he reached thirteen, nothing about him suggested that he was destined to become a political fanatic and rabble-rouser.

It was in 1981, the year in which Avishai celebrated his bar mitzvah, that a change occurred in him. During that year Israel began withdrawing from the eastern part of the Sinai Peninsula, in fulfillment of the terms of its peace treaty with Egypt. Raviv told his friends in the Labor Party's youth movement that the opponents of the withdrawal were right: It was a tragedy that would be mourned for generations. They watched in horror as he fell under the spell of the radical right. By age fourteen Avishai was proudly wearing the yellow T-shirt of the Kach movement. In light of his secular, leftist background, he never missed an opportunity to prove to his new comrades that he was one of them. He joined the Gush Emunim marches in the territories, distributed handbills, and tried to agitate the mourners at funerals of terror victims. He took to beating up activists from the dovish group Yesh Gvul ("There's a Limit").* Before reaching seventeen, Raviv had been arrested on suspicion of assaulting Arabs. By twenty-

*A protest movement formed during the Lebanon war that encouraged Israelis to refuse to do military reserve duty in Lebanon or the occupied territories.

three he had advanced to striking a Knesset member, Tamar Gozansky of the leftist Democratic Front for Peace, and was sentenced to nine months on probation. Of all the violent incidents for which Raviv was arrested over the years, the attack on Gozansky was the only one for which he stood trial. As a result of the assault, his prestige within Kach soared.

After joining the Givati Brigade, Raviv was wounded in the leg by a stray bullet, declared partially disabled, and discharged from the IDF. It was in 1987 that he was approached by the Shabak while waiting in a holding cell after being arrested at a Kach demonstration. Promised immunity from prosecution if he agreed to work as an informer, he agreed to pass on information about the radical right.

Avishai Raviv went to work for the Jewish Division of the Shabak, which was created at the start of the 1970s, after Meir Kahane had moved his headquarters to Israel. Between the suppression of the religious underground formed by Rabbi Mordechai Eliyahu in the early 1950s and Kahane's arrival, the security service had felt no need to gather intelligence on the right. The subjects of its surveillance were instead radical leftists. In the 1970s, however, alarmed by the formation of covert cells in the territories and plots to destroy the mosques on the Temple Mount, the Shabak turned its sights on the radical right. Monitoring it would prove a difficult task. The Shabak discovered the Jewish Underground in 1984 thanks to a tip from the inside. And it was only after interrogating the members of the Underground and the rabbis suspected of aiding them that the Shabak realized how inadequate its network of agents among the settlers really was. The problem was taken to Prime Minister Shamir, who approved an ambitious campaign to expand it.

Dozens of settlers were summoned for informal "chats" in nondescript "safe houses" and hotel rooms where recruitment officers appealed to their patriotic sentiments. As word of the Shabak's campaign spread through the settlements, briefings were held on how to resist the lures of the recruiters. Soon mutual suspicion was rife among the settlers. People in Hebron beat up neighbors suspected of being informers. One rabbi who abruptly turned radical was openly accused of collaborating with the Shabak. The word "informer" or "traitor" was sprayed on the houses of those deemed suspiciously eager to join vigilante raids. And one settler who had purchased a video camera was hauled before his neighbors and ordered to account for his sudden interest in home movies.

The problem was that the Shabak could not have it both ways, obtaining good intelligence while keeping the settlers on their guard. All this made Avishai Raviv a prize catch. He did not need a cover since he had been deeply embedded in the radical right since the age of fourteen. Though he did not live in the territories, he was associated with the group known as the Temple Mount Faithful, among the most extreme of the Land of Israel loyalists. Not only was he a familiar face in Kach, but because Kahane himself had a soft spot for Raviv, no one dared cast doubt upon him.

For eight years Avishai Raviv served the Shabak as a paid informer without arousing suspicion. At first he received only small sums, but his compensation grew in proportion to his indispensability. He drove an expensive Japanese car—bought, he told friends, with donations received from the United States. His tuition was covered by the Shabak, as were the bills for his cellular phone. Yet it wasn't until after the assassination that those closest to him reflected on the strange economics of his lifestyle. "Today, when I think about it, it seems strange to me that he had so much money. A new car, rented apartment, cell phone, beeper, television—and all in all he was just a student in the kolel [at Bar-Ilan]," mused Benny Aharoni after the assassination. "Today I know that this was on the Shabak's account."

In return for the Shabak's largess, Raviv mapped out the radical right for his handlers and identified its activists in photographs. He named people who had obtained explosives, coaxed detainees to open up to him, and occasionally wore a device to record incriminating evidence. Over the years he worked under a series of handlers, none of whom had him closely followed, although the last of them took the trouble to socialize with Raviv and pretend to be a personal friend.

After the Labor government was elected in 1992, Raviv became a prime source for the Shabak's Jewish Division. During these years he studied Jewish history at Tel Aviv University, where he was elected to the Student Council as a representative of Kach. But in the summer of 1993, after a Druze* was elected chairman of the Student Union, Raviv caused an uproar by denouncing him as a "fifth columnist." In response, the university's

---

*Member of a sect that split from Islam in the eleventh century. Unlike Israel's Muslim and Christian Arabs, Druze serve in the IDF.

rector, Professor Itamar Rabinovich (whom Rabin later appointed Israel's ambassador to Washington), expelled Raviv for racist incitement. The matter did not end there, however. After Raviv complained to his handler, the head of the Shabak asked Prime Minister Shamir to intercede. Shamir's chief of staff wrote Rabinovich a letter urging him to "help Avishai Raviv in every way possible to return to his studies." Rabinovich flatly refused. Ironically, however, the affair enhanced Raviv's credibility with the radical right and led him to Bar-Ilan University, where he met Yigal Amir.

The move took place just after the signing of the Oslo Agreement, and thereafter Raviv provided a wealth of information on the entire range of right-wing organizations. He filled in details about most of the bodies united in the Joint Staff: Women in Green, the Moledet party, Zo Artzenu, the Hebron Headquarters, and radical groups at Tel Aviv and Bar-Ilan universities. His handlers and their advisers in the State Attorney's Office were aware of the price the state was paying for his steady supply of information. Raviv enjoyed effective immunity from prosecution for his chronic violation of the law. By 1993 every time the police hauled Raviv into custody for his racist or violent actions, the Shabak immediately saw to his release.

Two points clearly emerge from the testimony of Raviv's handlers before the Shamgar Commission: They allowed but did not direct him to participate in antigovernment actions, and they did so to protect his credentials with the radical right. He was permitted, for example, to carry placards opposing the peace process. But Raviv strayed far beyond these guidelines. One of the handbills he disseminated threatened violent action against the army, warning: "The IDF must know that as soon as the Israeli government decides to return territory, dozens of strongholds of resistance will arise in Yesha and the Golan manned by hundreds of well-armed Jews. [If] any soldier tries to evacuate us by force, we will personally shoot him dead on the spot." In a subsequent press interview Raviv went a step further and exhorted Israeli soldiers to disobey orders. "It must be clear: No government formed in Israel has the right to return territory in the Land of Israel," he preached. "IDF soldiers must simply defy the orders of such a government. A soldier who does not do so is, in our eyes, like a *Kapo*, those who collaborated with the Nazis, and his sentence is death."

Shielded by the Shabak's promise of immunity, Raviv repeatedly committed acts of assault on Palestinians, using everything from barbed wire and the butt of a revolver to brass knuckles. He defaced road signs showing the names of Palestinian villages, smashed windows, trashed cars, slashed tires, and led teenagers on "raids" through Hebron in which they pummeled innocent bystanders and threw stones at windows and solar energy collectors. Raviv once incited a teenager to attack Faisal Husseini, the head of the Palestinian community in Jerusalem. He also plied journalists with reports of his escapades, which were published without verification. His brutal mischief did not spare Jews, either. He once sent his cohorts to puncture the tires of the chairman of the Kiryat Arba Local Council as a warning to stop "persecuting" the extremists in the settlement.

Raviv readily submitted to arrest—at least fifteen times—secure in the knowledge that he would quickly be released. All he needed to do was phone his handler, who promptly came to the rescue. In one instance, when the machinery of the law proved unusually efficient, Raviv was already in court, having been arrested for rioting. The judge was entering the hall when a Shabak agent burst through the door and ordered the police prosecutor to drop the charges. Raviv stood laughing as a policeman removed his handcuffs. Files were opened against him at least thirteen times for trespassing, disorderly conduct, incitement to racism, threats, and interfering with a policeman acting in the line of duty. For none of these crimes—with the exception of the assault on Gozansky—was Raviv prosecuted. Most of his offenses against Palestinians were never even reported.

After Raviv's association with the Shabak had become public knowledge, Carmi Gillon dryly characterized him as a "problematic agent." His personnel file in the Shabak's computer, which contains assessments of his character and memos from his handlers, offers a more vivid portrait. The personality profiles speak of him as "perfidious," "an overgrown child," "an introvert who aspires to lead and stand out," and a man who admires power of every kind. In closed meetings the directors of the Shabak—Ya'akov Perry and Gillon after him—expressed their view that the benefits derived from Raviv far outweighed the problems he caused. They regarded him as a good agent and approved his continued employment. But as time went on, his handlers grew increasingly frustrated by his behavior. More than once they suggested that he be fired but always dropped the idea when it proved impossible to replace him. Whenever Raviv was upbraided and warned to mend his ways, he would invariably apologize and promise to follow orders. But a memo written by his handler on April 30, 1992, reveals one agent's skepticism that the "Raviv problem" was likely to be solved:

> [I] made it clear to Raviv that his role, in terms of his association with us, is not to instigate actions but to defer, delay, and report on the actions of others. It was explained to the "subject" [Raviv] that as a result of his initiatives, we are essentially "chasing our own tail." Raviv was briefed and warned not to engage in illegal acts without first informing the Shabak [of his intentions]. The "subject" expressed his willingness to behave accordingly. The initiatives taken by the "subject" stem from his problematic character, and despite his agreement [to obey, expressed] during the meeting, it can be expected that he will continue his initiatives from time to time.

Avishai Raviv carried out his acts of thuggery under the cover of a number of fronts, which bore catchy Hebrew names like Dov, Nefetz, In, and Eyal.* He patterned these groups after the Stern Gang, the radical faction of the right-wing underground in Palestine in the 1940s, and he held Eyal's induction ceremonies at the grave of its leader, Avraham Stern.

One of these ceremonies was filmed by Israel's Channel One and broadcast on September 22, 1995. It showed a group of young men in black ski masks taking a vow on the Bible to do injury to Arabs and oppose by force any withdrawal from the territories. After the piece sparked a firestorm in Israel and was broadcast abroad, a right-wing group called the Public's Right to Know lodged a complaint with the police that the ceremony had been staged by the television reporter. The police inquiry found no evidence to substantiate the charge. The journalist who filmed it denied any misconduct on his part, and his superiors stood firmly behind him. However, the Shamgar Commission concluded, without citing its reasons,

---

*Dov means "bear," but in this case was an acronym for *Diku'i Bogdim* ("Repression of Traitors"). *Nefetz,* which means "explosion," stood for *Noar Facisti Tsioni* ("Fascist Zionist Youth"). "In" has the same social connotation as in English and was an acronym for *Irgun Yehudi Nokem* ("Jewish Vengeance Organization"). *Eyal,* the best known of these fronts, means "might" but was an acronym for *Irgun Yehudi Lochem* ("Jewish Fighting Organization").

that the ceremony had been staged by Raviv for the benefit of the documentary crew.

Various Shabak documents describe Raviv as an opportunist, but his friends insist that he genuinely believed in the fascist principles he practiced. After Rabbi Kahane was murdered, for example, Raviv donned a yarmulke and began observing all the injunctions of the halacha. He hoped to be chosen as Kahane's successor in Israel, not to serve his employers better but to fulfill his mentor's legacy. There is substantial evidence that he had his own agenda, unrelated to the needs of the Shabak. For example, he founded Eyal without informing his handlers in advance, and when he finally admitted to it, they were furious with him. In a memo written on June 29, 1992, a Shabak agent reported:

As is his wont, the "subject" reported on the formation of "Eyal" after the fact. Given his background and habit of post facto reporting, he was given a tough talking to. I explained to the "subject," at length, the problem that . . . someone reporting after the fact may err out of a narrow view of the matter; [that] he does not have legal backing for anything not coordinated with us; [and that] this constitutes a grave breach of discipline that hampers our ability to direct him to our important objectives. In light of his dependence upon us, I told him that after reviewing his file and considering my brief acquaintance with him, it is doubtful whether there's any point in continuing the connection with him when he exhibits behavior for which we cannot assume responsibility. This was said to the "subject" in the strongest of terms, and I believe he took it to heart. Nevertheless, it is doubtful that he will take it into account for long.

Raviv's handlers presented a similarly dismal portrayal of him to the Shamgar Commission, testifying that he had lied, deviated from orders, reported late, and was generally undisciplined. Twice the Shabak severed all contact with Raviv because of his unauthorized activities. Each time he shrugged off the rebukes. He was irreplaceable and knew that as well as the Shabak did. Each discussion on how to deal with Raviv always led to the same conviction: He was doing less harm than good. The problem of having a loose canon on the Shabak's payroll may have been untenable, but so was the situation that prompted it.

The massacre in the Cave of the Patriarchs proved to the Shabak—if that was still necessary—that its sources in Kiryat Arba and Hebron were not providing satisfactory intelligence. In an effort to remedy the situation quickly, Raviv was told to move to Kiryat Arba, where he rented an apartment in Block 306, one floor above Baruch Goldstein's family. There, according to testimony given at Yigal Amir's trial by Eyal member Eran Ojalbo (which the prosecutor tried repeatedly to have halted),* community leaders and members of Kach came and went at all hours. Amir was another regular visitor to the flat each time he came to Hebron.

Resettled in Kiryat Arba, Raviv was both farther from the oversight of his handlers and closer to the targets of his animus. He indulged his hostility by leading "pogroms" in the alleys of Hebron. When the Shabak discovered that he was victimizing Palestinians, he was summoned to Tel Aviv for a "strafing" that ended with yet another admonition to mend his ways.

Suspicions that Raviv was working for the secret service began to arise in February 1995, after Dmitri Goldin, a twenty-two-year-old student of mathematics and computer science at Bar-Ilan University, was arrested by the Shabak. Just before being seized, Goldin had been working on assembling bombs, for use in anti-Arab terror actions, in his apartment in a Tel Aviv suburb. As he was about to leave for the Yeshiva of the Jewish Idea in Jerusalem (an offshoot of the Kach movement), he received a call from Raviv. Asked what he was up to, Goldin spoke freely of his plans, then left for the yeshiva. He was stopped on the way by Shabak agents. The search of his car produced two knives, two bottles of acid and some mercury (for use in bombmaking), and leaflets calling for civil disobedience. At Goldin's trial for illegal possession of explosives, his lawyer argued that, at the Shabak's insistence, the prosecution had refrained from indicting his client for sedition because the leaflets confiscated in his car had been written by Avishai Raviv. To prevent the admission of testimony on Raviv, the Shabak

---

*Among Ojalbo's allegations in his testimony was that "Avishai said things to [Amir] on a certain Shabbat . . . Avishai said that Rabin is subject to *din rodef*, a death sentence, and whoever carries it out will be a saint. . . . In essence, Avishai organized and conveyed the order to Yigal and supervised him from above."

arranged a plea bargain for Goldin, who was sentenced to four months' imprisonment.

Reports of Goldin's arrest quickly reached the Hebron–Kiryat Arba community. Kach activist Itamar Ben-Gvir said that the only person who knew Goldin's time of departure and route that day was Raviv. From then on the word on the street in Kiryat Arba and Hebron was to avoid all contact with Raviv. But his final undoing did not come until September 1995, when, to shore up his listing credibility, Raviv had Eyal claim responsibility for the murder of a Palestinian in the town of Halhul, adjoining Hebron. The deed was done, his announcement stressed, for "nationalist reasons." Reaction from the left came swiftly in the form of cries to have all the settlers removed from Hebron. Soon thereafter, however, the police investigation found that the homicide had in fact been committed by Palestinians in the course of a robbery. Raviv emerged from the incident severely discredited. Throughout the territories settler leaders and rabbis warned against any contact with him, though they refrained from denouncing his violence against Palestinians.

The Shabak found itself in a more awkward position. In the summer of 1995, as Raviv's probable association with the service was bruited in settlements, yeshivas, synagogues, and Bar-Ilan University, not only did his usefulness wane, but the Shabak found its own probity being questioned. "I heard that Raviv was a Shabak agent from the people at Bar-Ilan about a month before the assassination," recalled Uri Elitsur of the Yesha Council. "This was one of the breaking points that caused [our] terrible crisis of confidence in the state's institutions. . . . It's hard for me to believe that Avishai Raviv operated without the knowledge [of the Shabak's senior echelon] when he carried out pogroms in Hebron and Nablus. This was a provocation [against us]. It caused us damage, and it drove us mad."

During a chance encounter with Carmi Gillon, one of the leaders of the Yesha Council came straight out and asked whether it was true that Raviv was on his payroll. Gillon ducked the question, and his evasion did nothing to dampen the rumors. His staff knew that Raviv had compromised himself with the settlers and Kach. But lacking other reliable sources of intelligence, they were loath to slash the knot tying them to an informer who, after all, had still not been thoroughly drummed out of the radical right.

In the autumn of 1995 the Shabak totally lost control of Avishai Raviv. Proof that the "problematic" agent had bolted its orbit came at the demonstration in Zion Square on October 5, where dozens of copies of a photomontage showing Rabin in an SS uniform were being passed through the crowd. The handout was unspeakably offensive by any standard. But it might have caused less of a sensation had Raviv not brought a copy to the correspondent covering the demonstration for Channel One and pressed him to report on it immediately. Had he been functioning as a conscientious Shabak operative, Raviv would have gone out of his way to avoid being even remotely associated with such an egregious act of incitement.

Jumping to conclusions, however, the leaders of the Israeli right accused Raviv—and, by extension, the Shabak—of creating the photomontage. Uri Aloni, the head of the Young Likud, who had organized squads to heckle Rabin, even declared, "I personally saw Avishai Raviv take the leaflets out of a backpack and distribute them." But a thorough check revealed that Raviv was not carrying a backpack that night. He had snatched a copy of the photomontage from an anonymous protester and rushed directly to the television reporter. Toward the end of December 1995 the police investigation revealed the creators of the montage to be two teenage *haredim* from Jerusalem who had photocopied a picture of Heinrich Himmler from a French encyclopedia, pasted Rabin's face on it, and photocopied the result at the printing press owned by the father of one of the boys. Like Raviv, they had been inspired by the doctrine of Meir Kahane, but that was the extent of his connection with them. Nevertheless, the lie crediting Raviv with the notorious handbill is still cited as a key element of the theory that Rabin was using the Shabak to discredit the political rights.

The suspicions about Raviv's connections with the Shabak also impaired his relations with Yigal Amir and thus the Shabak's chances of preventing the assassination of Rabin. On the basis of their informant's sporadic references to Amir, in August 1995 the Shabak told Raviv to keep a close eye on the law student. It proved an easy assignment, for he was a friend of Amir's and often consulted with him on campus, in Kiryat Arba, and at the weekend conclaves he organized. So close were the two, in fact, that at one point Yigal proposed to his two co-conspirators that Raviv be invited to join their inner circle. It was Haggai who squelched the idea because he had heard rumors that Raviv was a Shabak plant. Under interrogation Yigal referred to Raviv as "a good friend of mine" but also confirmed Haggai's reservations. "We suspected he was working for the Shabak," he said. "Each time I phoned him, [the Shabak] heard about it."

On directives from his handlers, Raviv held two long talks with Amir in which he tried to elicit his views on *din rodef*. Raviv also spoke with two friends who had studied with Amir in the Kerem D'Yavneh Yeshiva, and he came away with the impression that they believed Amir subscribed to right-wing views but was incapable of translating them into action. "A chatterbox and braggart" were the exact words Raviv used to describe his friend. On the basis of this assessment, the intelligence analysts concluded that it was no longer necessary to keep tabs on Amir. Raviv's report was not even circulated within the Jewish Division; it was simply shelved.

Amir by then had a file of his own in the Shabak's computer that described him as an "extremist" who "tends toward confrontation with Palestinians and with the regime." It also contained details on the demonstrations he had attended and his anti-Arab and antigovernment statements. Raviv apparently did not add much to this information. In their testimonies before the Shamgar Commission, Shabak agents described the material he supplied on Amir as "very rudimentary, general, and with no indications suggesting the possibility that he would take action." Haggai Amir had a more specific version of what Avishai Raviv knew about his brother. He told his interrogators that "Avishai Raviv heard Yigal Amir [say] that the solution [to the political situation] is the murder of the prime minister." Raviv did not deny having witnessed this statement. Behind closed doors he told the Shamgar Commission that he had heard Amir say that Rabin must be killed but had failed to report it because "I didn't believe him. I'd always thought he was a braggart."

While in custody after the assassination, Raviv was questioned for many hours about what he knew and believed about Amir's intentions. A lie detector test showed him to be telling the truth about dismissing Amir as a blusterer. It also satisfied the Shabak that he had had no knowledge of the explosives stashed away by the Amir brothers. After Abramovich's revelation there were naturally questions about what Amir had said to Raviv in the course of their joint endeavors and what Raviv knew but kept from his superiors. Was it possible that Raviv had discovered the plot to murder

Rabin but failed to report it to the Shabak? All the evidence suggests not. Thus the second widely discussed scenario—that Raviv reported the plan to his handlers but the Shabak deliberately ignored it—must be considered groundless.

Avishai Raviv and Yigal Amir met for the last time at Bar-Ilan University on October 30, 1995, and made a date to rendezvous on the following Saturday evening at the edge of the Kings of Israel Square, where the police had given permission for a small counterdemonstration. Raviv arrived only as the rally was drawing to a close and told his deputy in Eyal, Benny Aharoni, that he had overslept. He spent most of his time near the square talking on his cell phone and, immediately after the shots were heard, called Eran Ojalbo. The conversation is intriguing because it shows that, contrary to his assessment that Amir was incapable of taking any serious action, Raviv immediately suspected that Yigal was the assassin. We learn this from Ojalbo's reconstruction of his conversation with Raviv.

> About ten minutes after they began reporting that Rabin had been wounded, I received a phone call from Avishai, and he asked me how I was . . . [and] whether I was watching television. I said yes. He asked me if they had shown who shot [Rabin]. I take a look, see a short Yemenite guy, and was sure that he was the man they call Benny—a friend who more or less resembles [Amir]. I was wrong about the initial identification. Then Avishai asks me, "It isn't Yigal?" I told him I'd take a better look. . . . I looked at the picture again and identified Yigal clearly. "Avishai," I told him, "it's Yigal."

It was Aharoni who then suggested that In—another of Raviv's fronts—be "brought out of the cold" by using its name in a communiqué to the press taking responsibility for the shooting. (At the time the two men believed that Rabin had been only lightly wounded.) Apparently having forgotten the lesson of the Halhul blunder, Raviv agreed and sent Aharoni off to find a phone. By means of a beeper service, he sent the press an announcement boasting, "Next time we'll succeed." By the time Aharoni returned to the square, Raviv was nowhere to be found. He had gone home on orders from his handler to "lay low and continue passing on information." He talked to a number of journalists from his parents' apartment but insisted that he knew nothing about the assassination or about Yigal Amir.

Two days later Raviv was arrested by the Shabak and sent to coax Margalit Har-Shefi into opening up to him. Taken into custody the previous night, she had refused to talk to her interrogators. Raviv was sent into the room where Margalit was waiting and tried, as casually as he could, to draw out the exhausted Har-Shefi. But she remained evasive. There can be no doubt that she had misgivings about Raviv and sensed that whatever she said to him would be relayed to her interrogators. The conversation was in fact secretly being filmed and recorded:

HAR-SHEFI: "I didn't sleep. They held me all night. Do you believe that [Amir] did it?"

RAVIV: "No, I don't get it—"

HAR-SHEFI: "That he walked over nicely and shot him?"

RAVIV: "No, I don't get it. How is it possible to do such a thing? I don't get it—"

HAR-SHEFI: "I didn't know him. It's as if suddenly, I mean, I can't put the two together: Yigal until Saturday night and Yigal since Saturday night. No, it's as though the mind can't grasp it—"

RAVIV: "I don't get it—"

HAR-SHEFI: "That's not Yigal. It's as though it's—"

RAVIV: "He's a hero!"

HAR-SHEFI: "Oh, *really*? Give me a break!"

RAVIV: "He took all the responsibility on himself. All the responsibility, the whole country on his shoulders. He's going down in history—"

HAR-SHEFI: "He's going down in history, alright; the question is: as what?"

RAVIV: "He'll definitely be a hero!"

HAR-SHEFI: "What?"

RAVIV: "Definitely as a hero."

HAR-SHEFI: "Yeah, you and your heroes. . . . I have no strength."

RAVIV: "Whoever denounces him now simply has no Jewish pride—"

HAR-SHEFI: "It's Jewish pride that leads to things like this. . . ."

RAVIV: "They think they can break you."

HAR-SHEFI: "They talk as though Yigal said that I knew of his attempt and that they'll do me a favor. Come on—"

RAVIV: "This is one of their ways of breaking us, by waiting—"

HAR-SHEFI: "What do you mean 'breaking us'? What do they want? For me to say things were done? I don't believe this is happening to me. You know, [it's] as if Yigal knows I'm here now, and it seems that he's just laughing—"

RAVIV: "How does he know?"

HAR-SHEFI: "Because I heard voices yesterday. I spoke loudly and he spoke loudly. I think he sent me regards. . . ."

RAVIV: "He's lucky he wasn't killed."

HAR-SHEFI: "That's it. You know, if it were someone else, then everything would be so clear to me. But when it's a friend of yours who does this, it's a shock because he's my friend. I know I would treat the whole matter differently if it were someone else."

After a few minutes the Shabak agents apparently decided that the exercise was a waste of time because a voice can be heard off camera saying: "Okay, time's up. Come with me; you stay here." The futility of the ploy did not prevent the service from placing Raviv in Amir's cell, with the same purpose in mind. Their talk yielded little more than Amir's declaration "I've done my part. I'm pleased," and when Raviv told him that he could expect a life sentence, the equally sanguine statement "The Gemara [Talmud] is enough for me." Upon emerging from the cell, Raviv told his interrogators that Amir was in a state of euphoria.

The Shabak kept Raviv in custody long enough to subject him to a thorough grilling on whether he knew more about Amir than he had previously let on. It was during this interrogation that he took a polygraph test, which showed him to be telling the truth when he denied any knowledge of the plot or the explosives hidden behind the Amir brothers' home. Still, he was held for a total of ten days—perhaps because too swift a release would have aroused questions—after which he went with a friend to a hotel on the Sea of Galilee for a vacation. The Shabak provided him with a bodyguard to keep journalists at bay, and ever since then, once a week, a Shabak agent has phoned to warn him against talking to the media.

Since that time Avishai Raviv has had little contact with anyone outside his immediate family. He did not return to Bar-Ilan University. For a while he was employed in a hostel for the mentally retarded in Tel Aviv but left after being discovered there by the press. Two and a half years after the assassination he is an isolated and depressed man living off a disability pension from the army and a stipend from the Shabak. Every day he goes to work out in a gym in Tel Aviv, where some of the other regulars taunt and goad him. Stone-faced and silent, he works out for an hour or so and returns to his parents' apartment in Holon.

In June 1998 Raviv was still waiting to hear whether the state attorney would prosecute him for failing to prevent a crime and for suspicion of involvement in an illegal organization (Eyal). His is the only case related to the assassination that is still in abeyance. Other than the three co-conspirators and Margalit Har-Shefi, none of the students who were on the edges of the plot to kill Rabin, or to take violent action against Arabs, has been or will be tried. The delay in reaching a decision about Raviv stemmed from the Shabak's insistence that he enjoys immunity from prosecution. Clearly the service was concerned about having its agents and methods exposed in the course of criminal proceedings. "It would be a grave mistake to put Raviv on trial," Carmi Gillon warned the State Attorney's Office, not least because it would destroy the will of other informers and make future recruitment all the more difficult. If Raviv is eventually tried, the proceedings will undoubtedly be held behind closed doors. Never has there been an open judicial review of the Shabak's mode of operation.

After two weeks of fevered speculation following the article in *Hatsofeh*, portions of the secret appendix to the Shamgar Commission Report were released on November 13, 1997. They contained no surprises. The classified material reiterated that the commission had found no evidence of a conspiracy between Raviv and the Shabak or between Raviv and Amir. But it drew a damning picture of the way in which the service had managed Raviv by depicting the informer as a double agent who had repeatedly deceived the Shabak. His value as a source of intelligence, the panel concluded, was overestimated, while his protection from prosecution freed Raviv to engage in destructive and violent activities. "Raviv deceived, cheated, and kept information from the Shabak," the secret appendix stated, based on the testimonies of two agents. "His provocations, particularly in the form of physical attacks on Arabs and the show [he put on] about the existence of extreme and violent political bodies, clearly included a dimension of indirect but flagrant harm to legal and identifiable political bodies, which his handlers could not ignore."

Left unaddressed in the published portions of the appendix, however, are questions about the service's management of its wayward agent. The commission noted that Raviv's handlers permitted him to participate in radical activities in order to enhance his credibility among extremists. Unstated is how far they allowed him to go for this purpose. We know that he reported on the formation of Eyal only after the fact and was sharply rebuked. But what happened thereafter? Did he inform his handlers of Eyal's activities? If he did, why didn't they prevent him from leading rampages against Palestinians? Right-wing leaders were quick to allege that the Shabak had utilized Raviv as an agent provocateur to tarnish "half of the nation." But they didn't ask whether Palestinians had been forced to pay the price of protecting Shabak's tenuous inroads into the radical right, or worse, whether Eyal's actions had not only been tolerated but actually planned by the Shabak for that purpose.

Infiltrating subversive groups is integral to the work of secret services the world over. But it is incumbent upon such organs to circumscribe their agents' actions. They do so by clearly stipulating that only when operating within the approved limits are agents immune to prosecution.

"The rule is that an agent must not instigate actions," says Chaim Zadok, a former Israeli justice minister, in describing the guidelines applied to operatives planted within subversive organizations. "He is allowed to be a member of a group and join, when necessary, in its operations so as not to be exposed. But he must not act as an agent provocateur."

The Shamgar Commission's report indicates that Raviv's handlers disregarded this cardinal rule. The commission did not find the service directly responsible for his illegal activities, as a number of right-wing politicians continued to insist it should have. (Eitan, for one, ascribed its finding to not having received "all the information on Raviv's activities. If [it] had, [its] conclusions would have been harsher.") But the commission did determine that the damage Raviv had caused while in the Shabak's employ was not sufficiently considered.

The lack of control over an agent and the total backing he was given created the misleading picture of an identity of interests between him and his handlers that impaired and directly harmed the security service. . . . It is necessary to be wary of provocateurs who, because of ill intentions or personality disturbances, exploit the backing they receive to become the instigators of illegal acts . . . under the mantle of the regime. Such people also behave wantonly because they know they will not be prosecuted. The injurious results are borne by the state as a whole. The conclusion is that there must be effective control over an agent, and he must not be permitted [to engage in] mayhem.

The Shamgar Commission's statement that Raviv's activities contained a "dimension of indirect but flagrant harm to legal and identifiable political bodies" was plucked out of the secret appendix by the right and brandished as vindication that it was innocent of organizing the incitement against Yitzhak Rabin. It sought to focus public attention on the marginal issue of how a single agent was sloppily handled by the Shabak and also to peddle the notion that the incitement against Rabin was generated directly by Raviv on orders from the secret service. "Avishai Raviv functioned like an incitement machine whose chief operator was Carmi Gillon, and thus it is not surprising that [Gillon] is trying to play down Raviv's activity," Eitan charged in a television interview, while two other Knesset deputies (from the NRP and Tsomet) demanded that Gillon be tried for "activating Raviv against the right."

Incensed by these claims, Gillon responded: "To present Avishai Raviv as a man who carried a coffin on his back at the Ra'anana junction, drew tens of thousands of people into Zion Square, and cut off the loudspeakers while Rabin was speaking in Jerusalem is going too far. This is an attempt to help us forget the Action Headquarters and hang the entire incitement campaign, including *din rodef* and *din moser*, on a very problematic young man. That's ridiculous."

The public apparently agreed. After the release of the appendix, there was no popular pressure to try Raviv for orchestrating the incitement campaign against Rabin. Essentially Raviv had directed most of his energy against Palestinians. He had had no contact with the Political

Guidance Headquarters, the Joint Staff, or even kindred souls in the Action Headquarters (with the possible exception of Baruch Marzel). The Yesha Council had not consulted him, nor had rabbis made him privy to their discussions of *din rodef.* On the contrary, during the tumultuous months before the assassination it was widely assumed by the settlers that Raviv was working for the Shabak, and they kept their distance from him. What the secret appendix of the Shamgar Report should have laid to rest were the allegations that Raviv had pursued his sordid activities against Palestinians at the behest of the Shabak. It did not accomplish that. But in discounting the notion of a conspiracy, it did prove that Raviv had not been used as an agent provocateur to discredit Rabin's political foes. He appeared under the lens of judicial examination exactly as he did on the street: as a fascist who acted out of conviction rather than mercenary impulse.

The only point of substance that remained after the furor triggered by *Hatsofeh* was Amnon Abramovich's revelation, made two years earlier, that Avishai Raviv was working for the Shabak.

"Had I known in advance that the right would use the item to hang the incitement campaign on Raviv," Abramovich later confessed to colleagues, "I wouldn't have published it."

CHAPTER 9

FAILURE

W ord that the long wait was over passed through the swarm
of journalists standing outside Shalom House in the posh
Jerusalem neighborhood of Talbieh, where the Shamgar
Inquiry Commission had been meeting for five months. Video cameras
were hauled onto shoulders; microphones and tape recorders were thrust
forward to meet the line of grim-faced officials exiting the building. The
date was March 28, 1996. A day earlier Yigal Amir's trial had culminated,
predictably, in his conviction for the premeditated murder of the prime
minister. Now the commission appointed to investigate how that crime had
been allowed to happen was about to publish its detailed report.

Heading the three-man panel was retired Supreme Court Chief Justice
Meir Shamgar, who had chaired the commission of inquiry into the massacre in the Cave of the Patriarchs two years earlier. He was joined by
seventy-one-year-old Major General (retired) Zvi Zamir, a former head of
the Mossad, and fifty-one-year-old Tel Aviv University law professor Ariel
Rosen-Zvi. The panel's political proclivities were impeccably balanced:
Zamir was associated with the left, Shamgar with the right, and Rosen-Zvi
with the modern Orthodox community. They had held sixty-one sessions,
all of them in camera, and interrogated seventy-two witnesses, whose testimonies filled 6,387 pages. Their 214-page report was released to the public

on March 28, but a 188-page classified appendix was made available to only a dozen or so people before being locked in a safe in the Prime Minister's Office. Sections of this secret appendix, as we have seen, were eventually published as well.

The commission's mandate, as formulated by Shimon Peres's government, allowed the panel great flexibility in defining the scope of its investigation. Had they so chosen, the panelists could have ranged far beyond a technical examination of the intelligence obtained and protection provided by the police and the Shabak before and during the assassination. But they chose not to examine the campaign of incitement conducted against Yitzhak Rabin. Neither did they extend their inquiry to the rabbis who had ruled him subject to *din moser* or *din rodef.*

"The State of Israel after the assassination of the prime minister, Mr. Yitzhak Rabin, of blessed memory, will not return to what it was before," the Shamgar Commission declared in its final report. Yet its members held back from scrutinizing most of the factors responsible for that transformation. By limiting themselves to describing the shortcomings of the security forces, and primarily the Shabak, the commission gave undue emphasis to these factors. In effect, its report reduced the murder of the prime minister from a complex historical event to a simple lapse in security arrangements. As for the broader circumstances, the commission conceded that it had "not exhausted the need for an examination of Israeli society and a search for answers to questions [such as] how we reached the pass of the murder of a prime minister by a radical assassin and how violence has become a means of solving political disagreements." But it recommended that "society as a whole, and particularly its educational institutions," seek those answers on its own.

Justice Shamgar had taken a similarly restricted approach to circumstances two years earlier, when he had chaired the commission investigating Baruch Goldstein's massacre in the Cave of the Patriarchs. In that instance too the panel confined itself to a strict elucidation of the facts and performance of the security personnel, rather than an examination of the religious, social, and political conditions that had fueled the attack. While it is not difficult to appreciate why Justice Shamgar and his colleagues on both commissions chose to limit their inquiries so sharply, it is hard to escape the feeling that they did the Israeli public a disservice by doing so.

On the subject it did investigate—the performance of the police and the Shabak in regard to the assassination—the Shamgar Commission issued the most damning report ever on an official agency. It found that the resignation of the head of the Shabak, Carmi Gillon (which had already been tendered and accepted on January 5, 1996) was the only justifiable course. He had erred, the panelists concluded, in interpreting the intelligence available to him and bore responsibility for the inadequate arrangements for protecting the prime minister. Dismissed together with Gillon was the head of the Shabak's Security Division, identified by his initials, D.Y.; three other senior agents were also removed from their posts.

The Shabak's failure to prevent the assassination, the panel found, could be traced not to a specific lapse in judgment or performance but to a misguided approach to safeguarding the prime minister. The service had been alerted to the threat to the safety of public figures but had failed to deploy properly to meet it. Even though the Shabak's Intelligence Division had assessed the danger posed by radical opponents of the government, Gillon had failed to imbue his men with an adequate appreciation of its gravity. Some of Rabin's bodyguards, the commission noted, had not been briefed to anticipate the appearance of a Jewish assassin armed with a revolver. The commission believed that they had "focused more on the threat from stones and tomatoes." In a private conversation one of the members of the panel couched its findings in the simplest and saddest of terms: "The head of the guards fell asleep. That's why the prime minister was murdered."

The scion of a prominent Jerusalem family that produced three generations of leading lawyers, Carmi Gillon had been a late bloomer. Twice left back in high school, he shunned a law career and, after completing his military service, joined the Shabak instead. There he developed an interest in Jewish subversive groups, switched to the Shabak's Jewish Division, and ultimately wrote his master's thesis on *Ideologically Motivated Violations of the Law by the Radical Right in Israel.*

Gillon was appointed chief of the Shabak by Yitzhak Rabin on March 1, 1995. By that time he was head of the service's Jewish Division and had been considered a dark horse candidate for the critical post. He had never directed a large and complex organization, and his field experience, particularly in security operations, was limited. Rabin had been inclined to choose a retired army general to head the Shabak but ultimately accepted the recommendation of its outgoing director, Ya'akov Perry, that the assiduous and thoughtful Gillon be appointed.

The result of that decision would be supremely ironic. For although he was an expert on Jewish subversives, Gillon would fail to gauge the magnitude of the threat they posed. Essentially he misjudged both the likely nationality and psychological makeup of a potential political assassin. As in the case of other security blunders in Israel's history—notably the Yom Kippur War and the outbreak of the intifada—the Shabak's failure to prevent the assassination of Prime Minister Rabin could be traced to intellectual rigidity and overconfidence. The service believed that the prospect of fatal harm befalling Rabin at the hands of a Jew was minimal. This conclusion was based not on reliable intelligence and a thorough analysis of objective circumstances but on the assumption that a Jew would never murder a leading political figure in cold blood. If an assassin were lurking somewhere along Rabin's path, he would axiomatically be a Palestinian. The Shabak also believed that Jewish extremists would resort to the use of arms only if the government formally ordered the evacuation of settlements in the territories. Such an order, it held, would inaugurate a new phase of confrontation bluntly referred to in its closed deliberations as "a civil war."

Thus upon emerging from Shalom House pale and tense with anger, Gillon read a prepared statement condemning the commission for not "delving into the depth and scope of the responsibility borne by the Shabak and its commanders or the special problems involved in carrying out its tasks, particularly given [the circumstances of] a Jewish terrorist and murderer who is bone of our bone, flesh of our flesh. . . ." He also took the opportunity to argue that since the assassin was a nameless face in the crowd, it was impossible to pick him out.

Here, however, he misled the public on two counts. The murderer had not been hidden in the sea of people jammed into the square on the night of November 4; he had been loitering, alone, in an off-limits area, where he had been approached and addressed, on at least two occasions, by policemen. Neither was he an isolated and anonymous figure who, by the nature of things, would fail to attract the attention of any of Israel's security organs. He belonged to a small and well-defined circle; his name was passed on to the Shabak at least twice before the assassination by Avishai

Raviv; and the service kept a file on him. Yet he was never summoned for questioning because he did not fit the Shabak's set profile of a potential Jewish assassin as being a loner and mentally disturbed. Far from being a loner, the outgoing law student was the leader of a group of conspirators, to say nothing of being an energetic campus activist. The screenings he had passed in the army and before being sent to Latvia to work with Jewish youth gave no indication of emotional instability. Indeed, Yigal Amir committed his crime with a full and sober appreciation of its consequences. He repeatedly calculated the prospects and perils of getting close enough to Rabin to shoot him with a handgun, all of which proved to be perfectly accurate.

The source of the Shabak's miscalculation was a failure to acknowledge the new circumstances triggered by the Oslo Agreement: the possibility that the nationalist and messianist indoctrination of Orthodox youth, for more than twenty years, would lead at least some of them to reject the principle of democratic rule and resort to the use of force. In this the Shabak was a product of the society around it, many of whose members viewed the settlers as Jewish patriots. Leading lights of Israel's two main parties had lent the settlers their active support and even condoned their violations of the law.

Thus as the prime strategy of his defense, Carmi Gillon and his attorney, Eli Zohar, labored diligently to steer the Shamgar Commission's deliberations toward an appreciation of this broader social and political context. Gillon's testimony laid great emphasis on the climate of lawlessness in the territories that made it possible for subversive elements to act freely. He even suggested that Attorney General Michael Ben-Ya'ir had contributed to settlers' perception of being above the law by ruling, in April 1994, that Israeli law does not extend to any of the residents of the territories, Israeli or Palestinian, and blocking the establishment of civil courts for Israelis living beyond the Green Line. The panel, however, firmly rejected this line of argument.

Gillon felt that Rabin's two close friends on the commission, Shamgar and Zamir, were out to settle a personal score with him, and at one point he considered demanding that they disqualify themselves. There were also acrimonious exchanges over leaks to the press. The panel suspected Gillon of being the source of the chronic seepage of information, for which it publicly rebuked him, twice. Gillon, in turn, complained of tendentious leaks coming from the commission, a charge that Shamgar chose to deny in an especially sharp public statement.

In his defense, Gillon particularly stressed his dependence upon the judgment and skills of his subordinates, who had led him to understand that no one armed with a revolver could get within firing range of the prime minister. The problem, he argued, was not in the plan for protecting Rabin but in the negligence of the agents on the scene. The members of the VIP Protection Unit had been trained to thwart an attack under precisely the conditions in the parking lot—namely, preventing shots from being fired at the prime minister from within a range of fifteen yards. Gillon also testified that prior to the rally he had met twice with the group of body-guards assigned to the event, briefed them on the mission, and ordered them to be on high alert and adapt themselves to the circumstances. The bodyguards, he added, had assured him that they were capable of coping with a revolver attack at close range. "The tragedy was an isolated event," he told the panel. "It does not attest to deficiencies in organization, deploy-ment, readiness, or the alertness or the proper conduct of the unit."

The commission, however, concluded that the method of protecting the prime minister was antiquated. It noted that the Shabak had recently revised its strategy for protecting VIPs, following the recommendations of its own board of inquiry, appointed immediately after the assassination. Had Gillon and the head of the Shabak's Security Division made the neces-sary adjustments earlier, in response to the obviously ominous circum-stances, Rabin would not have died.

Gillon fought back, both during the commission's hearings and after the publication of its report. He insisted that its authors had chosen to dis-regard the complexity of guarding public figures in a democratic country. Even in the United States, despite the precedent of the Kennedy assassina-tion, his attorney said, the Secret Service had failed to prevent two attempts on the life of President Gerald Ford and a lone gunman from shooting President Ronald Reagan at close range. Israel had had no such experience, and its political lifestyle remained open and informal. Despite his retiring nature, Yitzhak Rabin was a man of the people, Gillon reminded the com-mission. He had demanded there be no barrier between him and the pub-lic. On Saturdays, when he regularly played tennis at a private court in Tel Aviv, the prime minister had refused to have more than one bodyguard accompany him. He would not wear a bulletproof vest and was always eager to greet groups of supportive citizens. Nor was he intimidated by hostile receptions. During his last visit to New York, a few weeks before the assassination, protesters were stationed outside his hotel shouting, "Rabin is a traitor!" As he moved to leave his car, Rabin's bodyguards signaled him to use the far door, away from the demonstrators. But he deliberately walked toward the crowd, gesturing his scorn for the protesters. Rabin was what his countrymen call a *jingi*,* hot-tempered and strong-willed, Gillon told the commission. It dismissed this argument, however, and stressed in its report that "The obstacle to implementing an improved method [of protection] was the result not of the statesman's need to have effective contact with the public but of conceptual routine."

All of Gillon's other efforts to defend the soundness of the Shabak's strategy met a similar fate. After three months of hearing testimony, the Shamgar Commission concluded that the agency's failure to prevent Rabin's murder was strategic as well as tactical—and that Carmi Gillon was responsible for both. Had Shabak's strategy not been flawed, the guards protecting the prime minister would have been able to deal with a lone gunman. And had the performance of the agents on the scene not been poor, the murder might have been prevented even by the existing, flawed strategy. It was the combination of faults at the senior command and the field levels that made for tragedy.

Yet it was primarily of Carmi Gillon's professional judgment that the commission wrote scathingly. He knew that the Shabak's Intelligence Division might not be able to provide prior warning of an assassination attempt. He was aware that the solution to this shortcoming was to enhance the protection accorded to VIPs. Yet he failed to take the most obvious steps in this direction. Gillon did not order his men to reappraise the method of guarding the prime minister or rehearse it under field conditions. Under his stewardship the service suffered from complacency and poor preparation. Intelligence gathering and analysis were handled negligently, and the existence of a clear and present danger to the prime minister was not brought home to his bodyguards.

Gillon's attorney had presented an alternative picture of his client's

---

*A redhead, from the English "ginger."

conduct, stressing both that the Shabak's Intelligence Division had done its job properly and that the protection for key government figures had been beefed up over the past year. New equipment, including an armored Cadillac for the prime minister, had been purchased. The number of bodyguards was increased, though not as much as the Shabak had wanted. "When I asked to enlarge the number of guards by a third, the Treasury refused to approve the budget for it," Gillon noted in his detailed analysis of the unit's operations during his ten months as chief of the Shabak. In addition, he pointed out that fifteen bodyguards had been assigned to cover Rabin at the rally.

Most striking of all, Gillon insisted that it was not his job to verify whether his policy was being carried out. He assumed that it was enough for him to raise the specter of a Jewish assassin emerging from a crowd for his subordinates to draw and act upon the necessary conclusions. In this sense he followed a style of management more appropriate to a corporate board of directors than a security service. Yet his attorney tried to persuade the commission that it was indeed the system practiced in the Shabak. "It is a fact that the head of the Shabak grew up . . . in the service and functioned for eight months as its chief," Zohar told the commission. "He behaved according to the norms he had learned . . . from the Shabak."

But Gillon's predecessor, Ya'akov Perry, took strong issue with his portrayal of the Shabak's mode of command, and the Shamgar Commission agreed. It found Gillon's constrained style of direction inadequate, saying that successful management means "carefully thought-out delegation of authority alongside command, supervision, and control."

"Gillon was not sacked because of [an isolated] blunder," observed an insider who had recently retired from a senior post in the military. "His dismissal wasn't punishment; it was a necessary organizational measure. In a country where it's customary to demand that officers and managers assume personal responsibility [for failures], Gillon might have been indicted for negligence, even criminal negligence. But in Israel it is rare for a senior official to pay a high price for his errors, even when they are fatal."

Since the Six-Day War, most of the Shabak's energies and resources have been focused on a single aim: foiling Palestinian terrorism. Until then the Shabak had been a compact intelligence service devoted to exposing subversive activities by Israeli Communists and Arabs. Prior to December 1966, in fact, Israel's four hundred thousand Arab citizens had been treated as potential fifth columnists, subject to military government control and required to obtain permits to travel within the country. This system too had been supervised by the Shabak.

It was the results of the June 1967 war that engendered a revolution in the service's size, structure, and tasks. Israel's decision to exercise tight control over the lives of the million and a half Palestinians in the West Bank and Gaza Strip caused the service to grow dramatically and its intelligence gathering to become more professional. Hundreds of its agents penetrated deep into Palestinian society, making their presence felt in every city, town, and village. They recruited collaborators and achieved excellent results in neutralizing scores of terror cells. Over the years the service earned a reputation for sophistication and resourcefulness as its more spectacular operations made headlines around the world. At least three times it saved Israeli airliners from being blown up in midair and once prevented an attack on an El Al plane by German terrorists on Kenyan soil.

The Shabak's record was not unblemished, however, and Carmi Gillon was not the first Shabak chief to leave the post under a dark cloud. One of his predecessors, Avraham Shalom, had been dismissed following a huge scandal known as the Shabak Affair.

The story began at the end of April 13, 1984, when four armed Palestinians hijacked a bus on its way from Tel Aviv to the town of Ashkelon and ordered its driver to proceed to the Gaza Strip. Stopped at a roadblock along the way, the hijackers demanded, in return for freeing the passengers, that the Israeli government release fellow terrorists from its jails. Negotiations continued throughout the night, though there was scant reason to believe that Israel would capitulate to such terms. Toward morning an elite military unit stormed the bus, killing two of the hijackers. Reporters witnessed the removal of the other two from the bus, but a few hours later the IDF published an official communiqué stating that all four hijackers had been killed during the rescue operation. When journalists pressed for an explanation, the army hedged, while the military censor quashed the publication of any details of the action. Defense Minister Moshe Arens was obliged to appoint a board of inquiry into the events. The investigation was to have remained a secret. But the daily *Hadashot* defied the censor's prohibition and published a photo of security men leading one of the hijackers off for interrogation.

The inquiry board was able to ascertain that two of the terrorists had been removed from the bus alive but not who had killed them. A second investigative team, working for the State Attorney's Office, found IDF Brigadier General Yitzhak Mordechai responsible for beating two terrorists, for which he was rebuked by his superiors, but not for their demise. It was not until the end of 1985 that Attorney General Yitzhak Zamir learned the truth of what had happened that night. Shabak chief Avraham Shalom, he discovered, had ordered Ehud Yatom, one of his senior commanders at the scene, to kill the two terrorists (who had already been severely beaten by security officers). Shalom then told his subordinates to forge evidence and lie when asked about the incident by inquiry teams. Zamir was again shocked when he learned that this was not the first time Shabak operatives had murdered Palestinian suspects or lied in legal proceedings. He resolved to end such practices by promptly prosecuting the errant agents, from Shalom down. But to his astonishment he found that Prime Minister Shimon Peres and Foreign Minister Yitzhak Shamir were determined to protect Shalom and his men by blocking legal proceedings.

For Zamir the hallowed tenets of the rule of law and equality before it were at stake. When he insisted upon prosecuting Shalom, however, he was elegantly eased out. Ultimately, Peres reached a compromise with the new attorney general whereby Shalom was dismissed and he and the Shabak staffers involved in the affair were granted a blanket pardon by President Chaim Herzog. Although the circumstances under its scrutiny bore no resemblance to this scandal, the memory of it undoubtedly made the Shamgar Commission far less disposed to take Shabak agents' arguments at face value.

The history of the Shabak's Jewish Division also can be traced back to the days following the Six-Day War. It was founded as a junior adjunct of the main corps, reflecting the perceived threat from Jewish extremists. Before the Oslo Agreement, the Shabak's last success in uncovering a subversive network was in 1984, when its agents rounded up members of the Jewish Underground just as one of its cells was about to blow up five Arab buses. Thereafter, however, the service failed in almost all its efforts to penetrate clandestine cells of Jewish extremists. It kept tabs on members of

Kach and thwarted the attempt of the Kahalani brothers to murder a Palestinian. But it failed to forestall Baruch Goldstein's massacre in the Cave of the Patriarchs, despite an eerily accurate prophecy of such an action by the chairman of the Kiryat Arba Local Council. It also, of course, failed to uncover the plot against Yitzhak Rabin. In essence, the Shabak misread the climate of violence. It did not know, for example, that there was talk of murdering the prime minister at the Sabbath conclaves organized for Bar-Ilan students by Yigal Amir. It was unaware that rabbis had issued judgments on *din moser* and *din rodef.* It did not maintain surveillance over most of the groups of zealots that were known to be gathering in settlements and yeshivas. And while it did keep an eye on certain Kach activists, it showed only mild interest in anyone beyond the most obvious figures and groups engaged in aggression and incitement.

Yigal Amir was surrounded by concentric circles of people who shared his worldview. The first circle of the plot against Rabin included nine students, from Margalit Har-Shefi to Aryeh Schwartz and Ohad Skornik. None of them was known to the Shabak. The second circle (as shown by research done in parallel to the Shabak's intelligence work) included hundreds of religious nationalists and *haredim* who professed themselves ready to commit acts of violence against left-wing politicians. The Shabak showed no interest in them. The third circle embraced countless right-wing activists engaged in an incitement campaign that drew in tens of thousands of sympathizers. Together they created an atmosphere that legitimized the act secretly being planned by Yigal Amir. But the Shabak ruled out a professional interest in so broad a collection of Jewish citizens.

Had the Shabak not assumed it unlikely that a Jew would assassinate the prime minister, or had it not adhered to its mistaken profile of a possible Jewish assassin, it would have had little difficulty identifying Yigal Amir as a danger. The garrulous law student was remarkably cavalier about observing the basic rules of circumspection. He was friendly with at least two Shabak agents. He shared his intentions with three people—Haggai Amir, Dror Adani, and Margalit Har-Shefi—and included two of them in planning its execution. In turn, this group asked other friends to help in obtaining arms and planning actions against Palestinians. Most startling of all, Amir casually spoke in the presence of dozens of students of the need to eliminate Rabin and, along with Dror Adani, consulted with rabbis on halachic sanctions for such a move.

An examination of the Shabak's work during the three months preced-
ing the assassination also leads to the conclusion that it had badly neglected
the prime minister's safety. At least four times during that period, it
witnessed incidents and received information that should have led to
measures to diminish the threat to Rabin.

The first alarm was set off by the startling data compiled in the summer of 1995 by sociologist Kalman Gayer, who was Rabin's personal poll-
ster and reported to him directly. Until Rabin became prime minister for
the second time, Israel's premiers had based their policies on the data and
assessments received from official intelligence organs. Rarely had decisions
been made on the basis of independent research conducted specifically for
the Prime Minister's Office. But upon returning to the Prime Ministry in
1992, Rabin directed his aides to create a new mechanism for planning and
assessment.

Kalman Gayer was part of this new arrangement. At Rabin's request, he
did a statistical analysis of the public's response to the government's peace
policy, focusing particularly on the potential for violence on the part of its
opponents. The first time he conducted a survey was in March 1994, before
the IDF's redeployment from Gaza and Jericho. At that point he gauged the
potential for violence as low. But his second poll, done in August 1995 after
the violent demonstrations by Zo Artzenu and about a month before the
Knesset was to ratify the Oslo II Agreement, showed an immense potential
for violent action against the government and Rabin personally. Extrapo-
lating from his data, Gayer concluded that no fewer than eight hundred
Israelis—many of them living within the Green Line—were prepared to
commit murder to bring the peace process to a halt. The number of Israelis
who supported the notion of assassination as a means of political expression was equally surprising: 12 to 15 percent of the respondents, the
majority of whom cited the government's disregard of the settlers' security
needs, insensitivity to their distress, and indifference to their fate. Finally,
Gayer assessed that some six thousand Israelis, about a third of them residents of the territories, were prepared to take up arms against the army and
the police. A close analysis of the responses convinced him that they were
sincere. He was forced to conclude that the potential for antigovernment
violence might be even greater than the raw figures indicated because many
respondents may have been reluctant to answer candidly.

Gayer rushed the results of the second survey to Rabin. "We're talking about a great number of people and a high level of extremism," he stressed. "I estimate that eight hundred to one thousand people are considering taking some sort of action." Gayer sensed that Rabin was not surprised by his findings and certainly didn't feel it necessary to respond to them with any urgency. He believed that most of the public would support the Oslo II Agreement and reminded the sociologist that after a suicide bombing by Hamas at Beit Lid the previous January, the poll numbers did not change drastically. Rabin took pleasure in comparing statistics. In one of his talks with Gayer, he contrasted the number of right-wing demonstrators who gathered outside his Tel Aviv apartment house each week with the number of leftist protesters who had stood vigil outside Menachem Begin's residence in the early 1980s and concluded that the opposition to the war in Lebanon had far exceeded the dissent over the Oslo Agreement. If public opinion had not turned heavily against the accord after an attack as brutal as the Beit Lid bombing, Rabin reasoned, the peace process surely enjoyed solid support.

After his meeting with Gayer, the prime minister passed the data on to his chief of staff, Eitan Haber, who showed it to Shimon Peres. Then Rabin personally conveyed Gayer's findings to Carmi Gillon. Gayer had asked his permission to meet directly with the Shabak's intelligence people, but Rabin turned him down. Apparently he was disinclined to reveal his personal sources of information to the security establishment.

After the assassination it transpired that Gayer's assessment and that of the Shabak were quite similar, although Gayer's conclusions were more explicit. This contrast also emerges clearly from the Shamgar Commission Report. The Shabak's Intelligence Division duly reported the potential for violence to the service's operational units. But its style of reporting did not emphasize the kind of urgency that might have jolted the field operatives out of their lassitude. When Gillon was informed of Gayer's findings, he had to judge whether the scope of the menace warranted a change in policy or procedures. As we shall see, he did take a number of deterrent steps, cautioning right-wing politicians of the possible consequences of the incitement and sharing this message with the press. He did not, however, order the VIP Protection Unit to go on high alert or reconsider its procedures. Moreover, he did not demand that the Jewish Division go systematically through its files and identify those who possessed the "potential for violence."

The latter effort alone might well have prevented the assassination, especially as the service had already received a tip about a would-be assassin who fitted Amir's description. The tip came from Shlomi Halevy, a Bar-Ilan student whose credentials as a veteran of the IDF's Intelligence Corps should have inspired a more serious response. Halevy had begun studying law at Bar-Ilan University in 1993, and it was in the kolel there that he became friendly with Yigal Amir. Like Amir, he wore a crocheted yarmulke. But in contrast to his friend, Halevy subscribed to moderate political views and backed the Oslo Agreement. Nevertheless, to satisfy his curiosity, he signed up for a few of the weekend conclaves held in the territories. There he had an opportunity to hear Amir's reasoning about the peace process, and although Halevy was not won over by it, he was impressed by his friend's intelligence and devotion to the Land of Israel.

It was at one of these conclaves that Halevy met Hila Frank, who belonged to the circle of young women drawn to Amir and helped him organize the seminars. (She was mentioned as one of the "gang" in the two letters Amir wrote to Margalit Har-Shefi while she was in custody.) Hila Frank and Shlomi Halevy began dating, and in June 1995 she made him privy to an intriguing piece of information: Yigal Amir was talking about murdering Yitzhak Rabin.

"Hila Frank told me about his threats to murder Rabin because we were friends," he explained in retrospect. "She didn't take them seriously, and neither did I. I knew him to be bright, and murdering Rabin was, to my mind, something stupid—even to Amir's way of thinking."

Yet the couple remained uneasy. "I thought perhaps I was wrong," Halevy recounted. "On the other hand, I didn't want to get [Amir] mixed up with [the law] for a remark that didn't seem serious. Had I known that my information could have prevented the assassination, I wouldn't have hesitated to tell the Shabak all I knew. But I was afraid of incriminating an innocent man, so I chose a middle road."

Halevy concocted a story that was deliberately vague and deflected attention from his source of information but contained enough nuggets of truth to warrant the Shabak's action. Then in June 1995 he went to the commander of his reserve unit in Military Intelligence and related the following tale:

I entered the bathroom of the Central Bus Station in Tel Aviv and heard two young men talking about murdering the prime minister. Both of them had standard Hebrew accents. One of the two—a short, young Yemenite wearing a crocheted yarmulke—was planning to shoot the prime minister at the first opportunity. The Yemenite said that he had already obtained weapons, was saying a confessional prayer twice a day, and had gone to the mikvah* to purify himself in case he dies in the attempt.

The intelligence officer took down the description and passed it on to the commander of the Special Crimes Unit in the Jerusalem District. The police relayed it to the Shabak, but Halevy was not summoned for questioning.

"To this day I don't understand why I wasn't called in for interrogation by the Shabak," he says. "I was sure they had managed to locate Amir, on the basis of the description I gave, and that was why they didn't summon me. Two days after I reported the matter [to the intelligence officer], I forgot the whole thing. Afterward I was at the [conclave] Amir organized in Netsarim [in the Gaza Strip]. . . . I saw Amir, and it didn't even cross my mind that he was someone who might kill the prime minister."

The Shabak's failure to question Halevy can only be explained as indolence. Had he been forced to repeat his story under the gaze of experienced interrogators, there can be little doubt he would have told the truth. And had Amir been arrested and a search done in his house, it's reasonable to assume that the explosives hidden behind his mother's kindergarten would have been discovered.

Instead, the information it received was disregarded because the Shabak rated an assassination attempt by a Jew as negligible. Gillon's subordinates would subsequently tell the Shamgar Commission that because Halevy was a sergeant in the Intelligence Corps, they took him at his word and believed that he could tell them no more than what he had already reported. "Had Halevy told us the truth about what Hila Frank heard Amir say, we would have acted immediately," the head of the Intelligence Division told the panel.

*Ritual bath in which Orthodox Jews immerse themselves as part of a process of spiritual purification.

Oddly, in this lone instance the commission accepted the explanation offered by the Shabak. It took Shlomi Halevy sharply to task for not telling the whole truth and thereby misleading the authorities. "It is likely that a more thorough investigation of Halevy . . . would have led to the discovery of the real information in his hands," the commission wrote. "But this does not detract from the [responsibility borne by] Halevy, who did not reveal the information at his disposal." Halevy was interrogated by the police and the Shabak immediately after the assassination and was released on bail. No charges were brought against him, and a year later his file was closed.

Carmi Gillon, as fate would have it, was not aware of Halevy's tip at all, since information of this sort rarely filtered up to the top. But the prime minister's media adviser, Aliza Goren, did steer his attention to the threats that reached the Prime Minister's Office by phone and mail. (In one instance an anonymous militant mailed a package containing dead doves.) At the beginning of August, in their weekly consultation, Gillon discussed with Rabin the possibility of an assassination attempt. It was then that he first proposed raising the issue of political violence with some of the leaders of the right and holding an off-the-record briefing for the press. Rabin was skeptical but ultimately consented, and Gillon went into action. On no fewer than four occasions he met with members of the Yesha Council to admonish them about the "wild fringe" associated with their constituency. He took the time to talk separately with Benjamin Netanyahu and Ariel Sharon of the Likud and then met with Zevulun Hammer of the National Religious Party, detailing the intelligence obtained by the Shabak and sketching its profile of a potential assassin.

Netanyahu reacted brusquely. He told Gillon that he had come to the wrong address because he himself had always made a point of denouncing the inciters at demonstrations. Afterward Netanyahu complained to one of his associates that Gillon had been recruited into the Labor Party. Sharon responded publicly, in an article published in *Yediot Ahronot* under the headline TYRANTS AT THE GATE, by accusing the government of spreading slander against the right:

Comparisons should not be drawn, but do we still remember Stalin's blood libels, by which he carried out the great purges, eliminated the veteran [political] leadership and top brass of the Red Army in the thirties? He liquidated many Jewish intellectuals in the forties and in the wake of the "Doctors' Plot" wiped out many Jewish doctors at the beginning of the fifties. Everything started then with "information" or "assessments" about alleged intentions to assassinate the despot. . . . Where are they leading with this new libel they're spreading? To smear the national camp, to abandon the settlers in Yesha, perhaps to a civil war?

A certain degree of antipathy to Gillon's démarche was anticipated, for many of the leaders on the right had been hostile to the Shabak's chief from the moment of his appointment. He had, after all, played a key role in the capture of the Jewish Underground in 1984, and the publication of his master's thesis on right-wing subversives had hardly endeared him to the more radical members of that camp. They pegged Gillon as a lackey of the Labor Party who was allowing Rabin to use him as a political tool in the service of his misguided peace policy.

Gillon's session with the press also yielded disappointing results. Meetings between the media and the head of the Shabak, whose name and photograph were then defined as "state secrets," were rare enough to merit special attention and treatment. Thus most of the media did feature his warning prominently. *Yediot Ahronot,* the newspaper with the widest circulation in Israel, gave the item a front-page headline, while Channel One interviewed Internal Security Minister Shahal (who repeated the information already provided by Gillon). But the coverage ended there. Neither the print nor the electronic media saw fit to assign investigative teams to piece together a portrait of a would-be assassin or even to evaluate whether the Shabak's alarm was justified. No one was dispatched to Hebron, Kiryat Arba, or Tapuach. No attempt was made to measure the mood in the more radical yeshivas or at Bar-Ilan. The media, no less than the Shabak, subscribed to the axiom that no Jew would go to the lengths of murdering another Jew for political or ideological ends. The notion was too grotesque to contemplate.

Throughout the summer the media had routinely covered the wave of right-wing demonstrations but barely noticed that the incitement against Rabin personally had reached intolerable proportions. Most of the vitriolic statements were unearthed only after the assassination. Few monitored the broadcasts of Arutz 7. Even fewer paid attention to the scurrilous articles in the *haredi* press and the handbills circulated in synagogues. (The Shabak itself read only a meager portion of this material.) From time to time one commentator or another wearily bemoaned the depths to which public discourse had fallen in Israel. But even as the opposing camps habitually charged each other with incitement, words were deemed innocuous. Even when they were translated into action, the Shabak refrained from going on high alert. There was ample reason to do so in September and October 1995, when protesters got to within revolver range of the prime minister on three occasions: at Kfar Shmaryahu, Mount Herzl, and the Wingate Institute.

The Kfar Shmaryahu incident, on September 11, 1995, occurred as Rabin was dedicating an underpass at a junction north of Tel Aviv infamously known as the "national cork," a daily nightmare for commuters entering the Tel Aviv metropolitan area. Unbeknownst to the security services, an assassination was planned for that day. Yigal Amir had loaded his gun and traveled the short distance from his home in Herzliya. But upon discovering that he had arrived a few hours too early, and fearing he would be spotted if he loitered in the area, he abandoned his plan and returned home. When the ceremony opened and the prime minister was invited to the rostrum, he was awaited by an audience of two hundred people, invited guests only. Suddenly an unidentified young man sprang out of his chair, just a few yards from Rabin, waving his hands in the air and shouting, "Traitor!" A policeman rushed toward him, struggled with the young man for a moment or two, and dragged him away.

Kalman Gayer, who witnessed the outburst, was deeply troubled that an interloper was able to infiltrate an area reserved for screened guests and that the zone immediately surrounding the prime minister was not protected. "At Kfar Shmaryahu it occurred to me that an assassination was a real possibility," Gayer later related. The next day he accompanied Rabin to another public ceremony—this one in Nesher, outside Haifa, where honorary citizenship was being conferred on the prime minister. Before the proceedings began, Gayer strolled through the crowd of local residents who had been drawn to the event mostly as curiosity seekers. "I heard harsh statements being made against Rabin, and I grew anxious," he recalled. "Then I noted how the security people were working closely around him, and I felt calmer. I left with the sense that the situation wasn't so terrible after all. It was only later, at the Wingate Institute, that I saw for certain how that ring of security too was broken."

The scuffle with Natan Ophir at the Wingate Institute has already been described in these pages. He was deflected by the head of the squad of bodyguards protecting Rabin as he rushed the prime minister. But had he pulled a gun while charging at his target, it is doubtful that Rabin would have escaped injury. Gayer, at all events, was horrified by the spectacle. "I know that psychologically we were all locked on [a threat coming from] Arabs, and I too feared primarily an Arab assassin. But here a Jew had managed to get close to the prime minister, right under his nose."

The most reasonable conclusion to draw from the two incidents was politically the least palatable: that Rabin should eschew appearances at large public events. Indeed, Justice Minister David Liba'i implored the prime minister to be more conscientious about his safety, as did Gayer.

"When I realized that Rabin was determined to take part in the open rally in Tel Aviv, I phoned and asked him, 'Why are you going?' Rabin mumbled something," Gayer later related. "I had no inkling that an assassination was coming [at that event], but I nevertheless feared for his life. A few days earlier the ideologue of the Islamic Jihad, Fathi Shkaki, had been shot dead in Malta. The foreign media attributed the assassination to the Mossad, and I thought the Islamic Jihad was capable of reacting to it by planting a bomb at the rally in Tel Aviv."

His gnawing apprehension drove Gayer to call Rabin again a few hours before the November 4 rally and make a last-ditch effort to dissuade him from attending. He failed then too, as did the director general of the Prime Minister's Office, Rabin's close friend and aide Shimon Sheves. At eight that evening, as he stood on the speakers' platform in the Kings of Israel Square, the prime minister seemed relaxed, despite indications that the situation warranted his friends' anxiety. At that same hour the Shabak relayed a warning to the police that Hamas might mount a terror attack that night. The commander of the police contingent at the rally, Deputy Superintendent Ya'akov Shoval, climbed the steps to the speakers' platform and passed the word on to the emcee, Shlomo Lahat, who took Rabin's hand and led him off to a corner of the platform to report the development. Rabin showed no sign of concern. He knew the difference between a blanket warning (which could, after all, have been a hoax designed to sabotage the rally) and well-sourced information that would have caused the Shabak to insist upon his immediate departure. He did, however, walk over to his wife and ask her quietly whether she wanted to return home.

"No," she said. "Why? Everyone here is family."

In retrospect, the warning of a possible terror attack makes the Shabak's behavior at the rally surprising. If there was reason to believe that any of the people on the speakers' platform were in peril, it is doubly curious that security was not particularly tight in the parking area below—to which Rabin would return at the end of the rally—as well as on the surrounding rooftops.

The security breach became even more obvious three days after the assassination when Israel's Channel Two opened its 8:00 P.M. news broadcast with an amazing sight: Yigal Amir, on videotape, shooting Rabin in the back. The tape had been filmed from a distance through a zoom lens by a man who had focused on Amir for forty-five minutes as he loitered in the parking area. The film showed him pacing back and forth on the sidewalk, then sitting on the edge of a concrete flower pot near the steps leading up to the square. As Rabin descended those steps and approached his car, the slight young man stood up, walked quickly toward Rabin's back, and drew his gun. Two shots can be heard and a flash of gunfire seen on the tape. At that point the cameraman apparently lost his equilibrium because his camera is no longer trained on the murder scene, the picture goes out of focus, and is cut off.

Unlike the footage of the Kennedy assassination taken by Abraham Zapruder, the video shown on Channel Two did not fuel conspiracy theories. More than anything, it sparked a series of questions about the amateur photographer, Ronni Kempler, a thirty-seven-year-old accountant in the Ministry of Finance who had positioned himself on a roof overlooking the parking area. Beyond the wonder of how he could have been allowed to stand on that roof with a direct view of the prime minister's car (had Kempler been sporting a rifle rather than a video camera, he could easily have shot Rabin) was Kempler's choice of subject. A hundred thousand people were gathered in the adjoining square. They were being addressed, under very unusual circumstances, by the prime minister, the foreign minister, and other prominent public figures who joined them toward the end of the rally in an emotional rendition of the "Song of Peace." Yet Ronni Kempler did not film any of this. Instead, his camera lingered for more than half an hour on an anonymous young man in a dim parking lot.

Why did the accountant choose to focus for so long on a man that trained policemen had concluded was a plainclothesman? In all fairness, it must be said that Kempler had come to the same conclusion. What drew and then locked his attention to Amir, he explained in an interview in *Yediot Ahronot*, was a "feeling that something bad would happen. . . . There was anxiety in the air. Maybe because in the [army] reserves I deal with security, I am more sensitive to that." Kempler also explained why he had not alerted the police about his qualm. "At first he looked suspicious to me as he sat by the plant," he said in an interview months after the assassination. "He stood out, and with all the talk of political assassination, attacks, he looked like a potential killer. Then I told myself that he was probably an undercover policeman, because otherwise the police would have dealt with him."

After interrogating Kempler, the Shabak was satisfied with his explanations. After all, the security service had made a similar error. Despite the "anxiety in the air" sensed by an ordinary citizen, a few days before the rally the head of the Shabak had left on a scheduled trip to Europe. Gillon was to have been accompanied by D.Y., the head of the Security Division. But the latter, concerned about the rally, canceled his plans and spent the evening of November 4 scouting the area below the speakers' platform. Toward the end of the rally, he descended to the parking lot and saw a number of unauthorized persons there. He testified to the Shamgar Commission that he had asked a police officer to have them removed. But the police contested that statement, saying that no such request had been made, and the Shamgar Commission accepted their version.

The commission held the Shabak responsible for what it termed the "minimal" cooperation between the service and the police. It also determined that the Shabak bore most of the blame for the fact that the sensitive parking area was not "sterile." The policemen stationed there had not been briefed on the comprehensive security plan. Nor had the Shabak shared with the police its fear of a possible attempt on Rabin's life by a Jewish assassin. These omissions, the panel concluded, accounted for the failure to clear the parking area. Had the imperative of absolute "sterility" been impressed upon the police, they would have demanded that Amir identify himself properly or at least, the commission presumed, have moved him farther away from the prime minister's car and thus diminished the peril to Rabin.

Even this failure would have been correctable had the number of body-guards around Rabin been increased. In previous attempts to get within shooting range of the prime minister, Amir had proved reluctant to take chances. If Rabin had been surrounded by a protective wall of five or six bodyguards, rather than the three attending him as he came down the steps, the assassin might well have been deterred again. And even if he had moved forward to shoot, it would have been easier to block him, as Natan Ophir had been blocked in the Wingate incident.

For all these sins of omission, the commander of the Security Division was held personally at fault. D.Y. had come up the ranks in the VIP Protection Unit, filling all its field and command positions, and was regarded as a seasoned expert. He portrayed himself to the Shamgar Commission (as had Gillon before him) as a strategist who did not concern himself with the details of individual operations. "The service's norm is that its commanders and division heads do not oversee operations," he told the commission, thus passing the blame downward. But the commission treated D.Y.'s case as it had Gillon's. It found his performance wanting on both the strategic and tactical levels. D.Y. had already resigned from the Shabak when the commission's verdict was issued.

The commander of the VIP Protection Unit, B.L., was another highly experienced operative, having worked in VIP protection for twenty-two years. He followed his commanders' example in trying to shift responsibility for the fiasco off his shoulders. But while Gillon and D.Y. had tried to pass the blame on to their subordinates, B.L. made every effort to push it on to his commanders. "The senior ranks of the service did not direct me to in any way enhance the level or change the method of protection," he protested to the Shamgar Commission. Although his superiors were aware of possible action by a Jewish assassin, they deemed the threat superficial because undefined "red lines" had not yet been crossed. Even so, B.L. pleaded in his defense, "I made improvements in the level of security."

The commission rejected this contention and judged B.L. responsible for most of the shortcomings on the night of the assassination. He had appointed as commander of the contingent at the rally an inexperienced subordinate, Y.S., who did not exercise adequate control over his men in the field. He did not ensure a satisfactory level of alertness, did not review the details of the plan prepared by Y.S., did not check the arrangements established for the parking lot and the roof of an adjoining building over-looking it, and did not ensure that the overall plan was free of defects. B.L. had already resigned from the Shabak.

B.L.'s immediate subordinate, A.A., the head of the Operations Branch of the VIP Protection Unit, also appeared before the commission. A few minutes before the shooting, he testified, he had accompanied one of the bodyguards down to the parking area to check whether it was indeed "ster-ile." The commission disputed the accuracy of this statement since Amir was in the parking area and was not accosted at that time. Its report attrib-uted full responsibility for the problem in the parking area to A.A. "He did not define what was required of the police; did not check the conditions in the field and the lighting at night; did not review the response of the police to the conclusions of the [Shabak's] preliminary meeting (sent to police headquarters); did not mention the parking area at the Orders Group; and ignored the situation he saw in the parking area when he arrived at the rally." For all these reasons, the commission disqualified him from serving in any command capacity for at least four years. A.A. was transferred to another division of the Shabak.

One of the more telling details of the Shamgar Commission's report was that most of the groundwork for the rally had been assigned to a junior officer, thirty-year-old Y.S., who had little experience in planning security at mass events. Y.S.'s advancement in the service had been swift. Before being placed in command of the force at the rally, he had been the head of the prime minister's bodyguards (and was the one who had scuffled with Ophir at the Wingate Institute). His commanders had expected that the commission would cast the full burden of censure upon him and were surprised to discover that it did just the opposite and criticized them for assigning him the task. Y.S. told the Shamgar Commission that he had not been properly alerted to the prospect of an attempt on the prime min-ister's life. "At most I feared the throwing of eggs or tomatoes, not a gun," he said.

Carmi Gillon was understandably intent on countering this claim. "We were conscious of [the possibility of] an assassination attempt," he assured the commission, relating that Shlomi Halevy's story had been placed in the files of all the bodyguards and that the commander of one of the squads had asked at an earlier briefing: "What's happening with the Yemenite in the bathroom?" At one point in the commission's proceedings, Gillon and Y.S. began to argue heatedly over failings in command. Y.S. contended that he had not been satisfied with the protection plan for the rally.

"I lacked [the necessary] resources," he complained.

"Then why didn't you speak up?" Gillon growled. "Did anyone prevent you from talking? You were appointed commander of the operation, and you had criticisms? Did anyone stop you from saying so? What is this? Are we in the Wehrmacht that you [were so scrupulous about] obeying orders?"

The clash between Gillon and Y.S. was of particular interest to the commission because of its suspicion that evidence had been suppressed. About a week after the assassination, when all the members of the Security Division convened to discuss the findings of the Shabak's internal-inquiry board, an argument broke out between the service's commanders and their field operatives. At least four bodyguards criticized the *modus operandi* dictated from above, and some of them angrily dubbed the board "a field court-martial." The meeting was recorded on tape, and a copy of the cassette was subsequently turned over to the Shamgar Commission, which discovered that a few sentences uttered by Y.S. had been erased from it. Outraged by what it saw as an attempt to destroy evidence, the commission demanded the full transcript of the meeting and in its report rebuked the Shabak for "contradictions and conflicting versions of the testimony given by commanders of the VIP Protection Unit" and for "deficiencies in the immediate transfer of all the material relevant to the commission's work."

Although the commission found that the bulk of the blame for failures at the rally lay with Y.S.'s superiors, it censored him for not making a satisfactory tour of the area together with the police, for not reviewing the police plan for security, and for the lack of clarity in his understandings with the police. Having failed to appreciate the sensitivity of the parking area, he did not take the precaution of filtering out those who would be allowed to enter the "seam" around the lot or take action to have that seam cleared when a crowd had gathered at the foot of the steps. He did not deploy the bodyguards in a way that would have allowed the VIPs to leave the area safely, nor did he consider an alternate route for the prime minister's departure. That the roof of the building adjoining the parking lot did not receive appropriate attention and the lighting in the parking area was not scrutinized in advance were also blamed on Y.S. The commission barred him from holding any command position for two years.

The commander of the Shabak's Intelligence Division, H.K., was reprimanded (as he had been by the Shabak's internal board of inquiry) for failing to convey the information received from Shlomi Halevy to the police. In his defense he argued that the intelligence he handled was extremely sensitive and could be distributed only within restricted circles. He had, however, provided the police with a wealth of information about the threat of attacks on public figures. The commission believed he should have done more but did not recommend any action against him.

Finally, the Shamgar Commission did not limit its criticism to Shabak. "Our findings and conclusions . . . reflect conceptual and operational flaws in many areas and a weakness in the management culture of government authorities," it stressed. "In this respect, this report serves as a signpost and warning for many other institutions." In so writing, the commission echoed a criticism that Rabin had voiced about Israeli society not long before his death. He deplored the prevailing attitude that, despite a slapdash approach to an appointed task, "Everything will be fine," undoubtedly thanks to the grace of God. There could be no greater irony than the fact that this methodical man with a legendary appetite for details lost his life as the result of oversight and neglect, compounded at every level by men from whom he expected consummate professionalism.

Following the assassination, the Shabak dramatically improved security for the prime minister and other top officials. Some members of the press have even complained of "overkill." But the more stringent policy remains an imperative because threats to the prime minister's safety are as potent as before. In the winter of 1997, when Israel was to have turned over additional territory to the Palestinian Authority (following the provisions of the Oslo Agreement), posters appeared in Jerusalem showing Prime Minister Netanyahu in a keffieh, while others pronounced him a traitor. At the end of that year State Attorney Edna Arbel conceded that "there are fears a similar murder will take place." And in July 1998, for the first time in its history, the Shabak formally warned the prime minister that in the event of a further withdrawal from the territories, Jewish extremists were prepared to mount armed actions against political leaders and government institutions. While the breakdown of the peace process had halted the resurgence of incitement and violence from the far right, there was no guarantee that the phenomenon had been silenced for long.

CHAPTER 10

FLIGHT

No one can say how momentous the assassination of Yitzhak Rabin will prove to be for Israel's future. Nor is it possible to know today whether the change of course Rabin introduced will prove any more than a brief deviation from a national policy long colored by suspicion, pessimism, and ideological rigidity. What does seem certain, however, is that historians will view this period as a complex and nuanced story of a society that turned against itself and, when it had the opportunity to move from tragedy to catharsis, fled from that prospect with all possible speed.

One explanation for that flight has been offered by an astute observer of the Israeli scene, U.S. Assistant Secretary of State Martin Indyk. Upon ending his tour as U.S. ambassador to Israel in September 1997, Indyk referred in a *Ha'aretz* interview to the frenetic pace of Israeli life. "I have the feeling that part of the energy with whose aid you move from crisis to crisis, part of the rhetoric with which it is done, derives from a desire to escape from a situation that is too brutal," he observed. "I think this is also true of the Rabin assassination. The country bounced back too quickly and moved on to the next crisis, and thus it lacked the ability to truly cope, to digest what happened."

Indyk saw and diplomatically phrased what many Israelis are loath to admit: that rather than address and assimilate, reflect and rehabilitate, they chose to repress the Rabin assassination and treat any serious examination of the affair almost as a national taboo. Safely protected from the light of scrutiny were the individuals, parties, and organizations that had organized and funded the incitement against Rabin; the rabbis who had ruled on *din moser* and *din rodef*; the national figures who had made thinly veiled references to the fate due a "traitor," "Nazi," and "collaborator"; the extremists who had called for discarding the democratic way of life; and the leaders of the moderate right who had allowed radical elements to dictate their program of action. Fateful questions were buried together with the body of the slain leader. The assassination was erased from the public agenda so quickly that the processes of conciliation and reform never had a chance to begin.

Before Yitzhak Rabin had even been laid to rest, the Israeli right began complaining that it was the object of a cynical campaign to lay responsibility for the violence at its doorstep. Its indignation soon spawned a spate of popular conspiracy theories that blamed Rabin for his own death. The left, consumed by shame over its complacency and failure to protect and defend Rabin prior to the assassination, fought back by portraying itself, rather than Israeli society and democracy, as the injured party. And both sides felt that an honest examination of their behavior would only aggravate the divisions within Israeli society and should thus be carefully avoided.

Indeed, hardly had the week of national mourning ended when the imperative of "national unity" was raised as a supreme value. It quickly became clear, however, that the assassination of the prime minister was not an event around which such unity could coalesce. For the dictates of solidarity would require Israelis to penetrate dark corners of religion and politics, basic halachic issues, the relationship between religion and state, and the country's commitment to the core value of democratic rule. Paradoxically, Rabin's murder confronted them with questions deemed far more menacing and potentially divisive than any policy he had promoted during his life.

Avoidance of these questions was initially chosen by Shimon Peres as the best way to preserve the peace process, and in this case his decision was right. In the weeks following the assassination, he managed to withdraw Israeli troops from six Palestinian cities in the West Bank without any protest from the opposition. It was embraced by Benjamin Netanyahu as the means for distancing himself from his own connection to the incitement. Both camps prescribed it as the solution for healing the national rift. But it has merely allowed them to cling more tenaciously to their opposing positions.

There was a brief moment of respite. In his postelection victory speech in June 1996 Prime Minister Netanyahu pledged to be the prime minister of all the people of Israel. A year and a half later, however, a radio microphone picked up his voice whispering into the ear of an influential Sephardi mystic: "The leftists have forgotten what it is to be Jewish." Little wonder, then, that by the second anniversary of the assassination, the incessant friction and use of the tragedy as a political weapon brought the historian Professor Shlomo Ben-Ami, a Moroccan-born immigrant who grew up in the northern development town of Kiryat Shmonah and is today the leading intellectual in Israel's Labor Party, to describe the gravity of the crisis in writing:

> The ties that hold Israel together as a united society have long been in a tragic process of disintegration. What we have here is not a society but cells inimical to one another in a state of potential civil war. Israel will not be able to stand this way before an enemy or confront the difficult challenges of peace. . . . Two years after the assassination we have learned nothing and forgotten nothing; we are in exactly the same place. This nation is not even capable of mourning together.

It will be argued, and justly so, that Israel was no less factious under Rabin's tutelage. But even as its people clashed over the course of the peace process, the country as a whole was reaping its benefits. After the Oslo Agreement Israel emerged from the diplomatic isolation of the 1980s to find itself crowded with official visitors from the Americas, the European Union, the CIS, the Far East, and the Arab world. Israeli businesspeople plied the routes between Tel Aviv and Egypt, Jordan, North Africa, and the Persian Gulf, developing new markets as the walls of the Arab boycott crumbled and Arab regimes established diplomatic ties with Israel. Foreign investments poured into the country as the future technological and financial hub of a "new Middle East," bringing the national growth rate to 5 to 6 percent per annum. Israelis even began to fear for the ecological health of their country were it to become a crossroads of heavy commercial traffic.

Two years after the "national camp" narrowly won the 1996 election, little of this picture remained. The peace process was stalled, and the Oslo Agreements were frozen. Negotiations with Syria had not been renewed, and the Arab world had severely curtailed its contacts with Israel. The growth rate had fallen to 1 to 2 percent, and the optimism that was to have launched a thriving Israel into the twenty-first century had evaporated, casting the economy into a deep recession. The country had slid back into a "Fortress Israel" mind-set, shunned by the Arab states, at loggerheads with the European Union, and bickering with its staunchest ally, the United States, over the administration's resolve to keep the peace process alive.

On the domestic scene no consensus had been reached by the broad political center to isolate the extremists. At the same time the violence perpetrated against the nation's leader seemed to have become infectious, as the rates of murder and domestic violence rose markedly in the intervening years. Tempers were shorter than ever; life in Israel was less tranquil (if it could ever have been described as such). Practically every sector of society, from religious and political groups to new immigrants, women, and Arabs, complained of a lack of tolerance. Antigovernment incitement continued as well, especially whenever the prospect of a further withdrawal from the territories returned to the headlines.

Historians are likely to characterize the post-Rabin period as a time of deep anxiety. There are many indications that racist and separatist philosophies are gaining ground, especially among the *haredim* and national religious population. One particularly troubling development is the recent waves of verbal assaults on the High Court of Justice by religious circles of both tendencies. The threats made against Chief Justice Aharon Barak have already been described. In May 1997 a crowd of *haredi* protesters rushed the Supreme Court building on the day it was hearing arguments, inter alia, against a decision to indict a leading *haredi* politician. Knesset member Aharon Cohen of the ultra-Orthodox Shas Party, which in the past decade has grown from a marginal political force to a major power, characterized the court's justices as "foreign priests of modern, primitive idolatry." Shas's spiritual mentor, former Sephardi Chief Rabbi Ovadiah Yosef, went a step further in urging all Israelis to boycott the secular courts, "which are not for Jews," and agree to be judged only before rabbinical tribunals.

The desire to reconstitute Israel as a halachic state has also enjoyed a highly public revival since the 1996 election, in which the three religious parties won a total of twenty-three Knesset seats. The unsettling result is that over a fifth of Israel's legislature advocates a philosophy that would effectively strip the Knesset of authority. Over the past year the uproar over an amendment that would formally recognize only those religious conversions performed in Israel by Orthodox rabbis has drawn the greatest coverage, primarily because of the intense antagonism it has sparked among the majority Conservative and Reform streams of Judaism in the United States. But within Israel itself the creeping legitimization of a halachic state is the more alarming phenomenon because of the stature of the people now promoting it.

One of them is Rabbi Yitzhak Levy, who became chairman of the National Religious Party at the beginning of 1998 after the death of Zevulun Hammer. As minister of transport in Netanyahu's government, the soft-spoken Levy, who represents the far-right position within the NRP, made his first official visit as a cabinet minister to the yeshiva at Joseph's Tomb in Nablus and the settlement of Bracha to encourage the zealots who study or live there. In November 1997 he told an interviewer from *Ha'aretz* that he too sides with the notion of Israel's becoming a state ruled by the halacha (provided this change comes about by consensus). He does not see a conflict between a halachic state and a democratic one, he added, because the ancient law provides sufficient protection of individual rights. This view, which fifty years ago was confined to the margins of the body politic, is now being advocated at the very heart of the political establishment. Today Rabbi Levy is Israel's minister of education and culture. His colleague Hanan Porat is also strategically placed as chairman of the Knesset Constitution, Law, and Justice Committee, with considerable influence over the fate of civil rights legislation.

Yet another barometer of Israeli ambivalence about the health of its democracy and the rule of law is the fact that the fanatic groups that were active in the incitement campaign against Prime Minister Rabin continue to thrive. Kach and Kahane Chai, which were outlawed by the Rabin government after the massacre in the Cave of the Patriarchs, pursue their activities under new names. Both have found a home in the Yeshiva of the Jewish Idea in Jerusalem. Most of the hard core of Kahane Chai is concentrated in the Samarian settlement of Tapuach and publishes a weekly newsletter, the *Way of the Torah*, that is circulated in synagogues and from distribution points at heavily frequented sites, such as the Mahane Yehudah open market in Jerusalem. Since Rabin's assassination Kahane Chai has framed its messages more gingerly. But each time there are rumors of possible movement in the peace process, threats against the government, and specifically against Netanyahu, reappear in its publications, usually under the guise of verses from the Bible.

To circumvent the ban on the two organizations, in November 1996 some of their members joined forces in establishing a new group called the Ideological Front. Four hundred people showed up for its founding meeting. They included Itamar Ben-Gvir, who tore the Cadillac symbol off Rabin's car and threatened to "get to" the prime minister as well; Natan Levy, who was one of Avishai Raviv's deputies in Eyal; Rabbi Yitzhak Ginzburg of the yeshiva in Joseph's Tomb; and Shmuel Sackett of Zo Artzenu. A few of the group's leaders were subsequently interrogated by the police in connection with an attack on senior officials of the Palestinian Authority. Similar sources were suspected of being behind the death threat made against the Irish singer Sinead O'Connor, who consequently canceled a concert in Jerusalem on behalf of the Jerusalem Link, a joint Palestinian-Israeli women's peace group. Ben-Gvir publicly boasted that he had scared the singer away.

Avigdor Eskin, who pronounced the *Pulsa da-Nura* curse on Rabin, continues his provocative activities. Along with a handful of followers, Eskin has introduced a new custom by annually celebrating Yigal Amir's birthday, replete with champagne, outside the prison where the assassin is serving his life sentence. A Beersheba taxi driver who dared protest the celebration was badly beaten by Eskin.

The Action Headquarters also continues to exist, with Ya'akov Novick on constant alert to take on the Netanyahu government if and when it votes to cede additional territory under the provisions of the Oslo Agreement. Novick's friend Baruch Marzel is as influential as ever in Hebron, where tensions periodically explode into violence and the latest strategy of the Jewish settlers is to prod Israeli troops to enter the Palestinian sector of the city, thereby wrecking the withdrawal agreement signed by Netanyahu. And Elyakim Ha'etzni of Kiryat Arba, who compared Rabin to Marshal Pétain, has now trained his sights on Netanyahu and reached beyond French history all the way back to the Talmud in warning in a *Yediot Ahronot* interview:

> If Netanyahu, heaven forfend, turns over responsibility for areas of Judea and Samaria to Arafat . . . it can be expected, by simple logic, that what happened to Rabin and Peres will happen to him as well. If the Land of Israel is lost, we will fight him as we did his predecessor. In the Talmud [it is written that] an ox that has gored three times must be put to death. The Likud gored in Camp David and in Madrid, and if it gores in Oslo, then it must be put to death.

Given the experience of November 1995, should rhetoric of this sort be defined as incitement to murder? Well after the assassination some leaders of the opposition, who were by then back in power, felt secure enough to admit that criticism of the Rabin government had been stretched beyond the limit of what is permissible in a democratic society. But the Israeli legislature and legal system were still reluctant to define the line separating the exercise of free speech from the practice of illegal incitement. Before the Rabin assassination the law enforcement authorities had approached this matter with caution and restraint for fear of trampling on the cardinal right of democratic protest. Attorney General Michael Ben-Ya'ir had also advanced the pragmatic argument that trying offenders for incitement would only provide them with a platform for disseminating their views to an ever-wider audience. Immediately after the murder, stung by criticism that they had been too lenient with offenders and had misjudged the powerful influence of fanatics, the authorities initially overreacted and went to the opposite extreme. In one case a settler from the Hebron area who expressed his satisfaction over the assassination to foreign news networks was arrested and remanded for a week without bail. The newfound zeal was at any rate short-lived.

Since then some jurists and legislators have moved to amend the law and draw a clearer distinction between the right of free speech and its abuse. They propose to define incitement and sedition as explicit calls to engage in violence or perpetrate crimes against the regime, as the creation of a climate conducive to such crimes, and as defiance of the democratic and legal order. Obviously, criticism of the government or passive resistance to its policies would not be categorized as crimes, as the motivation behind new legislation is to protect the democratic system, not debase it.

One advocate of such an amendment is the Hebrew University law professor Mordechai Kremnitzer. Known for his liberal outlook, Kremnitzer nevertheless believes that in times of emergency, as when the democratic system itself is under assault, society is entitled to place constraints on freedom of speech. In various articles he has expressed deep concern over the stability of democratic rule in Israel, explaining that:

> Yitzhak Rabin was murdered because of the weakness of Israeli democracy, because of the delegitimization of the government he headed and the political line he advanced. I am not speaking of criticism, which is the life breath of democracy, but of the denial of legitimacy, whence the distance to political murder is short. . . . Not only did the assassination expose the weakness of Israeli democracy, it considerably enervated [that democracy], and the support for the murder and the murderer, which is hardly marginal, continues to weaken it. Israeli democracy today is not something to be taken for granted; it is frail.

Contrary to initial expectations, then, the short-term effect of Yitzhak Rabin's assassination has been a rise in violence, rather than a sober reconsideration of its efficacy. It has also generated a decline in national self-confidence. Israelis recurrently express the fear that their country will ignite in civil war—a specter that weighs more heavily than fundamentalist terrorism or war with its neighbors. Sadder but not necessarily wiser for the experience of November 4, 1995, they are also prepared to believe the worst of themselves. As many as 70 to 80 percent of the respondents in public opinion polls believe that a political assassination can recur. (Between 18 and 24 percent of the respondents in other polls have said that they support, or at least do not oppose, a pardon for Yigal Amir.) More than 50 percent of Israel's citizens believe that the country's leaders have not drawn the necessary conclusions from the Rabin assassination. When a Gallup poll done for *Ma'ariv* on the second anniversary of the murder asked whether the country was closer to unity or civil war, more than twice as many respondents (56 compared with 21 percent) answered the latter. Four months later the Tami Steinmetz Center for Peace Research asked Israelis to rate the issues on which there is a "high chance of violence breaking out." Almost four-fifths (79 percent) of the respondents cited relations between the secular and religious camps, with friction between the left and the right coming in a close second (70 percent).

How should we interpret these disturbing data? All we can say is that as the state celebrates its jubilee year, scholars of the Jewish past and present are divided on their assessment of the future. One school views the murder of Prime Minister Rabin, the election of Prime Minister Netanyahu, and the derailing of the Oslo process as a progression that augurs the demise of Zionism as a classically secular, democratic movement. Noting that the messianic strain in Israeli life is growing increasingly militant, the members of this school see compromise with the extremists as unlikely. One of them, Hebrew University sociologist Professor Moshe Lissak, has gone so far as to characterize the secular Jewish state established in 1948 as "largely a fleeting episode."

The opposing school takes a more sanguine view. It argues that the present crisis, though particularly grave, does not necessarily foreshadow the collapse of the original Zionist design. Instead, secular Zionism will rally and begin working toward a kind of synthesis with the fundamentalist forces in Judaism. As Professor Yaron Ezrachi, a Hebrew University political scientist, writes in his 1997 book *Rubber Bullets*:

If the agreements with our Arab neighbors indeed reduce regional tensions and the sense of siege in Israel, the focus of the relations between religion and politics may shift from issues of territories, settlements, and power to the related yet more complex issues of values, culture, and identities. As a civilization Judaism cannot be reduced to religion (certainly not to Orthodox Judaism) and as a way of life democracy cannot be reduced to a set of political and legal procedures. The more direct encounter between Judaism and democracy in Israel is likely to trigger processes of selection and adaptation that could transform them both.

Yet this development too is predicated on the assumption that Israel must settle its conflict with its neighbors before it can resolve its dispute with itself.

Finally, the optimists believe that Israel's elites have essentially accepted the historic decision to share the Land of Israel with the Palestinians. The debate now, they say, is not over the principle of making peace but merely over the price as measured in territory.

Aryeh Naor, who as government secretary under Prime Minister Begin was an outspoken champion of the settlement movement and has since had a change of heart, is a prime example of this thinking. He believes that Yigal Amir's attempt to redirect the course of history with three bullets has already proved a failure. For not only does Israel's recognition of the PLO remain in place, but the post-Oslo right-wing government has withdrawn from most of Hebron—the place of deepest Jewish significance in the West Bank—and has pledged to carry out further withdrawals from the occupied territories. Thus on the second anniversary of the assassination Naor was moved to write:

> The mutual recognition reached in the Oslo agreement is a recognition of reality. Peace follows from the recognition of reality, is an imperative of reality, and thus will overcome obstacles and inhibitions. The sun will yet rise to lighten the morning, and when we together bring the coveted day, we will all—Jews and Arabs, Israelis and Palestinians—stand before the grave of the late Yitzhak Rabin, the victor in war and in peace, and say: Thank you.

That day, if it ever arrives, will come too late for Yitzhak Rabin. We cannot predict how he will be remembered by his country. But in a speech to the U.S. Congress in July 1994 Rabin gave a clue about the epitaph he would have written for himself in saying: "I, military I.D. number 30743, retired general in the Israel Defense Forces in the past, consider myself to be a soldier in the army of peace today." Whether or not Yitzhak Rabin is remembered as a soldier of peace and a bold statesman who made hard decisions for the sake of his country's future will depend largely upon the kind of society Israel's citizens forge for themselves and for posterity.

BIBLIOGRAPHY

BOOKS AND ARTICLES

Almog, Shmuel. *Zionism and History: The Rise of a New Jewish Consciousness.* New York: St. Martin's Press, 1987.

Avinery, Shlomo. *Varieties of Zionist Thought.* Tel Aviv: Am Oved, 1980 (in Hebrew).

Ben-Sasson, H. H., ed. *A History of the Jewish People.* Cambridge, Mass.: Harvard University Press, 1976.

Ben-Simon, Daniel. *A New Israel.* Tel Aviv: Arie Nir Publishers, 1997 (in Hebrew).

Benvenisti, Meron. *The West Bank Handbook: A Political Lexicon.* Jerusalem: Jerusalem Post, 1986.

Black, Ian, and Benny Morris. *Israel's Secret Wars: A History of Israel's Intelligence Services.* New York: Grove Weidenfeld, 1991.

Ezrachi, Yaron. *Rubber Bullets: Power and Conscience in Modern Israel.* New York: Farrar, Straus & Giroux, 1997.

Friedman, Robert I. *The False Prophets: Rabbi Meir Kahane.* London: Faber and Faber, 1990.

————. *Zealots for Zion: Inside Israel's West Bank Settlement Movement.* New York: Random House, 1992.

Goldberg, J. J. *Jewish Power: Inside the American Jewish Establishment.* Reading, Mass.: Addison-Wesley, 1996.

Harkabi, Yehoshafat. "The Controversy Over the Settlement and the Crisis Thereafter," in Rachel Pasternak and Shlomo Zidkiyahu, eds., *A New Era or a Lost Direction: Israelis Talk About Peace.* Tel Aviv: Itiav, 1994 (in Hebrew).

Hertzberg, Arthur. *The Zionist Idea: A Historical Analysis and Reader.* New York: Atheneum, 1972.

Kapeliouk, Amnon. *Rabin: Un assassinat politique.* Paris: Le Monde Editions, 1996.

Laqueur, Walter. *A History of Zionism.* London: Weidenfeld and Nicholson, 1972.

Milstein, Uri. *The Rabin File.* Tel Aviv: Yaron Golan Publishers, 1995 (in Hebrew).

Peleg, Muli. *Spreading the Wrath of God: From Gush Emunim to Rabin.* Tel Aviv: Hakibbutz Hameuchad, 1997 (in Hebrew).

Rabin, Yitzhak. *The Rabin Memoirs.* London: Weidenfeld and Nicholson, 1979.

Raviv, Dan, and Yossi Melman. *Every Spy a Prince: The Complete History of Israel's Intelligence Community.* Boston: Houghton Mifflin, 1990.

Rubinstein, Amnon. *From Herzl to Rabin: 100 Years of Zionism.* Tel Aviv: Schocken Publishers, 1997 (in Hebrew).

Rubinstein, Danny. *On the Lord's Side: Gush Emunim.* Tel Aviv: Hakibbutz Hameuchad, 1982 (in Hebrew).

Segal, Haggai. *Dear Brothers.* Jerusalem: Keter, 1988 (in Hebrew).

Shafat, Gershon. *Gush Emunim: The Story Behind the Scenes.* Beit El: Beit El Publishers, 1995 (in Hebrew).

Shragai, Nadav. *The Temple Mount Conflict.* Jerusalem: Keter, 1995 (in Hebrew).

Slater, Robert. *Rabin of Israel: Warrior for Peace.* New York: Harper Paperbacks, 1996.

Sprinzak, Ehud. *Political Violence in Israel.* Jerusalem: Jerusalem Institute for Israel Studies, 1995.

Talmon, Jacob L. *The Age of Violence.* Tel Aviv: Am Oved, 1977 (in Hebrew).

Weiss, Hillel. "En Route to the Redemption from Post-Nihilism," in Pinhas Ginossar and Avi Bareli, eds., *Zionism: A Contemporary Controversy.* Sede Boker: The Ben Gurion Research Center, 1996 (in Hebrew).

NEWSPAPERS AND PERIODICALS

Algemeiner Journal, New York, weekly.

Baltimore Jewish Times, weekly.

Forward, New York, weekly.

Gilayon, Tel Aviv (Religious-Zionist Movement of Halacha Believers), April 1996.

Ha'aretz, Tel Aviv, daily.

Hashavua, Bnei Brak, weekly.

Hatsofeh, Tel Aviv, daily.

Jerusalem Post, daily.

Jewish Press, New York, weekly.

Jewish Week, New York, weekly.

Kol Ha'ir, Jerusalem, weekly.

La-Ge'ula (Chai ve-Kayam Movement).

Ma'ariv, Tel Aviv, daily.

Nekudah, Beit El.

New York magazine, weekly.

The New York Times, daily.

Outpost, New York (Americans for a Safe Israel).
Shabbat be-Shabbato (National Religious Party).
Viewpoint, New York (The National Council of Young Israel).
Village Voice, New York, weekly.
Yediot Ahronot, Tel Aviv, daily.

INDEX